EVAGRIUS PONTICUS

D1599955

Evagrius Ponticus (c.345–99) was a seminal figure for Eastern monasticism and had a strong influence on Western monasticism as well. He left more writings than any other father from the Egyptian desert. However, many of his writings were lost after he was condemned as an Origenist in the sixth century. During the twentieth century, numerous works were recovered (especially in ancient oriental translations from the original Greek) but very few of these works are available in English translation; many of them are not readily available at all.

This collection presents complete works drawn from the full range of his writings, many of which have not previously appeared in English, offering translations of some of Evagrius' letters, his notes on various books of the Bible, his treatises and his 'chapters' (a genre popularised by Evagrius that consists of condensed, interconnected sentences). All of the works included here are translated in full.

The translations aim to present the material accurately and accessibly. The volume is prefaced by a substantial introductory essay that presents Evagrius, his works and influence, and modern scholarship about him in a way that is of great use to students and also comprehensible to beginners.

Augustine Casiday is Leverhulme Fellow in the Department of Theology, Durham. His research primarily concerns Christian monasticism during the first millennium. He has published several articles on Evagrius and other early monastic authors.

THE EARLY CHURCH FATHERS
Edited by Carol Harrison
University of Durham

The Greek and Latin Fathers of the Church are central to the creation of Christian doctrine, yet often unapproachable because of the sheer volume of their writings and the relative paucity of accessible translations. This series makes available translations of key selected texts by the major Fathers to all students of the Early Church.

CYRIL OF JERUSALEM
Edward Yarnold, S.J.

EARLY CHRISTIAN LATIN POETS
Carolinne White

CYRIL OF ALEXANDRIA
Norman Russell

MAXIMUS THE CONFESSOR
Andrew Louth

IRENAEUS OF LYONS
Robert M. Grant

AMBROSE
Boniface Ramsey, O.P.

ORIGEN
Joseph W. Trigg

GREGORY OF NYSSA
Anthony Meredith, S.J.

JOHN CHRYSOSTOM
Wendy Mayer and Pauline Allen

JEROME
Stefan Rebenich

TERTULLIAN
Geoffrey Dunn

ATHANASIUS
Khaled Anatolios

SEVERUS OF ANTIOCH
Pauline Allen and C.T.R. Hayward

GREGORY THE GREAT
John Moorhead

THODORET OF CYRUS
István Pásztori-Kupán

EVAGRIUS PONTICUS
A.M. Casiday

EVAGRIUS PONTICUS

A.M. Casiday

Routledge
Taylor & Francis Group

LONDON AND NEW YORK

First published 2006
by Routledge
2 Park Square, Milton Park, Abingdon, Oxon OX14 4RN

Simultaneously published in the USA and Canada
by Routledge
711 Third Avenue, New York, NY 10017

Routledge is an imprint of the Taylor & Francis Group, an informa business

© 2006 A.M. Casiday

Typeset in Garamond 3 by
Florence Production Ltd, Stoodleigh, Devon

British Library Cataloguing in Publication Data
A catalogue record for this book is available from the British Library

Library of Congress Cataloging in Publication Data
A catalog record for this book has been requested

ISBN13: 978–0–415–32446–5 (hbk)
ISBN13: 978–0–415–32447–2 (pbk)
ISBN13: 978–0–203–35697–5 (ebk)

For Fr Gabriel

Πλὴν εἰ μετήλθες ἐκ καλῆς ἀπληορίας
καὶ τοῦ ταπεινοῦ τρεῖς βίβλους Ἐυαγρίου
οὐδὲν βλαβήσῃ, μᾶλλον ὠφέλεια σοι
γενήσεται καὶ γνώσεως ὄψῃ βάθος
ἐκ πράξεως ὑψοῦν σε πρὸς θεωρίαν.
Εἰ δὲ βλέπεις ποῦ σῖτον ἐν ζιζανίοις·
ἀλλ᾽ οὖν ἄριστος ὡς γεωργὸς ἐκτρέπου
ἐκεῖνα, σῖτον συλλέγων εἰδημόνως·
ἔνεστι γὰρ καὶ κρεῖσσον ἐκ τῶν χειρόνων.

Anon. (c.12th–14th century), 'Iambs on the
words of the holy fathers', ll. 52–60
(Amaduzzi [1773]: 2: 29–30)

CONTENTS

ACKNOWLEDGEMENTS

This project has been several years in the making and would not have come to bear such fruit as it does without the support, assistance and encouragement of many parties, who are of course in no way responsible for the views expressed herein (or, indeed, the mistakes that they may very well have warned me about). I am therefore happy to confess my indebtedness to the following persons: Revd Dr John Behr, Prof. Peter Brown, Revd Dr Adam Cooper, Revd Dr Jeremy Driscoll OSB, Revd Dr Luke Dysinger OSB, M. Paul Géhin, Prof. C.T.R. Hayward, Revd Dr Daniël Hombergen OSCO, Revd Prof. Andrew Louth, Dr Barbara Müller, Dr Sara Parvis, Prof. Lorenzo Perrone, Revd Prof. Mark Sheridan OSB, Revd Dr Columba Stewart OSB, Dr M.K. Törönen, Revd Dr Tim Vivian, Rt Revd Dr Kallistos Ware, Mrs Josephine Williams and the audiences who have, with great patience, endured talks on matters pertaining to this book that I have delivered in Durham, Edinburgh, Oxford, Pisa and Rome.

I am also grateful to the hardy souls in the Greek reading group of the Durham Patristic Seminar, who indulged me by spending a term looking over Evagrius' *Scholia on Job*.

During the course of this work, it was my great pleasure to be able to consult several volumes from the extraordinary library bequeathed to the University of Durham by Dr Routh; the Staff of University Archives and Special Collections in the search room at Palace Green Library were indefatigably helpful in this connection.

Deserving of special thanks are Dr Carol Harrison, who graciously entertained my first mention of this proposal when I was up to my eyeballs in writing a doctoral thesis and was thus unable to offer her any convincing reasons for thinking I would ever bring it off, and Dr Richard Stoneman, who has been a model of reliable support and civility even as I allowed several deadlines to slip past unheeded.

My wife, Rachel, has cheerfully tolerated an interest in Evagrius that must seem obsessive and perhaps unhealthy; our children have regularly obliged me with welcome distractions.

But my profoundest debt in all matters Evagrian is assuredly to Fr Gabriel Bunge. His publications have been constantly illuminating and rewarding, the interest he has shown in this project, humbling. This book is therefore respectfully dedicated to him.

Durham
Christmas 2004

ABBREVIATIONS

CCR	*Coptic Church Review*
CPG	*Corpus Christianorum Clavis Patrum Graecorum*
CSCO	Corpus Scriptorum Christianorum Orientalium
CSEL	Corpus Scriptorum Ecclesiasticorum Latinorum
DP	*Doctrina patrum de incarnatione Verbi*
GCS	Die griechischen christlichen Schriftsteller der erster Jahrhunderte (Berlin: Akademie-Verlag)
HL	*Historia Lausiaca*
HM	*Historia Monachorum*
KG	*Kephalaia Gnostica* (Gnostic Chapters)
LCL	Loeb Classical Library (Heinemann: London)
LXX	Septuagint
Mus	*Le Muséon*
OCA	Orientalia Christiana Analecta
OCP	*Orientalia Christiana Periodica*
OUP	Oxford University Press
PG	Patrologia graeca
PIOS	Pontificum Institutum Orientalium Studiorum
PO	Patrologia orientalis
PTS	Patristische Texte und Studien (Berlin: Walter de Gruyter)
SA	Studia Anselmiana (Rome: Sant' Anselmo)
SC	Sources chrétiennes (Paris: Cerf)
SM	*Studia Monastica*
SP	*Studia Patristica*
TU	Texte und Untersuchungen

Evagrius Ponticus, as depicted on p. 778 of MS 285 in the collection of the Library of the Armenian Patriarchate of Jerusalem; on this manuscript, see further Nira Stone, *The Kaffa Lives of the Desert Fathers: A Study in Armenian Manuscript Illumination* (Leuven: Peeters, 1997), in which this image appears as illustration 43, plate 18. The author wishes to thank His Beatitude, Archbishop Torkom Manoogian, the Armenian Patriarch of Jerusalem, as well as Dr Stone, for their permission to reproduce the image here.

Part I

INTRODUCTION

1

WHY EVAGRIUS
MATTERS

Evagrius was, and still is, the teacher of prayer par excellence for the Greek Christian tradition.[1] That fact alone justifies the study, transmission and perpetuation of his writing. But there are further reasons to read his works. Evagrius lived in the Egyptian desert during the age of the great desert saints. In fact, he was the disciple of Macarius the Great and also studied with Macarius of Alexandria; he visited John the Seer of the Thebaïd; his teaching influenced Palladius and Cassian, who were both important witnesses to the desert saints. Unlike most of the desert saints, however, Evagrius left behind a substantial collection of writings. He thus provides us with firsthand evidence for what the theology of the desert fathers could be like. Evagrius lived during a period of great flourishing for Christian literature; among his contemporaries are numbered Augustine, Jerome, Basil the Great and John Chrysostom. Even more significantly, Evagrius' own life intersected the lives of Basil, Gregory Nazianzen, Rufinus and Melania the Elder. The last three of those people, at least, maintained correspondence with Evagrius, even when he was set up in the desert. In this way, Evagrius kept involved in intellectual exchanges that were foundational for the development of Byzantine spirituality. Thanks to Rufinus' Latin translations of his works and Cassian's dissemination of what he had learnt from Evagrius, he also exercised some influence on the development of the spiritual life of the Latin Middle Ages. Finally, Evagrius' name figures prominently (and, regrettably, much to his detriment) in a series of debates about how Christian piety could or should relate to pagan learning during the transitional period of Justinian's reign. In a small way, then, Evagrius' fate – whether justifiable or not – is indicative of the cultural negotiations that accompanied the birth of the Christian Roman Empire of the east.

Apart from the inherent interest of his writings – which any translator is more or less bound to feel with respect to an ancient author – and the light that it helps shed on the golden age of patristic literature, Evagrius deserves to be better known because it is no exaggeration to say that the recovery and re-construction of his works is a success story for modern scholarship. For centuries, Evagrius was known only, if at all, as a discredited Origenist theologian and (notwithstanding the high regard that some of his works enjoyed pseudonymously) he languished on the margins of respectability. Over the last century, however, dozens of previously lost works have been discovered, edited and studied, with the result that the clouds that have long darkened Evagrius' reputation have been at least somewhat dispersed. Even if he has not yet been swept up to the lofty heights of being a 'classic' fourth-century author on a par with Athanasius or Augustine, at least Evagrius has been retrieved from the dustbins of history. Research into all aspects of Evagrius' life, thought and works has proceeded steadily and this research has brought together scholars at the international level (most of the great contributions have been made by French and German scholars). Although there is still much to do, future research can build on a broad basis of primary sources and when future researchers carry out their work, they will be able to do so while perching on the shoulders of giants. But to understand why this work is necessary, and to appreciate its significance, what is needed is an overview of Evagrius' life and the reception of his works.

2

EVAGRIUS' LIFE
AND AFTER-LIFE

'One who prays truly will be a theologian, and one who is a theologian will pray truly.' Evagrius makes that claim at *On prayer* 61 and, in so doing, he stated in lapidary form the patristic ideal of how theology relates to the spiritual life that was taken up in due course by the Byzantine Fathers and subsequently enshrined in Eastern Orthodoxy – to say nothing whatever of his impact on the Latin West, as mediated through John Cassian.[1] For Evagrius, theology and prayer are mutually implicated in the Christian life; spiritual growth and maturity are necessarily connected to good theology. Evagrius speaks with authority regarding theology as well as prayer. The earliest writing of his that we have is a letter (*On the faith*) written from Constantinople to the brethren he had left behind in his native Cappadocia. In it, Evagrius expounds very clearly and very precisely on the orthodox confession of the full divinity of the Son and of the Holy Spirit, as against those who were challenging those claims (the Arians and Pneumatochians, respectively).[2] As the deacon and assistant of Gregory the Theologian, Evagrius accompanied him to the First Council of Constantinople in 381, where he aided Gregory in the fight against the Arians;[3] so it is plausible to think of *On the faith* as Evagrius doing his bit for the cause. The bedrock, then, of his whole literary production is this confession of doctrinal orthodoxy. More specifically, the bedrock of Evagrius' writings is the confession that he will have learnt from his time with Basil the Great and Gregory Nazianzen. Although the full extent of their impact upon his development remains at present an open question, a strong prima facie case can be advanced for supposing that Evagrius was, in every sense, a product of Cappadocia.

5

Cappadocia: birth to 379

Around the year 345, Evagrius was born in Ibora, Pontus, a city that was probably not far from Annisa, where Basil retreated in about 358 to establish his monastic life and, indeed, where Basil's sister Macrina had retired into monastic life.[4] Evagrius was the son of a *chorepiskopos*, or 'country bishop', whose responsibilities are aptly summarised in the gloss on that term in an ancient Latin translation of the *Lausiac history*: 'a priest responsible for many churches, whom they call *periodeutês* [i.e., "circuit-riders"]'.[5] Evagrius may well have been named after his father, if we take Gregory Nazianzen's *Letter* 3 as referring to Evagrius Ponticus.[6] Some manuscripts further describe Evagrius' father as being 'a nobleman, of the better sort in the city' and it is possible that he owned an olive grove.[7] What can be inferred about Evagrius' education would support the conclusion that he came from a family of some means: even though his later writings are not ostentatious (as one would expect from a monk), it is possible to find evidence in them that he benefited from training in philosophy and rhetoric, and had a gentlemanly appreciation of mathematics, medicine and astronomy.[8]

Evagrius need not have gone far from home to acquire this learning. We know that in about the year 375 the people of Neocaesarea had invited Basil to teach there – as, indeed, Basil's father had done before him.[9] We can therefore deduce that it was a sufficiently large city for instruction to be possible there. Located near Ibora, Neocaesarea seems a likely place for Evagrius to have studied as a youth. In view of how advanced his education seems to have been, he probably completed the standard cycle of liberal studies. If this is correct, then he would have studied in Neocaesarea from 352/3 until perhaps as late as 373. He would have been a precocious student: at the tender age of fifteen, he already impressed Gregory Nazianzen as needing no further eloquence.[10] (Gregory was in the vicinity around that time collaborating with Basil on their anthology of Origen, the *Philokalia*, and his association with Evagrius during this period probably accounts for Evagrius' first exposure to the great Alexandrian master.)[11] Attaining eloquence was a critical element in the classical liberal education, since it fitted the youth for a life in the public domain. Education in the post-classical world was the domain of the wealthy, or at least the aspirant who could gain patronage from the wealthy.[12] In either case, it is fair to suppose that Evagrius came from a reasonably affluent background.

Even without the ability to be more precise concerning the social situation of Evagrius' family, it seems overwhelmingly likely that his family would have moved in circles that overlapped with those of Basil's family – if for no other reason than that Evagrius' father was a clergyman and Basil came from a prominent Christian family.[13] It is entirely possible that Evagrius would have encountered Basil during his days as a student. In any event, Evagrius seems to have fallen in with Basil's set during the 370s. In his capacity as bishop of Cappadocia, Basil made Evagrius a reader.[14] Presumably, Basil would not have ordained Evagrius, even to a minor order, without knowing him quite well – and this certainly fits with the warm terms that Evagrius will later use to describe Basil.[15] It is also likely that Basil brought Evagrius into the monastic life.[16] Indeed, it is more than likely that when Evagrius left Cappadocia for Constantinople upon Basil's death in 379, he did so as a monk.[17]

Constantinople: 379–82

Moved by an unexpected event that he tantalisingly fails to disclose, Evagrius left Cappadocia and made his way to Constantinople. It was likely Gregory Nazianzen's transfer to Constantinople that attracted Evagrius, a small-town boy who was well aware that the Devil's deceits are thickly strewn throughout cities,[18] to the capital on the Bosphorus. In explaining to unnamed countrymen why he tarries so far from home, Evagrius alludes to 'a certain longing for godly teachings, and for the philosophy pertaining to them' that led him to study with Gregory, 'the mouthpiece of Christ' – and it may be significant that, in pleading tones, he writes, 'a little time, I beg you, grant us a little time!' He indicates that his conversation with Gregory (and perhaps others, since he refers to 'the society of holy men') is instilling in him 'a habit of contemplation that is not easily lost'.[19] In his plea, several characteristics of Evagrius' theological programme are in evidence. For Evagrius, theology is an undertaking that occurs within a community (it is social), as a learned and experienced teacher instructs a disciple (pedagogical) about how to live (practical) in such a way as to be constantly orientated toward God (contemplative). The foundations of Evagrian theology are therefore edifying dialogue and the habit of moral reform, both of which facilitate communion with God.

To that end, Evagrius had an excellent teacher in Gregory. If, as seems plausible, Evagrius had known Gregory since he was a child;[20] if his requests for 'a little time' are not pure rhetoric;[21] if we take seriously his claim to be advancing in understanding thanks to Gregory – then it would seem likely that Evagrius came to Constantinople expressly for the purpose of pursuing advanced instruction at Gregory's feet. For his part, Gregory was in all likelihood only too happy to have at his disposal such a precociously talented assistant, because things were going rather badly for him in his new see. In fact, Gregory may very well have invited Evagrius to join him, in anticipation of the theological controversies that lay ahead.[22]

The thirty-odd months of Gregory's tenure in Constantinople were characterised by tenacious advances among the various opponents of Nicea, and brilliant ripostes by Gregory on behalf of the small and beleaguered proponents of Nicea. It would appear that Gregory was induced into coming in order to pave the way for the new emperor, Theodosius, a Spaniard of unmistakably Nicene leanings, in a staunchly anti-Nicene city.[23] Evagrius proved his worth in fighting at close quarters. As is evident from *On the faith*, Evagrius thoroughly assimilated the Cappadocian perspective on Nicene theology – so thoroughly, in fact, that he was in all probability involved in the drafting and editing of the great orations that earned for Gregory the sobriquet 'the Theologian' (an exceedingly rare honour among the Greek fathers).[24] His many brilliant accomplishments notwithstanding, Gregory was harried out of Constantinople as a result of the Council of 381. His successor, Nectarius, was a devout man of senatorial rank but an unseasoned candidate, designated for the archbishop's throne though as yet unbaptised.[25] Surrounded by hostile Eunomians, Anomoeans, Macedonian Pneumatochians and, perhaps, an Arian or two, Nectarius was surely happy to have at his disposal such a 'skilled dialectician' as Evagrius.[26]

The up-and-coming controversialist from Pontus must have cut a dashing figure in Nicene circles, with his clerical dignity, handsome appearance and elegant clothing.[27] But Evagrius' time in Constantinople was not entirely about pummelling heretics, and his good looks precipitated his downfall. He initiated an ill-advised, if unconsummated, romance with the wife of a prominent functionary, in consequence of which he had to leave the city very quickly.[28] But where to go next? Because he had compromised himself – and that with the wife of a powerful politician from Cappadocia! – Evagrius would have found it impossible to return to his community near the Black Sea. Perhaps it was in a spirit of repentance, pricked in conscience as he would have been at having come so perilously close to adultery, that he set his face to the holy city of Jerusalem.

Palestine en route to Egypt: 382

When Evagrius arrived in Palestine, he was deeply troubled in spirit. Tormented in turn by thoughts of lust and of his reputation, he appears to have abandoned his monastic vocation for nearly six months.[29] But brooding silently over the problems did not help him. Eventually, Evagrius confided his woes to the indomitable Melania the Elder, who had herself expressed concern about his protracted sickness. Daughter of a Roman consul from the patrician Antonia clan and widow of a Roman prefect, Melania had settled in Jerusalem after passing through Egypt and divesting herself of huge amounts of money there.[30] In the Holy Land, she founded a double-monastery (i.e., a monastery for men joined to one for women) with a mandate to care for pilgrims. Her patronage also supported scholarly endeavours such as Rufinus' translations from Greek into Latin; Melania herself was steeped in the works of Origen and was doubtless a formidable theologian. She therefore stood in continuity with the kind of highly literate asceticism that Evagrius would have come to know in Cappadocia. And this is to say nothing of her commitment to promoting Nicene orthodoxy, which would have further strengthened the bonds between her and the wayward Evagrius. This affinity gave weight to her counsel when, upon learning of Evagrius' sad story, she exhorted him to 'give me your word before God that you will have as your goal the monastic life'.[31] Encouraged by her, Evagrius gave his word, received his monastic habit anew from Melania (or rather, from Rufinus) on Easter Sunday, 9 April 383[32] and resolved to travel to the world's foremost centre for the monastic life – the deserts of Lower Egypt. One imagines that Melania had a hand in Evagrius' choice of Egypt for his next destination and undoubtedly her contacts there were very useful for him.[33]

Egypt: 383 to death

If Evagrius' purpose in coming to Constantinople was to increase in wisdom and virtue while assisting Gregory Nazianzen, then his decision to set up in Nitria, Egypt, can be understood as furthering that goal – less the unwanted distractions and temptations of city life, of course. Desert life, as Evagrius would come to learn, has enough distractions and temptations of its own. It also has an intensity that Evagrius would have been little prepared for. Regardless of such attainments as having been Gregory's theological right hand, having been made a monk by Rufinus, or perhaps even bearing letters of introduction from Melania, Evagrius would have to learn quite quickly that he was an outsider who had come among the Egyptians to learn their wisdom.[34] It was probably this wisdom, and indubitably the means of attaining to it, that Evagrius sought to promote in his monastic writings as will be evident from the translated texts that appear below. So it will be worthwhile to consider in some detail what this life was like.

At Nitria, Evagrius entered one of the fifty or so 'monasteries' – by which we understand individual residences – under the supervision of an abba, or 'father'.[35] The abba would have been the seniormost of the eight priests at Nitria and, as such, would have the prerogative of celebrating the divine offices, preaching and maintaining discipline.[36] The eight priests together would have presumably made up the governing assembly of the community, also known as 'the Elders' or simply 'the Fathers.'[37]

Daily life in Nitria aimed at promoting structure, order and discipline, but we have precious little specific information about it.[38] Most of the Nitrian monks' time was spent in one of their 'monasteries': even the office of the Ninth Hour was recited, not in the church (which was reserved for the weekend synaxes), but in the cells.[39] Manual labour was certainly practised there, though, in Evagrius' case, this would have meant scribal work – rather than the usual business of weaving flax.[40] As for their food, seven bakeries provided bread, there was a kitchen and a garden: these services appear to have been run by the monks themselves and, as such, seem to have fallen under the jurisdiction of the steward.[41] Wine and cakes were also available for purchase, though it may well be the case that the purveyors were merchants from outside the establishment.[42] (Such merchants would not have been the only visitors to Nitria: there was also a guesthouse, where pilgrims could lodge for up to two or three years.) Physicians – some of whom may have been monks – attended to the sick.[43] It has been observed of a neighbouring settlement that 'the life of a monk in Scetis was ordinarily barren of incident, and years would pass with little or nothing to vary the ordinary routine'.[44] So it was, it seems, for Evagrius in Nitria.

Evagrius remained there from 383 to 384/385, whereupon, in keeping with an established convention, he retired to the remoter location of Kellia.[45] There, Evagrius apprenticed himself to Macarius the Great; his days with Macarius set the seal on Evagrius' monastic life and on his theological outlook.[46] As his disciple at Kellia, he would have lived within the same small complex as his teacher and attended to his needs. The relationship of teacher and disciple was tremendously important, and the relative isolation of life at Kellia insured that this was so. (Monastic cells were sufficiently far apart in Kellia that chanting the psalter in one cell ought not to be audible to the nearest neighbour.) The monks only gathered on the weekend, with some of them travelling up to four miles to meet at the church in Kellia. Privacy – and thus, to some extent, autonomy – characterised the monastic life there. There was a priest in charge of the communal worship, as was Macarius the Great, and this priest could exercise authority over the monks there. For instance, Isaac the Priest is reported to have expelled a dandified monk.[47] But Isaac also knew that the priest's instructions could be ignored.[48] Rather more authority, we may suppose, rested with the spiritual guide of a 'synod' or 'fellowship', such as Macarius the Great was or, indeed, as Evagrius himself became.[49] From scattered references in Palladius' account and in the *Coptic life*, it seems that these groups would assemble for mutual encouragement and exhortation, as well as to discuss Scripture, prayer and the spiritual life. Their discussions in all likelihood provided the first venues for most of Evagrius' theological work. These theological reflections were focused, and so intensified, by the way of life that they shared. In keeping with the stricter regimen at Kellia, however, there is no evidence of wine-sellers or guesthouses in Kellia during Evagrius' day. Such pilgrims as arrived would have sought accommodation with the monks they visited.

Evagrius stayed in Kellia for the remainder of his life, from 385 to 399/400.[50] He gave himself over chiefly to asceticism (about which, more anon), to hospitality, to teaching and to the study of Scripture. As we have already noted, Evagrius became a respected teacher in his own right, with a 'synod' or 'fellowship' learning from him.[51] He had two particularly noteworthy disciples: Cassian, whose Latin writings popularised Egyptian monasticism for the West, and Palladius, who dedicated to the Emperor's chamberlain a book that recorded his memories of what life among the desert saints was like. These two were not the only ones to seek out Evagrius for his teaching and advice. In the *Coptic life of Evagrius*, we read that pilgrims flocked to his cell to seek counsel and knowledge.[52] The stream of pilgrims was such that Evagrius had a steward who maintained a purse of some 200 gold coins so as to defray the expenses incurred through hospitality.[53]

Evagrius' teaching ministry was extended, too, through his writings. Although he had maintained a steady stream of theologically informed correspondence with numerous friends in Palestine, his greatest outpouring of literary effort belongs to this period. His account of the monastic life, *Praktikos*, was written at the request of a certain Anatolius who seems to have been at Melania's establishment in Palestine;[54] his exhortatory *Virgin* was, in my view, quite possibly intended for the redoubtable desert mother, Syncletica, and it was almost certainly this that he sent to the Deaconess Severa when she was unable to make the journey from the Holy Land to Kellia; his most concise account of the mystical heights of theology is a letter written to Rufinus in Palestine (the *Great letter*). He wrote a beginner's guide to the monastic life (*Causes*) that is of such general applicability that it could have been despatched almost anywhere to anyone. His treatise *Thoughts* showcases a remarkable talent for introspection and discernment that would be of use to advanced practitioners of monasticism. Evagrius also left behind a massive corpus of notes (or 'scholia') on various passages from Scripture. His preferred method of expositing the deep meaning of a given passage is, as like as not, through allegory: his notes lead the reader to the 'spiritual sense' of the passage through the method of interpretation that had been familiar in Egypt from at least the time of Philo. Commenting upon this sense, or level of meaning, more often than not provides Evagrius an opportunity to say something about Christ. And it is this Christocentric reading that provides, for Evagrius, the 'real' meaning of Scripture. But this is not to say that he had no interest in the text as such. His *Notes on Job*, in particular, demonstrate quite clearly that Evagrius was aware of the fact that his Bible – that is, the Jewish Greek translation known as the Septuagint – could, and in some cases should, be compared to other versions in order to establish his reading of it.

The level of Evagrius' productivity during his years in Egypt is unmatched by any other desert father of that age, which makes him an invaluable primary source for the theology of the desert. All the evidence suggests that he was an admired teacher whose works were in great demand. Certainly he was popular enough to have attracted unfavourable notice.[55]

Evagrius also maintained an outspoken apologetic for Nicene orthodoxy. When three demons cleverly disguised themselves as clergymen and came to him to discuss matters pertaining to the faith, he promptly undid them 'with spiritual wisdom' and revealed the errors of their respective Arian, Eunomian and Apollinarian beliefs.[56] He also travelled on occasion to Alexandria in order to confute the philosophers.[57] He would sometimes leave Kellia for other reasons. Once he went to Alexandria to persuade an errant monk to return to the desert. On another occasion, Evagrius accompanied Ammonius on an eighteen-day journey from Kellia to consult the great Seer of the Thebaïd, John of Lycopolis, for his explanation of a mystical experience. At the peak of his renown, Theophilus of Alexandria sought to make him the bishop of Thmuis, but Evagrius avoided such a fate by fleeing to Palestine.[58] Clearly, Evagrius did not have an insurmountable preference for staying put.[59] As an accomplished ascetic, he would have had considerable discretion in matters related to the struggle and could therefore have decided under certain circumstances that travelling into a city (for instance) was appropriate.

About his ascetic practices, it can confidently be said that Evagrius devoted himself to a regimen so rigorous that his health was seriously damaged; this may well have contributed to his early demise. (In an age when famous ascetics like Anthony were renowned for longevity, Evagrius' biographer seems to have been acutely conscious that a span of only about fifty-five years seems paltry – which probably accounts for the haste with which he mentions that Evagrius filled up those few years with tremendous accomplishments.)[60] He ate only once per day.[61] When he did eat, his diet was extremely limited. He assiduously abstained from lettuce, green vegetables, fruit, grapes and meat; he refrained from bathing and took no cooked food; eventually, he ruined his digestive tract and probably suffered from urinary tract stones.[62] He slept no more than a third of the night, devoting the rest of his time to prayer, contemplation and study of Scripture.[63] To keep himself awake, he was in the habit of walking in the courtyard of his cell. He scrupulously attended to his thoughts and, based on these observations, prepared a dossier of verses from Scripture to be cast in the face of attacking demons.[64] If Evagrius fell victim to such an attack, he would mortify himself by undertaking spectacular measures to expose his body to the ravages of nature.[65] This remarkable lack of self-regard took its toll and in due course Evagrius was firmly instructed by his elders in Kellia to moderate his habits. But by the time some vaguely described symptoms became manifest and Evagrius' health was obviously deteriorating, the physical harm had been done. Shortly after receiving communion in the Church at Kellia on the feast of Epiphany, Evagrius died.

The aftermath: controversies from the fifth to mid-sixth centuries, and beyond

The evidence that can be gleaned from the dedications of Evagrius' writings, his lines of correspondence, the reports of the Palestinian pilgrims in the *Historia monachorum in Aegypto*, Palladius' recollections and the theological vision of Cassian, all point to the conclusion that Evagrius was a respected spiritual master. There are some indications that he was not entirely free from criticism, but nothing from his lifetime suggests that he was considered theologically suspect.[66] But all of that changed abruptly in the years after his death.

In fact, it would appear that as early as one year after his death, things began to go badly for Evagrius' peers. Disputes about the appropriation of Origen's theological legacy (not least his technique of Scriptural interpretation, and his Trinitarian theology) began to break out in the monasteries of the desert.[67] The responsibility for pacifying the situation fell to Theophilus, the pope of Alexandria. A consummate politician, he appears to have changed his loyalties: first he supported Origen's supporters, but later he allied himself to Origen's detractors. His precise motivations are difficult to determine and the records preserve accusations and counter-accusations that range in topic from theological minutiae to financial malfeasance. What is reasonably clear is that he inaugurated a campaign of clearing out the monks who were, on the evidence of Palladius' *Lausiac history*, kindred spirits to Evagrius. These monks were chiefly from the circle of Ammonius and his brothers, Dioscorus, Eusebius and Euthymius (who were collectively known as the 'Tall Brothers' because of their unusual height), and they were ultimately driven out of Egypt by Theophilus; they took shelter with John Chrysostom in Constantinople.[68] In furtherance of his campaign, Theophilus articulated a dichotomy that has become deeply influential over the centuries as a way of characterising the controversy. In a letter he sent to Constantinople concerning 'such things as Origen blasphemously claims about the Son and the Holy Spirit',[69] Theophilus denounced a group of body-hating heretics inspired by Origen, and contrasted them to the pious, if perhaps a bit too simple, native Egyptian monks who were susceptible to theological crudities – both of which groups needed archiepiscopal intervention and correction:

> We anathematise not only Origen's heresies, but also the other attempt to stir up trouble in most monasteries. Even

if some savage and stupid people have babbled that it is necessary to conceive of God anthropomorphically, we have not kept silent but (since Christ has given us watchfulness) we overturn this heresy, too, with instructions written in ecclesiastical letters.[70]

It is obvious that the trouble being stirred up in the monasteries came from the fact that these monasteries harboured both Origen's admirers and the rude and simple:

It is utterly clear that the thick spreading of Origen in the monasteries of the desert has not yet been prevented from sustaining those fond of the vomit of Origen's rash saying that 'the first man had no body' and, 'had his mind not sunk with sins, one [presumably, a body] would not have been dispatched'.[71]

Theophilus' references to the 'rash sayings' by Origen anticipate the ultimate condemnations of Origenism – a process in which it is often claimed that Evagrius' writings played a determinative role.[72] Specifically, Theophilus was castigating the claim that bodily existence resulted from a fall into sin, but for which creation would have been non-material.[73] It is easy to imagine how this view could have attained some currency among monks (if indeed we are to accept Theophilus' allegation that it did): an ascetic approach to Christianity could easily accommodate a belief that embodiment is in a very serious way a reminder of the fall of a 'mind . . . sunk with sins'. If that claim is accepted, it is very easy to imagine how Evagrius himself, a monastic theologian who promoted an allegorical interpretation to Scripture in the manner of Origen, could have embraced such a perspective about embodiment (and its corollaries: the Incarnation, Christology, salvation, eschatology . . .). But we shall need to consider what, if anything, this accusation tells us about Evagrius in due course.

What can confidently be said at once is that this dichotomy proved to be remarkably tenacious, inexplicably enduring even to the modern day. Perhaps the simplicity of this view recommends it to people – but it is untenable for several reasons. First, we can be quite confident that the contrast fails to do justice to the broad intellectual horizons of Coptic monasticism.[74] Second, it is clear even from anecdotal evidence that would initially seem to support Theophilus' dichotomy that things are much more complicated. The case of Abba

Arsenius is instructive: here we find a man competent to tutor the Emperor's sons who, upon finding himself in Kellia (at the same time as Evagrius, it can be noted), is asked why he has come to study at the feet of peasants; in response, Arsenius notes that he has not even 'learned the alphabet' of the Egyptians.[75] The salient claim is not that Arsenius is cultured and the peasants are not – that is an utterly banal point; what matters is that Arsenius (and others, no doubt, such as Evagrius) came to Egypt to learn from their experience. It is not so much a mistake to stress the difference in culture between Arsenius and the peasants, as it is a misleading thing to focus on. Even canny old peasants could very well have imbibed enough theology to preach effectively on the spiritual life. Third, although there undoubtedly were some philistine Egyptians in the monasteries of the day, it is far from clear that we ought to take at face value the pious ideal of being 'taught by God' and free from the baleful influence of secular culture.[76]

There are, then, several good reasons to decline from thinking that intellectual culture can be inferred from ethnicity – or, to put it otherwise, from thinking that educated Greeks such as Evagrius represent a Hellenistic intrusion into pure Coptic simplicity. It does not do to imagine that the monasteries in the desert were inhabited by an uneasy mixture of Coptic bumpkins and Greek philosophers. Whatever else one thinks of Theophilus and his politics, it is clear that his dichotomy is merely one way of characterising the situation – and it is also clear that his way does not correspond adequately to the rich diversity of the intellectual scene.

The impact of Theophilus' controversial writings was matched by Jerome's. His long friendship with Melania and Rufinus had soured and he had become embroiled in a letter-writing campaign and pamphlet warfare about the acceptability of Origen's theology. In this context, Jerome enjoys the dubious distinction of being the first person to implicate Evagrius in the sordid affair. In a letter written c.415 to Ctesiphon, Jerome drew Evagrius into the web of his sharp criticism of Origen and (perhaps more to the point) of his erstwhile friend, Rufinus.[77] In an accusation that is actually more substantial than it might seem (albeit one that is inapplicable in this case), Jerome claimed that Evagrius' spiritual counsels were untenable because they attempted to eliminate a constitutive element of human life – emotions. It is worth noting that, even in condemning Evagrius, Jerome does not avail himself of accusations that Evagrius spewed heresies of the sort that he claimed were found in Origen's

First principles; instead, Jerome contents himself with the far more circumspect allegation that Evagrius' theological anthropology is skewed.[78]

Guilt by association has a regrettable staying power. Between Theophilus' overly simplistic schematisation of the desert monks and Jerome's caustic insinuations of Origenist heresy, Evagrius' reputation was dealt a staggering blow. Even so, when the 'First Origenist Controversy' began with Theophilus attacking the errors of Origen that were embraced in various monasteries, Evagrius was a marginal figure at best.[79] It has been said of Evagrius (with a nod to Tacitus' *Agricola*) that he was *felix opportunitate mortis* – he died in good time – and some have supposed that only his death shielded him from being personally implicated in the debates.[80] But Evagrius' date of death is only conjectured and it is inadvisable to make too much of it: granting that Evagrius vanishes from the historical record *c.*399 is not enough to conclude that, had he been alive, he would have been revealed as the husbandman chiefly responsible for thickly sowing the seed of Origenian theology in the desert monasteries. And, in any event, what grounds have we for thinking that Evagrius' death would have preserved him from criticism? Origen's death as a confessor was not shielding him, so it is hard to see why a recently deceased monk ought to fare better. It should also be noted that all the surviving claims lodged against him during the First Origenist Controversy are explicable in purely topical terms and none of them ever accuses him of the metaphysical aberrations that have been associated with his name by modern scholars. (These claims are derived from the 'Second Origenist Controversy', and will be described below.) Even taking into account the extremely vague and remarkably vitriolic aspersions cast in Jerome's letter, Evagrius himself was not specifically accused of propagating Origenist errors for another century and a half.[81]

In the intervening time, his writings circulated from the Holy Land and it is probably also to this period that several anthologies of Evagriana are to be traced.[82] In addition to the original Greek, his works also spread in translation. We know that Rufinus translated some of Evagrius' works into Latin (and it seems that someone else did, too, since there are two Latin versions of *Virgin*), that numerous works were available in Coptic, and that a massive collection of Evagrian material appeared, probably before the sixth century, in Syriac. Thanks to the Syriac translations, Evagrius' works (in whole or in part) spread across the Christian Orient as far as Mongolia:

we have evidence for further translations into Arabic, Armenian, Ge'ez, Georgian and Sogdian.[83] For reasons that will emerge, that flurry of translations has in due course proved to be providential.

This intense rate of translation allows us to infer that Evagrius' works enjoyed considerable demand. Apart from this, we know rather little about how his reputation fared in the fifth century. But by the sixth century, his name was overtaken by controversies that are still very much alive. The first evidence that all was not well comes from the correspondence of Barsanuphius, the Great Old Man of Gaza, and the Other Old Man, his disciple John. In four letters in particular, the two respond to the question of how – or indeed, whether – one may read Origen, Didymus and Evagrius.[84] It is clear from these letters that the third and most theologically advanced instalment of Evagrius' great trilogy, the *Gnostic chapters*, was causing quite a stir. Both Barsanuphius and John dissuade the brother in question from the 'speculation of the Greeks' and from this we are to understand that the controversies surrounding Origen's name and legacy were beginning to flare up again.

Barsanuphius' rejection of the three authors was categorical, but John's was more qualified: John could envisage that some good might be found in their works, but could more readily envisage that a monk's reading time would be more profitably spent in the study of Scripture. Sensing John's rather more generous attitude, the brother sent him another question, plaintively requesting clarification: 'But ought we not to read even Evagrius' works?'[85] John acknowledged that with care it could make for spiritually profitable reading. John's moderate response recalls the temperance with which delicate issues could be handled by spiritual guides.[86] Though it may seem strange to say so, John's response also demonstrates a frankly unfortunate development in the reception of Evagrius' writings: by quietly accepting the distinction of Evagrius' works into the practical and useful on the one hand and the speculative and questionable on the other, John endorses a bifurcated view of Evagrius that subsequently became historically normative for the Greek tradition. The great pitfall in this moderate advice is that it may well not be possible to separate out Evagrius' (supposedly salutary) ascetic counsels from his (putatively problematic) mystical theology. But this is to anticipate a problem that only becomes truly acute after the Greek originals are lost, and we shall need to return to it in due course. And, in any case, one has to appreciate John's discretion.[87]

An altogether different approach is found in the *Life of Kyriakos*, written by Cyril of Scythopolis. Cyril relates how, in the callowness of his youth, he ventured an opinion not unlike Barsanuphius' when he met the old monk Kyriakos. Kyriakos' response is explosive.

> The teachings about pre-existence are not neutral and free of danger, but dangerous, harmful and blasphemous. To convince you, I shall attempt to describe their manifold ungodliness in a few words. They say that Christ is not one of the Trinity; they say that the bodies we have from the resurrection will pass to complete destruction, and Christ's first; they say that the Holy Trinity did not fashion the world and that at the Restoration all rational beings – even the very demons – will be able to fashion universes; they say that our bodies will be raised ethereal and spherical at the Resurrection, and so too they claim that even the body of the Lord was raised thus; they say that we become equals to Christ at the Restoration. What hell, then, spewed out these things? They have not learnt them from the God who spoke through the prophets and apostles – not so! – but they have retrieved these filthy and irreverent teachings from Pythagoras and Plato, from Origen, Evagrius, and Didymus.[88]

This tirade elegantly summarises the claims which from that time on will constitute 'Origenism' – and which will also exercise a tremendous influence upon modern scholarly evaluation of Evagrius in particular.[89] With reference to philosophical theology, the salient dimensions of 'Origenism' thus condemned may be summarised as follows: a sharp distinction is made between Christ and the Trinity – or, more specifically, between Christ and the *Logos*, because implicit in the further accusations is an emphasis on the evil of material (hence, the assertion that there will be a non-material resurrection, and that the Trinity is not answerable for creation) and this emphasis compromises any possibility of straightforwardly identifying Christ as the *Logos*; corresponding to this view of creation and of Christ is the assertion that, when creation is purged of matter and restored to God, all the rational creatures will eventually enjoy a status equal to that of the rational being Christ.[90] In historical terms, what is most notable about Kyriakos' fiery rejection of Evagrius (along with Didymus and Origen) is that it was contemporaneous with a shift in how Christians were thinking of their monastic heritage. The comparison of Evagrius and associates to Pythagoras and Plato is telling: around the same time that Justinian cut imperial funds to the Platonic Academy and thus in effect drove the Platonic Diadochus and his handful of colleagues into the Syrian Orient for some years, Cyril and other likeminded people (such as the anonymous redactor of the *Sayings of the desert fathers*) were busy re-imagining a history of monasticism in which intellectual culture was irreconcilably at odds with God-given sanctity.[91] One of the lingering after-effects of this age, then, is that to this day people are disposed to perceive a tension in Evagrius between his intellectual accomplishments and his moral teachings; the former are regarded as neo-Platonic accretions that compromise the integrity of the latter. But it is to be doubted whether the tumultuous cultural transformations that marked Justinian's reign actually provide a meaningful insight into the events of an earlier age.

Justinian's efforts to re-fashion the Roman Empire into a wholly Christian society were not the only factors that influenced the debates that increasingly centred on Evagrius' writings. The question of Evagrius was driven further, no doubt, by a raging controversy that was (again) being fought within the monasteries – the 'Second Origenist Controversy'. Quite apart from the description of the controversy as found in the records preserved by Cyril of Scythopolis, we know that around 512–15 a scribe and monk from Edessa named Stephen bar Sudaili, who had settled in the Holy Land, was drawing unfavourable attention to himself owing to his purportedly pantheistic writings.[92] Stephen has been provisionally identified as the author of the *Book of Hierotheos*, a work that attributes itself to the teacher of Denys the Areopagite.[93] The teaching of that book – and indeed the teaching for which Stephen is sharply criticised by Philoxenus of Mabbug – can be described as a heady cocktail of neo-Platonic cosmology (as mediated through Christians such as Denys and Origen) and pantheistic eschatology, with a stiff dose of dubiously monophysite Christology.[94] If it is correct that the *Book of Hierotheos* originated from this milieu (whether by Stephen's hand or not is irrelevant), one can readily appreciate why a vigorous response by guardians of orthodoxy such as Philoxenus and Kyriakos seemed in order. In the *Book of Hierotheos*, one reads of precisely the kinds of speculative flights that Kyriakos warned Cyril of Scythopolis about. Given the turbulence already manifest in Palestine, Stephen's mere presence would have been a provocation. And it is not without significance that Stephen's writings are identified using categories and language characteristic of the condemnations of 'Origenism'.

Now the church historian Evagrius Scholasticus follows Cyril in identifying the epicentre of the turbulence as the New Laura of the Monastery of St Sabas,[95] where the in-fighting became so fierce that

the Emperor was eventually obliged to intervene. The imperial intervention took the form of condemning the excesses of 'Origenism'
(or perhaps the speculations of Origen himself),[96] and this condemnation was one of three that were made in fairly rapid succession.
Consequently, condemnations of Origenism were re-iterated at
Constantinople III (= Sixth Ecumenical Council, 680/1), Nicaea II
(= Seventh Ecumenical Council, 787) and Constantinople IV (869).[97]
The unhappy Alexandrian trio – Origen, Didymus, Evagrius – were
seen as central to the problem and were consequently anathematised.
So, for a period of some three and a half centuries, Evagrius' reputation was roundly trounced. In more recent times, it has been argued
in a scholarly article and, subsequently, in a tremendously influential book, that the phrases used to represent Origenism in the
condemnation are to be traced back to Evagrius' *Gnostic chapters*.[98] In
due course, we will come back to the revival of Evagrian studies in
the modern period and the impact of the condemnations on the
modern studies; for the moment, it suffices to say that Evagrius'
reputation was deeply compromised by the events in Palestine.

But not everyone despised Evagrius after this. The temperate view
expressed so judiciously by John of Gaza still found its adherents
among those who wanted to retrieve elements of Evagrian asceticism.
His monastic writings continued to be read and valued for centuries,
as is evident from occasional references to 'Abba Evagrius' in such
classic compilations of Byzantine monasticism as the eleventh-
century *Synagogê* of Paul Evergetinos and the *Philokalia* of Nikodimos
the Hagiorite (published in Venice in 1782). Nikodimos, in particular, seems to have valued Evagrius for his psychological insight,
since he selected for inclusion in his *Philokalia* Evagrius' *Thoughts*
and *Causes* (and, in fact, *On prayer* – though Nikodimos ascribed
it to Neilos of Ancyra). If it is the case that Evagrius' thought was
influential in the development of later 'mystico-pantheism' as repre-
sented by Stephen bar Sudaili, it is no less the case that Evagrius
was influential in the development of orthodox Byzantine ascetic
theology.[99]

To mention but one name, Maximus the Confessor's theology is
unthinkable without the precedent of Evagrius' path-finding work.[100]
In Maximus' theology, Evagrius' theology is clarified and rendered
more profound; here, a comparison to Maximus' treatment of
Gregory Nazianzen's theology might be ventured. Be that as it may,
what is most important is that one need not think of this as always
being a process of recovering the good bits of an erstwhile heretic
from his overall excesses; that way of looking at things is heavily

laden with undefended presuppositions to the effect that the heretical tradition stemming from Evagrius' works is somehow more
authentically Evagrian than any other tradition. What happened
here, as elsewhere, amounts to nothing more or less than the creative
and critical reception of earlier material that is the driving force of
theological tradition.

In a syllabus of ascetic theology written perhaps in the twelfth
century, we find a good statement of this process:

> But if from good greed and humility
> you seek the three books of Evagrius,
> you will be hindered by nothing; rather,
> they will be useful to you, who shall see
> the depth of wisdom elevating you
> from ethical deeds to contemplation.
> And if you should see some grain 'mongst the tares,
> like an excellent farmer turn aside
> to them, gathering the grain skilfully:
> for better things come from the lesser ones.[101]

The implied caution is surprisingly gentle – skill is needed, but
nothing hinders the reader from following Evagrius' programme of
spiritual development.

Evagrius' works were not always treated with such tact and discretion. Even though there is no justification for presupposing that
Byzantine theologians categorically believed that Evagrius was a
heretic in need of correction, one can nevertheless sometimes find
outspoken criticism, or outright denunciation, of Evagrius in works
deeply indebted to him. John Climacus, for instance, sharply disowns
Evagrius even as he propagates so much of Evagrius' ascetic theory
– a remarkable backhanded compliment.[102] Similarly, the seventh-
or eighth-century compiler of the *Doctrina patrum de incarnatione Verbi*
culled several definitions from Evagrius, but explicitly labelled him
as being 'accursed'. This gloss tells us much about how complex were
later Greek attitudes toward Evagrius. He was accursed perhaps, but
still too valuable to be simply eliminated. Under such ambivalent
circumstances, it is hardly surprising that the bulk of his corpus in
Greek simply vanishes.

3

EVAGRIUS' WRITINGS
AND HIS THINKING

The loss of the Greek originals notwithstanding, we have obviously
not been altogether deprived of Evagrius' works. Thanks to the
ancient translations of Evagrius' works (particularly the Syriac translations) mentioned earlier, many otherwise lost letters and brief
treatises are available. Obviously, working from the ancient translations has to be done with great care, and not just because we have
lost the author's original words. Evagrius was the mystical doctor
nonpareil for the Christian Orient, as is revealed by occasional
remarks in the works of the great Syrian theologian and scholar of
the thirteenth century, Gregory Barhebraeus, for whom Evagrius
was 'the greatest of the gnostics'.[1] So sometimes it happened that
the writings of lesser authors were ascribed to Evagrius in the Syriac
tradition, to increase their reputation.[2] A good example is the case
of Abraham of Nathpar, several of whose writings were ascribed to
Evagrius in the Syriac manuscript used by Frankenberg for his
edition.[3] This inclusion of this material within the Evagrian corpus may well have contaminated the transmission of Evagrius' own
works. The ancient translations also sometimes enable scholars to
restore to Evagrius certain Greek texts that were wrongly attributed
to Nilus or to Basil the Great. For instance, Evagrius' *On prayer*
survives in Greek under Nilus' name; and his *On the faith* is
preserved as *Letter* 8 in the collection of Basil's letters. It has also
been possible to extract Evagrius' scholia from lengthy chains of
scholia on various books of Scripture (e.g., his particularly interesting *On Psalms*).[4] Taken together with the surviving Greek texts
found, for instance, in the *Philokalia*, these various sources make
up a respectable collection. As a result of this textual work, we can
now study a dossier of primary material from a writer whose significance – for good or ill – is indisputable. As far as we can tell, this

23

opportunity has not been paralleled since Evagrius' own lifetime. We can now re-evaluate Evagrius' writings and come to conclusions about them while being critically aware of the historical limitations of the sixth-century condemnations. It is worth thinking about how this is done.

Retrieving the writings

We begin by thinking about one of the challenges that faces textual critics and scholars. Editing a manuscript is a complicated business. Palaeographic competence can be objectively evaluated and even if there are debates about the precise reading of some text or other, there are agreed standards to which appeals can be made. But not all of the business of recovering ancient material is so theoretically straightforward. A considerable amount of expertise and discretion is necessarily brought into the process whenever an attribution has to be established. The criteria used here are rather subtler than the palaeographer's tables of Greek hands. When one of the greatest twentieth-century scholars of Evagrian manuscripts, Joseph Muyldermans, addressed the difficulties of determining which of the Syrian Evagriana were actually written by Evagrius himself, he appealed to somewhat elusive qualities such as 'the breath of doctrine that animates the unedited material and the technical vocabulary that characterises it'.[5] Muyldermans is not alone: to take two examples from works translated in this volume, Hans Urs von Balthasar's arguments concerning the authenticity (or otherwise) of the *Notes on Luke* hinge on evaluations about technical language and style; and Robert Devreesse's argument against Evagrius' authorship of *scholion* 1 *on Job* 1.5 ('On the divine names') rests on the presupposition that Evagrius would not have taken an interest in Hebrew vocabulary.[6] It is wrong to imagine that, in pointing out this element of professional judgement, we are tacitly making an invidious comparison to the objective standards of exact sciences; without digressing into a discussion of philosophical hermeneutics, we are simply noting that expectations of what counts as Evagrian are operative when scholars decide which texts are legitimately ascribed to him.[7] It is important to be aware that ascribing to Evagrius a system of thought is not simply a useful heuristic device for organising, evaluating and presenting his writings – it is also a potential limitation to what is admitted as Evagrian. In this way, heuristics evolve into prejudices with the result that a conservative bias develops and restricts scholarly attention to writings that conform to (and, in so doing, confirm) the supposed system of thought.

Discerning their meanings

This point is relevant because a number of leading scholars have attributed to Evagrius a highly specific intellectual system that they have then used to reconstruct his teaching and even to infer Evagrius' positions in matters for which no direct evidence is available. In some cases, this has had a direct effect on any of a number of important questions. The most central question is how Origenist Evagrius was, but other less spectacular questions are relevant, too. For instance, whether one thinks Evagrius' theology provoked the First Origenist Controversy is in large measure a consequence of whether one thinks that his theology was exceptionally unusual in the context of late fourth-century Egypt (not to mention whether one thinks Evagrius had enough clout to stir up such an intense reaction). But there is no need to resort to hypothetical situations here, when there are a few examples at hand. We will take them in turn and redress some imbalances in them. In this way, this exercise will provide an overview of recent developments in scholarship,[8] and also an orientation toward Evagrius that aims to prepare the reader to make sense of the texts here translated.

'An iron-clad system'

The first item for consideration is to what extent it is legitimate to think of Evagrius as being bound to a system of thought. There is no better place to begin than by quoting Balthasar:

> In constructing his system Evagrius has not merely taken over the terminology and system of Origen (as the majority of investigators suppose). His approach has been bolder: he has brought the loose, flowing and changing system of Origen to a final, mathematically exact precision. In doing this, he has sacrificed Origen's versatile thought to an iron-clad system to which he holds fast, come what may, to its final consequences. Origen is a cathedral filled with perspectives, towers, statues, pillars, intersecting forms, where everything is as allusive as the discontinuous lines which, like so many waves of thought, press upon each other. But

this rich structure withdraws from the field of vision of the monk of the desert to become an attenuated, single, clear silhouette thrown up against the horizon in stark outline. He is more of an Origenist than Origen himself, and Bousset is indeed correct when he states that it is from this Origenism that we must begin if we are to understand the mystical theology of Evagrius.[9]

Whereas one can only smile sympathetically at the metaphor of Origen as a cathedral, it is monstrously unjust to say of Evagrius that he pitilessly reduced the splendours of Origen's supple thinking to a severe and formulaic precision. One only need spend time reading Evagrius' pragmatic and open-ended *Thoughts* or his fluid and elusive *Great letter* to know that he did nothing of the kind. The false step is in supposing that intellectual symmetry or simplicity is the prime factor motivating Evagrius, and the great mistake is in taking for granted that Evagrius sacrifices complexity on the altar of abstraction.

This mistake can be seen at work in specific points of interpretation no less than in overarching analyses. For instance, Irénée Hausherr in his comments to *On prayer* 63 argues that the Spirit does not in fact visit the undeserving (Evagrius' explicit claim to the contrary notwithstanding!), on the grounds that such a visitation would violate the fundamental system of Evagrius' thought.[10] The problem here, as with the problematic attitude expressed by Balthasar, is that expecting to find in Evagrius' works an 'iron-clad system' disposes scholars to constrain Evagrius so that he fits neatly into the schema of an intellectualist monk. By contrast, the great merit of contemporary research is evident in its emphasis on Evagrius' goal of cultivating a way of life that leads to understanding, rather than (say) constructing an airtight philosophical worldview.[11]

It is entirely possible to see Evagrius' writings – particularly his 'Chapters' – as a training-ground for understanding, rather than a metaphysical jigsaw. In the words of one scholar, Evagrius aimed chiefly 'to stimulate meditation' and to inculcate virtues that would lead one to approximate to the life exemplified by Christ; and this is explicitly contrasted to the attempt to read Evagrius' works as 'a sort of systematic, even cartographic guide to a quasi-philosophical territory of intellectualist monastic life'.[12] In keeping with the metaphor of terrain, one might say that Evagrius' writings aim to promote the essential skills for mountaineering, thus enabling the adepts to scale the mountain. The mountain's peaks are permanently veiled in the clouds, but (as it is the same mountain) one can expect that the successful climbers will arrive at the same peaks. Emphasising the techniques (rather than the view from the top) does not mean, then, that the exercise is unanswerably subjective. Two teams of climbers might ascend the mountain along different tracks, but their destination is the same mountaintop.

If we take that view of Evagrius' programme of teaching, then we will incline to think of him as a guide, perhaps a trainer, instead of the kind of systematician described by Balthasar. This does not mean that there is no system. Instead, it means that the system is to be sought – not in the crystalline beauty of a well-defined theory – but rather in the exhortations and practices that prepare one to undertake the long journey to God. That is to say, the Evagrian system is fundamentally pedagogic and consists in the threefold division of ascetic practice, natural contemplation and theology (or ethics, physics and theology, as Pierre Hadot rightly interprets the scheme).[13] The system is *not* basically speculative and metaphysical in the way that Balthasar suggested. To be sure, Evagrius is not content to advocate a bare outline and he certainly has specific views about how best to follow that programme of spiritual living. But, in contrast to Balthasar's claim, Evagrius is notoriously unsystematic in his presentation of the sacred mysteries of Christianity. We will want to come back to that point shortly, but for the moment we need to consider that the reason for the unsystematic approach could well be that his presentation is meant to be incomplete and evocative and only lightly descriptive.

On this reading, Evagrius – like Thomas Aquinas long after him – was content 'by stammering' to 'echo the heights of God as best we can'.[14] In the end, it is clear that Evagrius' *Gnostic chapters* is not a closed theological system from the fact that the six centuries are actually incomplete, and indeed deliberately incomplete (which, it may be noted, also bears comparison to the Angelic Doctor's decision to leave his *Summa* incomplete).[15] For Evagrius, in the words of a commentator, 'the incompleteness is not due to chance, it represents the incompleteness of the unlimited ignorance of *theologia*. *Gnosis* can only be indicated, not explained; it is more a *state* of knowing, than any amount of knowledge.'[16]

The appeal of a neat system is very strong – and rightly so. Without some sense of what counts as Evagrian, one faces tremendous difficulties in coming to a defensible position about which writings are his. But in the case of Evagrius' supposed system, it is important to think about why the lineaments of the system are drawn as they are. The source of this system leads to a second problem.

Condemnations as criteria

Following his discovery of a second, markedly more Origenist, version of Evagrius' *Gnostic chapters*, Antoine Guillaumont argued very influentially that the version previously published by Wilhelm Frankenberg had been edited for content because the original version (that is, the version Guillaumont discovered) was directly responsible for the Christological controversies that resulted in the anathemas against Origen promulgated in 553.[17] Guillaumont's analysis has met with such widespread acceptance that, even in Straub's critical edition of the acts of the Fifth Ecumenical Council for the series *Acta Conciliorum Œcumenicorum*, one is referred to Guillaumont for the sources of the condemnations. It would not be too much to say that Guillaumont's perspective is currently dominant.[18] So it will be worthwhile to ensure that the reader is familiar with it.

Evagrius is supposed to have taught that, once creation has been reconciled to God, the qualitative differences between Christ and other rational beings will gradually disappear with the result that ultimately even Satan will be equal to Christ (in Greek, *isochristos*).[19] The heretical nub of this claim is that Christ is presumed to have been different to all other rational beings only insofar as the human soul of Christ is further along the spectrum of spiritual progress that all rational beings must inevitably make. Now the arguments in support of attributing this view to Evagrius are ingenious and Guillaumont has made an unarguably important discovery about where the Palestinian Origenists looked for their inspiration. But it must be noted that this view relies on configuring Evagrius' disconnected utterances in a specific way and (perhaps more troublingly) claiming that hostile statements resolving the Second Origenist Controversy provide the correct template for this reconfiguration. What justification have we for thinking that the later crisis provides us with the best pattern for Evagrius' beliefs?

If it were the case that the interpretation advanced by Stephen bar Sudaili (and by Kyriakos, though of course they would not have evaluated the works in the same way) was the only available platform for re-assembling Evagrius' thought, then clearly we would need to rely on it, *faute de mieux*, and base our interpretation on it. But it has not yet been sufficiently recognised that there are multiple trajectories of interpreting Evagrius. As we have seen from the survey above, the impact of Evagrius is evident in a range of later writings, from Stephen's pantheistic musings, through John of Gaza's word of warning and the anonymous endorsement of Evagrius' trilogy, to Kyriakos' syllabus of errors. What we have, then, are multiple traditions – some in direct competition with each other – that look back to Evagrius for inspiration. The history of the reception of Evagrius' works is convoluted, but one thing is clear: it does not support the idea that a privileged insight into his thinking was preserved by a single school of thought. So the prudent conclusion to draw from it is that Evagrius was a complex and evocative teacher.

As for the Second Origenist Controversy as a point of departure for Evagrian studies, there are further points to be kept in mind. It certainly seems to be the case that the *Book of Hierotheos* and the accusations by Kyriakos and Philoxenus tend to converge on a 'mystico-pantheistic' synthesis in which Evagrius' *Gnostic chapters* play an important part. But this is relevant only for the Second Origenist Controversy and, even so, it is exceedingly difficult to re-construct the 'Origenist' side of that controversy.[20] The most detailed source for the controversy – Cyril of Scythopolis' hagiographical sketches of contemporaneous Palestinian monks – is deeply suspect, despite the confidence that has been placed on it for generations, and we must acknowledge that Cyril's biases radically reduce the usefulness of his evidence for our purposes.[21] In view of how hopelessly thin our evidence about the Origenists is, we would be rather poorly served if it were our only source of information about Evagrius' beliefs.

But, of course, it is absurd to lament that fact, since we have a major fund of information about Evagrius' beliefs in his own writings. As we have already observed, it is important to have some principles when we are faced with difficult decisions about attributing some particular writing to Evagrius. But we are no longer talking about textual criticism in the narrow sense; now we are talking about interpreting his work as a whole. For that purpose, it is surely better to rely on the core of undisputedly authentic texts, to follow their lead and to buttress their witness whenever possible with reference to other ancient sources. With dozens of primary sources at our disposal, there is no longer a need to look back to the sixth century for a sweeping narrative of Evagrian theology. It is in any case out of keeping with contemporary methodology to rely on evidence from heresiologists when re-constructing the beliefs (or indeed the writings) of their opponents. In some cases, it can be very helpful to have recourse to a hostile view because one partisan viewpoint can counterbalance another. But this is not the same as endorsing the insights of the opponent and basing one's own views on those insights. A helpful parallel may be found in the case of the Gnostics.[22]

Before the explorations of Bruce and, even more importantly, the discovery of the cache of documents at Nag Hammadi supplied a veritable treasure-trove of primary evidence, scholars looked to Irenaeus and other opponents of the Gnostics for information about their beliefs. Subsequent to the discovery of primary sources, however, scholars have been able to evaluate the accuracy of various claims about Gnosticism and come to conclusions that are significantly independent from traditional claims. We are in rather a similar situation with the modern recovery of Evagrius' works. It is no longer necessary for us to identify Evagrius as 'the Origenist condemned by the Fifth Ecumenical Council' (as he would have appeared to the eyes of the great patristic historian, Le Nain de Tillemont, for instance). In fact, that is a tendentious claim, regardless of what the various partisans of the sixth century may have thought. No one has yet shown that the condemned beliefs are identical to Evagrius' beliefs, merely that the condemned beliefs draw inspiration from him.

By the same token, it is no longer necessary for us to begin with the sixth-century condemnations – or even with the presumption of Evagrius' heresy – in evaluating his works or reconstructing his teaching. In the light of how trenchantly orthodox Evagrius is shown to have been by his letter *On the faith* – in which, incidentally, he has already begun to use the categories for the mystical contemplations that are found in his *Great letter* and *Gnostic chapters*[23] – it seems more sensible to begin our attempts to understand his admittedly obscure writings from the presumption of Cappadocian orthodoxy rather than to work backward from the presumption of Origenist heresy. This is not to cast doubt on the claim that Evagrius himself drew inspiration from Origen, which is beyond dispute.[24] It simply means that we are now able to work forward from Origen (via the Cappadocians and Egyptians) to Evagrius and reconstruct Evagrius' thinking with reference to a reasonably large corpus, without having to rely upon subsequent interpretations or evaluations of Evagrius' writings.

Esoteric teachings

A third and final consideration about Evagrian theology is in order. It concerns Evagrius' marked propensity to hold back information and what to make of that propensity. The conventional hermeneutic problems that arise when we take up ancient writings are intensified by finding in them specific references to secrecy on the author's part. And there can be no doubt that Evagrius appreciated the value of discreet silence and was reluctant to 'cast pearls before swine'. Some evidence that this reticence is present across the corpus can be had from the fact that he approvingly quotes Mt 7.6 in his *Praktikos*, intro. §9 (a foundational work) and from his obscure worrying about entrusting certain teachings to the written word at *Great letter* §17 (an advanced work). Encountering this secrecy, scholars naturally want to know what it is that Evagrius forbears to write out. We will therefore want to pose two related questions: what are the reasons for identifying his esoteric teachings as Origenist speculation, and are there any alternative explanations?

At *Great letter* §1, Evagrius writes:

> You know that when those who are separated far from each other by a great distance (which many different necessities may occasionally bring about) want to know – or to make known to one another – those intentions and hidden secrets that are not for everyone and are not to be revealed to anyone except those who have a kindred mind, they do so through letters.

Commenting upon those words, Martin Parmentier has written:

> Evagrius 'has something to hide'. His teaching is, he realizes, easily misunderstood and rejected. This is why he refrains from showing the back of his (Origenistic) tongue in his ascetic-practical works, which are addressed to a wider and less intellectual public.[25]

In view of the foregoing discussion, it is no surprise that Parmentier has supposed that Evagrius was concealing Origenist metaphysical speculation.

These comments conform splendidly to the idea that Evagrius was a bold thinker who found it necessary to hold back information that would not be intelligible to the great unwashed – indeed, a bold thinker whose ideas would eventually attract an explicit condemnation. Parmentier is certainly not the only scholar to come to such a conclusion. In fact, the view is quite commonly expressed that, in the *Great letter*, Evagrius has at long last spoken clearly and without riddles. In particular, scholars have often resorted to the *Great letter* in search of confirmation that Evagrius was responsible for Origenism as condemned in Justinian's era.[26] But there is a fundamental flaw in this approach to Evagrius. The best way to see this is to compare two relevant passages from Evagrius – *Praktikos*, intro. §9 and *Great letter* §17. Here, then, are Evagrius' words at *Praktikos*, intro. §9:

> Now, concerning the ascetic and gnostic life, what we shall fully describe (instead of such things as we have seen or heard) are such things as we have learned from [the Elders] to tell to others, setting out in concise form the ascetic teachings in one hundred chapters on the one hand, and on the other the gnostic teachings in fifty followed by six hundred. We shall veil some things, and obscure others, lest we 'give holy things to the dogs' and 'cast pearls before swine' (Mt 7.6). But these things shall be clear to those who have set out on the same path.[27]

We must carefully note that Evagrius is not simply flagging his intention to be secretive. Instead, he says that he 'shall veil some things, and obscure others' only after promising to give a full description of the ascetic and gnostic teachings that he learnt from the Egyptian elders. Even more importantly, Evagrius claims that the veiled and obscured points 'shall be clear to those who have set out on the same path'. This claim effectively indicates that Evagrius does not believe that some people are intrinsically unable to attain to the 'secret teachings'; nor does he believe that scholarly research is required in order to understand the 'secret teachings'. In principle, the 'secret teachings' are available to everyone who undertakes the Christian life with diligence, attentiveness and understanding.[28] Furthermore, we are not to seek the veiled and obscured teachings from some other source; rather, we are to follow Evagrius' ascetic instructions so that, setting out on the same path, we may come to understand the fullness that is veiled and obscured in the concise form of the chapters. For those with eyes to see, then, the trilogy of *Praktikos*, *Gnostikos* and *Gnostic chapters* contains all that is required for a full description of the ascetic and gnostic teachings of the desert fathers. But, of course, the *Gnostic chapters* are notoriously difficult to understand. Many scholars turn to the *Great letter* in hopes of assistance on that front, and so shall we.

At *Great letter* §17, we read the following:

> Now if letters, in service of those far away, can signify what has happened and what will happen, how much more can the Word and the Spirit know everything and signify everything to their body, the mind. I can truly say that many pathways full of various distinctions meet me here – but I am unwilling to write them down for you because I am unable to entrust them to ink and paper and because of those who might in the future happen to come upon this letter. Furthermore, this paper is overburdened with presumption and it is therefore unable to speak directly about everything.

At this point in the letter, Evagrius is bringing to a close an elaborate simile about how the universe is like a letter from God, by returning to the claim that letters reveal hidden secrets (from §1, as cited above). In considering how the Word and the Spirit communicate God's purposes to the mind, Evagrius acknowledges that many possible avenues of further theological research are open to him – but he pointedly declines to take any of them, reiterating instead his belief that some secrets are best kept. Because of the ramifications of that latter point, one feels that the significance of this passage has been lost on most of Evagrius' readers.

First, it is immediately after he has expressed deep reservations about committing the 'wondrous distinctions' to writing that Evagrius embarks on a discussion of the mystical union of creatures to the Creator. It makes no sense to suppose that Evagrius would clearly disclose the intimate and lofty heights of his theological insights immediately after refusing to speculate on how the Son and the Spirit communicate to the mind (and that on grounds that the letter might fall into unknown hands). It is therefore implausible to think that the remainder of the *Great letter* reveals the closely guarded secrets of heretical speculation. We can conclude from Evagrius' own words that, regardless of whatever bold things he may have written in the *Great letter*, his 'secret teachings' are not to be found there. In view of his anticipation that the letter will circulate beyond his control, we must infer that he included in it only such content as he was willing to have noised abroad – and that ought to give us pause. Evagrius was willing to allow an unknown and uncontrolled readership to share his metaphorical account of the mystical union as so many rivers flowing to the sea. Consequently, we cannot suppose that Evagrius was trying to hide his views about how humans will be reconciled with God and we therefore ought not to cling to the suspicion that the 'secrets' are heretical Origenist speculation about the final restoration. Once that suspicion dissipates, we lose a great deal of motivation for assuming that Evagrius' thinking about the mystical union is a secretive, esoteric and individualistic insight that has to be guarded from the masses who would not understand (and who might well repress such thinking).[29] The relatively straightforward way of avoiding that problem is simply not to assume that the union being described is ontological. Instead, the letter can be taken as a description of the relational and moral consequences of reconciliation with God. With this alternate interpretation in hand, we should be very cautious about asserting that Evagrius is reconnoitring the trail of pantheistic speculation that Stephen bar Sudaili will later follow.

Second, the reconciliation of creation to the Creator cannot be what Evagrius is keeping from those who are not likeminded. This much is clear from the context at *Great letter* §17. The mystical teachings that Evagrius declines to put in writing concern how the Holy Spirit and the Son communicate insights to the mind. Throughout the letter to that point, Evagrius describes the human mind as the body of the Son and the Spirit. But he is unprepared to develop that line of analysis in a letter that could fall into anyone's hands. The question of how God the Son relates to the human mind is an important one for Evagrius and it is that question, rather than some esoteric speculation about the final fate of creation, that Evagrius pointedly refuses to discuss. As yet, that question has not received the attention it deserves – probably because many scholars have devoted their time to configuring Evagrian Christology along Origenist lines, and few have studied it for its own sake – and further research along those lines is urgently needed.[30] At present, it is possible to offer some provisional observations about why Evagrius would have held his peace about that subject. Conveniently, these observations centre on what we can learn about Evagrius' 'secret teachings' from the tradition to which he belongs.

He had at least two illustrious precedents for referring to 'secret teachings': Basil the Great and Origen.[31] The point of departure for both Basil and Origen was an emphasis on the spiritual dimensions of liturgical practices that are available (at least in principle) to the whole Christian community. The central question, then, is less about separate groups of intellectuals on the one hand and plebeians on the other than it is about which Christians are prepared to understand in a profounder way the significance of liturgical actions or other ritual performances.[32] The trajectory of understanding is identical to that traced by Origen in his discussion of Numbers 4.17–20: 'First let us understand what is meant word for word; then, with God's help, we will ascend from verbal knowledge to spiritual under-standing.'[33] To put it otherwise, the basic subject matter is widely available within the community, but for a variety of reasons not everyone is prepared to understand it deeply. Whereas Basil and Origen are preoccupied with the implications of public worship, Evagrius' attention is directed toward ascetic practices. (This is not to foreclose discussion of Evagrius' understanding of public worship, which is another important topic in serious need of further study.) In conjunction with *Great letter* §17, what this suggests is that Evagrius wanted his readers to contemplate how God communicates with them; as for his teachings about the restoration of creatures to their Creator, it falls within the public domain.

4

EVAGRIUS
THE GUIDE

The foregoing remarks about some standard presuppositions have aimed at creating a reasonable doubt about the propriety of reading backward from the Second Origenist Controversy and taking that controversy as the hermeneutic key to Evagrius. A brief word about an alternative view is therefore in order.

In place of a metaphysical system, we have argued that Evagrius' theology is better approached as a structured and disciplined way of living. That approach enables us to appreciate Evagrius' intellectual accomplishments within the frame of reference of his ascetic doctrines: thinking is, after all, a part (but only a part) of living. To be more specific, Evagrius' system is a three-part programme of spiritual development whereby one progresses from ethical and ascetical practices, to a renewed understanding of the universe and its meanings, and thence to the vision of God. The programme describes a journey, so Evagrius' writings can profitably be thought of as signposts. It is quite clear that the journey is complex and not all of the sojourners arrive at the same destination, as we see from the history of reception of Evagrius. Some suggestions for following Evagrius' guidance are thus appropriate.

It is important to try to come to grips with his writings by studying the whole corpus and seeing how he uses language – not least language drawn from Scripture – across his writings. With the newly recovered works at our disposal, we can now begin to evaluate Evagrius by looking at how he exposited Scripture in his scholia and by using Scripture as a kind of framework for organising his occasional remarks. Similar use can also be made of his doctrinal letters, *On the faith* and the *Great letter*, although it is as well for the reader to know at this point that they are not systematic treatises. As for the ascetic corpus, it is crucial to pay very close attention to the principles Evagrius sets down in them. Very few of even his most ardent admirers will be able to enact them fully, but it is obvious that Evagrius has a serious expectation that ascetic undertakings are prerequisite to understanding. I am aware of no reason for supposing that we can ignore his expectations and still understand his teaching. After making a serious effort to come to terms with (even to embrace) Evagrius' ascetic principles, after closely studying Evagrius' technique of spiritually interpreting Scripture, after familiarising oneself with Evagrius' extended treatises and letters, one is prepared to make sense of his epigrammatic 'chapters'.

The present volume aims to facilitate such study of Evagrius. To that end, it contains specimens of the major genres in which Evagrius wrote. Since it cannot be assumed that the reader will have recourse to an Evagrian abba when difficulties emerge, the texts are arranged in what seems to be a pedagogically sound order: the easier, more explicit and comparatively fulsome works come first, gradually leading on to the more complicated, elusive and rather elliptical works. Thus, the letters appear first because they include historical information and are in some instances reasonably expansive; the treatises are likewise broad in scope and presentation; the notes are terse and sometimes quite difficult to understand, but are linked back to the biblical text; the chapters are often (probably deliberately) difficult because they are advanced teaching for the proficient. The reader who follows the pattern set down in this book may well still feel perplexed, but it is hoped that the initial readings will provide a good foundation for understanding Evagrius' more challenging pieces. The sequence of writings ends with *On prayer* – Evagrius' luminously brilliant 'kephalaiac' work. Though *On prayer* can certainly be approached without such lengthy preparation, the exposure to Evagrius' style of thinking that comes with reading many of his other writings first will contribute to an enriched appreciation of that sublime work.

The decisions about what to include were motivated by several factors. Among these factors were the desire to make available some of his writings that are difficult to find, the conviction that a broad range of primary material is necessary for a good understanding of Evagrius and the preference for including complete works (rather than extracts). As regards the principles of translation, I have tried to adhere to Evagrius' style as it varies from work to work, so that *On prayer* is terse, *Virgin* is given in blank verse and *Thoughts* is expansive. Without trying to offer a word for word translation of the Greek (or Syriac or Coptic), I have nevertheless aimed at consistently translating key terms like *logos*, *theoria* and *katastasis*. (A select glossary is given in an appendix to this introduction.) The overarching design is that the translation should enable readers without knowledge of the ancient languages to have a faithful representation of Evagrius in comprehensible English, while still being useful to readers who have the ancient languages. If this collection helps further the study of Evagrius, it will have served its purpose. By that token, the collection may very well raise more questions than it settles. Perhaps the greatest of those questions will be the one with which this introduction began, and to which we now return by way of a conclusion.

Why, then, does Evagrius matter? He matters because his writings have not yet received the attention they fairly scream out for. They open on to a host of concerns that are extremely important for patristic studies. For instance, the dramatic afterlife of Evagrian theology serves as a valuable lesson in how the people who lived during the generations that come between us and what we study are able sometimes to divert our attention away from earlier history onto their own concerns. In this case, the sixth-century debates about intellectual culture in Christian monasticism had the result of sorting out early documents into ideological categories that were not obviously relevant before that time. So Evagrius' works are important because they prompt us to look more closely into the history of monasticism during that period, while questioning the conventional assumption that holiness and intellectual culture are antithetical. Evagrius can be seen to subvert that assumption in that he is a person of evident godliness and deep learning. In fact, Evagrius' writings are also significant because they clearly demonstrate that theology can be thoroughly infused by prayer in a way that is no longer immediately available to us, and they demonstrate a way of finding enduring meaning in Scripture that is similarly foreign to us. Evagrius' writings also show us how doctrinal orthodoxy can be closely connected to mystical experience. In all these ways, Evagrius' writings are representative of countless other texts from Christian antiquity – so these eminently readable works can enable us to appreciate aspects of ancient theology that are not self-evident to the twenty-first-century reader. For all these reasons, Evagrius is important because his works prod us into thinking more carefully about how the mind and the heart can, and should, co-operate in Christian theology.

APPENDIX

SELECT GLOSSARY
OF TERMS

I have made a serious effort to translate key terms consistently and it may therefore help the reader to keep the following conventions in mind.

akêdia	despondency
apatheia	imperturbability, whence
apathês	imperturbable; free from perturbation
autexousion	self-determination
dianoia	thinking
enkrateia	self-control
epithumia	concupiscence
gnôsis	knowledge, whence
gnôstikos	gnostic
hêgemonikon	governing faculty
katastasis	disposition
kephalaion	chapter
lypê	grief
logismos	thought
logos	reason, meaning
misos	anger
mnêsikakia	grudge-bearing
noêma	concept
nous	mind
organon	organ of perception
orgês	wrath
physikê	natural contemplation
pragma	thing (which need not be a physical thing)
praktikê	ascetic struggle, whence
praktikos	ascetic

prosochê	vigilance
theôria	contemplation
thumos	irascibility
typoô	to imprint, to make an impression
stasis	status, standing

It is notoriously difficult to translate some of these words, but it seems to me that providing a translation (even an imperfect one) is better than simply transliterating and thus putting an additional burden on the reader. For further consideration of these terms, the reader may profitably consult Miquel (1986), Lampe's *A patristic Greek lexicon* or the excellent glossary provided in the English translation of the *Philokalia* (by Palmer *et al.* (1979–)).

Note that I do not claim my choices are exhaustive or perfect; I can only invoke the old Italian adage, *Tradittore, traduttore* – or, to paraphrase, translation is an act of treachery. Let the reader beware!

Part II

TEXTS

LETTERS

INTRODUCTION

Evagrius was involved in numerous lines of correspondence. A collection of more than sixty letters (three of which are fragmentary)[1] survives in the Syriac tradition. One of the letters survives in its entirety in Greek (*Faith*) and fragments in Greek from several others have been identified on the basis of comparison with the Syriac. Two of the letters – *Faith* and the *Great letter* – are unusually long and involve sophisticated theological discussion. They both occur at the end of the collection. The others are occasional pieces. Though not lacking in theological content, they are particularly interesting for the light that they shed on Evagrius' daily life, his role as a spiritual father and other such concerns. As such, they are important for our understanding of how Evagrius perceived himself and what sort of counsel he offered. The evidence from the letters has also been used to describe Evagrius' position within various social networks.[2]

Since *Faith* appears as *Letter* 63, but can be confidently dated to the earliest period of Evagrius' literary career, the arrangement of letters within the corpus is clearly not chronological. Another question that arises in connection with the corpus is to whom they were written, since only four of the letters mention the addressee by name.[3] Gabriel Bunge, in his seminal volume *Briefe aus der Wüste*, argued on the basis of their content for specific addressees in thirty-three cases; his arguments have been generally accepted. On the basis of his analyses, we find that twenty-three of the letters were dispatched to Jerusalem (for Melania, Rufinus, Anatolius, Severa or John of Jerusalem), one was sent to Theophilus of Alexandria, and three to Gregory Nazianzen.[4]

For the volume in hand, six of the letters have been translated: *On the faith* (*Letter* 63), the *Great letter* (*Letter* 64), *Letters* 7–8 and

43

19–20. The rationale for including these letters in particular is that *On the faith* is the earliest datable writing by Evagrius and it summarises his fundamental beliefs pertaining to Christ and to the Holy Trinity. The *Great letter* expresses his mystical teaching and as such represents the highest reaches of Evagrian theology. The contents of *Letters* 7–8 and 19–20 are typical of his pastoral activities. According to Bunge's widely accepted analysis, those four letters refer to Evagrius' *To the virgin* (also translated in this collection), so their witness to the dissemination of that text is valuable.

On the faith appears first since it is in all likelihood the earliest of the letters. Next follow *Letters* 7–8 and 19–20. Since they form a coherent unit, they are printed together. The *Great letter* is given last, chiefly because of its advanced subject matter. The letters are prefaced by some introductory remarks.

Bunge has translated the entire corpus into German, providing useful notes and helpful internal divisions. His divisions have been adopted for this translation.

Texts: The Syriac corpus: Frankenberg (1912), 564–619; the *Great letter*: Frankenberg (1912), 610–19 and Vitestam (1964); *On the faith*: Gribomont (1983). Additional Greek texts: Géhin (1994), Guillaumont (1987).

Translations: Bunge (1986): German translation of the whole corpus; Bunge and di Meglio (1995): Italian translation of the Greek fragmentary letters; Frankenberg (1912): Greek retroversion from Syriac.

ON THE FAITH

(CPG 2439)

INTRODUCTION

The following letter is in many ways unusual. First, it is far longer than most of Evagrius' letters. Second, it is one of the very few letters that survive in Greek. Third, on the basis of its contents it can be dated relatively securely to Evagrius' early years in Constantinople – and is thus the earliest datable writing of his. Fourth, it outlines the basic categories of Nicene theology as understood by Evagrius. The first point is somewhat trivial, but the other three call for further comment.

Several of Evagrius' works survive in Greek only pseudonymously. Of these, most were preserved under the name of Nilus of Ancyra (the most famous instance being *On prayer*). The letter here presented is unusual in that it passed into the collected letters of Basil the Great, as *Letter* 8. We can be confident that the letter was in fact written by Evagrius, however, because it is ascribed to him in the Syriac corpus and because it is consistent with Evagrius' style of interpreting Scripture (among other things).[1] It is tempting to suppose that, as Evagrius' reputation began to suffer, a copyist simply struck Evagrius' name and replaced it with Basil's, thinking perhaps that the content of the letter ought not to be lost simply because Evagrius fell into disfavour. And indeed the content of the letter is remarkable. It features classically Cappadocian affirmations of the divinity of the Son and of the Spirit, thus highlighting Evagrius' susceptibility to the influence of his elder contemporaries, the great Cappadocian fathers.[2]

We read in Palladius' account of the life of Evagrius that, after Basil's death, he went to Constantinople for a time to study with Gregory (*HL* 38.2). The letter's references to abandoning the homeland and seeking out Gregory (§§1.1, 1.3) fit well with Palladius' account; since Gregory's own time in Constantinople was rather brief, we can date this letter, with more precision than is usual for Evagrius' works, to c.379–80. Since Evagrius spent the first thirty-five years of his life in Asia Minor – and several of those years, presumably, working at close quarters with Gregory and Basil – it is not surprising that *On the faith* rests on terms important to Cappadocian theology, such as 'nature', 'number', 'circumscribed' and 'like'. It was more than likely in the auspicious company of Basil and Gregory that Evagrius acquired his first knowledge of Origen and, as this letter shows, he was able to put his learning to such good effect in their causes.[3] So it is encouraging that scholarly attention has turned now to *On the faith*.[4] In many ways, it provides a surer foundation for re-constructing Evagrius' ideas than do any of his other writings.

Source: Gribomont (1983).

Translations: Gribomont (1983); Deferrari (1926), 47–93 (with a facing Greek text); Bunge (1986), 284–302; for the translation in hand, the numbers in square brackets correspond to the internal numbering of Gribomont; the other numbers are those of Bunge – which I have included for the sake of greater precision.

TRANSLATION

[1] 1. Often I have wondered what you have felt for us; why you have so yielded to our wretchedness, smallness, insignificance and even lack of lovability; and exhorted us with words reminding us of friendship and homeland – as if you were trying with bonds of nostalgia to draw a fugitive back to his own people. I confess, and do not deny [cf. Jn 1.20], that I have become a fugitive – and now you may learn the reason why, which you have long seemed to want to know.

2. First and foremost, I was caught out by an unexpected event and could not keep hold of my thoughts, as happens when by sudden noises people are utterly taken by surprise; but fleeing, I travelled far away [cf. Ps 54.8] and have dwelt for some time away from you. Furthermore, a certain longing for godly teachings, and for the philosophy pertaining to them, overtook me. 'For how', I asked, 'could we conquer the evil that dwells within us? Who would be my

Laban, freeing me from Esau and leading me to the highest philosophy?'[5] **3.** But since, with God's help, we have as far as possible attained our goal by having found a 'vessel of election' [Acts 9.15] and a deep well-spring – I mean Gregory, the mouthpiece of Christ[6] – a little time, I beg you, grant us a little time! We ask this, not because we welcome life in the cities (for it has not escaped us that the Evil One devises deceit for men by such means) – but rather because we judged that the society of holy men is most helpful. For in speaking a bit about godly teachings, and more frequently in listening, we are acquiring a habit of contemplation that is not easily lost. This is how it currently is with us.

[2]**4.** As for you, o divinely noble ones whom I love beyond all, beware of the Philistines' shepherds, lest one of them block your wells unawares [cf. Gen 26.15] and contaminate the purity of your knowledge concerning the faith. For it is always their business, not to instruct the largely uncontaminated souls from the divine Scriptures, but to displace the truth through outsiders' wisdom. For one who introduces 'unbegotten' and 'begotten' into our faith, who teaches that he who always was, once was not; that he who naturally and always was Father became a father; that the Holy Spirit is not eternal – is he not an outright Philistine? He envies our Patriarch's sheep, wanting them not to drink the pure water which springs up to everlasting life [cf. Jn 4.14], but to win for themselves the words of the prophet, who says: 'They have abandoned me, the fountain of living water, and have dug themselves broken cisterns which cannot hold water' [Jer 2.13]. One must confess God the Father, God the Son, and God the Holy Spirit, as have taught both the divine words and those who have understood them more sublimely.

5. To those who insult us on grounds of believing in three gods, it must be said that we confess that God is one, not in number, but in nature.[7] In fact, not everything that is called one in number is really one, nor is it simple in nature. Furthermore, God is universally confessed as simple and uncompounded [cf. Ps 146.5]. Nevertheless, God is not therefore one in number.

6. This is what I mean: We say that the universe is one in number, but not one in nature, nor yet simple. After all, we divide it into the elements from which it is composed, that is, into fire, water, air, and earth. Again, a man is said to be one in number, as when we frequently speak of one man. But, as a composite of body and soul, he is not simple. Likewise, we say an angel is one in number, but not one in nature, nor yet simple; for we understand an angel's person as essence plus holiness.

7. If, then, not everything which is one in number is one in nature; and what is one in nature and simple is not one in number; and we say that God is one in nature, how do they impute number to us? And this despite the fact that we exclude number altogether from that blessed and spiritual nature! Number is a property of quantity; and quantity is linked to bodily nature; therefore, number is a property of bodily nature. We have affirmed our faith that our Lord is the fashioner [*demiourgos*] of bodies. So every number designates those things that have been allotted a material and circumscribed nature; but 'One and Only' is the designation of the simple and uncircumscribed essence.[8]

8. So anyone who introduces number or creature when confessing the Son of God or the Holy Spirit, introduces a material and circumscribed nature unawares. By 'circumscribed', I mean not merely that which is enclosed by space, but also what has been comprehended in the foreknowledge of him who will bring it from non-existence into being (and can therefore be comprehended by knowledge). Therefore everything holy that has a circumscribed nature has holiness added to it; and since it has holiness added to it, it admits of evil. But the font of holiness, from which every reasoning creature is made holy in proportion to its virtue, is the Son and the Holy Spirit.

[3]9. And yet we, in keeping with right reason, do not say the Son is either like or unlike the Father; each term is equally inapplicable. For the terms 'like' and 'unlike' are used only with respect to qualities, whereas the divine is free from quality. But as we confess the identity of their nature, we also accept the identity of their essence and disavow the idea of a composite nature – for the Father, who is God by his essence, has begotten the Son, who is God by his essence. Thus, the identity of their essence is shown: for one who is God by essence has the same essence as another who is God by essence.

And yet even man is called a god, as in the passage, 'I have said, "You are gods"' [Ps 81.6; Jn 10.34]; demons are likewise called gods, as in the passage, 'The gods of the pagans are demons' [Ps 95.5]. The former are called gods through grace, and the latter, falsely; and only God is God by essence. 10. Now when I say 'only', I clearly indicate the holy and uncreated essence of God. Sometimes the term 'only' is used both for a given man and for undifferentiated common nature. It is used for a given man, for instance, when it is said of Paul that only he was 'snatched up to the third heaven and heard ineffable words which it is not appropriate for man to utter' [2 Cor 12.4]. But it is used for common nature as when David says, 'man's days are like grass' [Ps 102.15] – for here he means, not some particular man, but rather human nature in general (and, indeed, every man lives briefly, then he dies).

Likewise, we understand these things to have been said in reference to nature: 'the only one who has immortality' [1 Tim 6.16]; and 'to God who alone is wise' [Rom 16.27]; and 'None is good, save one – that is, God' [Lk 18.19] (for here the word 'one' means the same as 'only'); and, 'the only one who spreads out the heavens' [Job 9.8]; and again, 'You shall honour the Lord your God, and serve only him' [Dt 6.13; Mt 4.10]; and 'there is no other God than me' [Dt 32.39] (which means the same thing as 'only'). 11. Yet, in Scripture, the designation 'One and Only' is applied to God, not as distinct from the Son and the Holy Spirit, but as from those who are not really gods but are falsely called gods. Thus: 'Only the Lord lead them, and there was no foreign god with them' [Dt 32.12]; and, 'Israel put away the rites of Baalim and the sacred groves of Astaroth, and served the Lord alone' [1 Kgs 7.4]; and again Paul writes, 'But although there are many gods and many lords, yet for us there is one God – the Father, from whom everything exists – and one Lord – Jesus Christ, by whom everything exists' [1 Cor 8.5–6].

12. Now here we may enquire why, after he said 'one God', he was not content with that word (for we have said that 'One and Only' refers to God's nature), but also added the Father and mentioned Christ. Well, then, I suppose that Paul, the vessel of election [cf. Acts 9.15], reckoned it was not enough here simply to proclaim God the Father, God the Son and God the Holy Spirit – which he clearly indicated with the phrase 'one God' – unless he also clearly indicated him 'from whom everything exists' by adding the Father and designated him 'through whom everything exists' by recalling the Son – and indeed announced the Incarnation, asserted the Passion, and declared the Resurrection by including 'Jesus Christ'. For the name 'Jesus Christ' brings to our mind such considerations as these.[9]

13. In fact, it was for that reason that the Lord Jesus refused to be proclaimed as Christ before the Passion, and 'He commanded his disciples that they should tell no one that he is Jesus the Christ' [Mt 16.20].[10] For he intended to permit them to announce him as Jesus the Christ, once he had 'fulfilled the dispensation', 'after the resurrection from the dead and the ascension into heaven'.[11] This is what the passages mean which say, 'That they may know You, the only true God, and the one You have sent, Jesus Christ' [Jn 17.3]; and 'Believe in God, and also believe in me' [Jn 14.1] – the Holy

Spirit all the while protecting our understanding, so we do not fall from one idea while grasping for another; and despise the dispensation while focusing on theology; and our incompleteness become impiety.

[4]14. But by unfolding the very words of divine Scripture that our adversaries seize and distort to their own purpose before presenting them to us to debase the glory of the Only-begotten, let us examine their meaning insofar as we can.

Our first set text is 'I live through the Father' [Jn 6.57]; for this is one of the darts fired against heaven by those who have used it impiously. But here this expression does not describe his life in eternity, as I think (for everything that lives through another cannot live in itself – just as what is heated by another does not heat itself – whereas Our Lord has said, 'I am the life' [Jn 11.25; 14.6]), but rather that life in the flesh that came to be in time which he lived through the Father. For he dwelt among men in this life by his own will; and he did not say, 'I have lived through the Father', but 'I live through the Father', thus clearly designating the present time. 15. He can also mean by 'life' that life which Christ lives in that he has God the Word within himself.[12] And we see that this is so from what follows. 'And whoever eats me', he says, 'will live through me' [Jn 6.57]. For we eat his flesh and drink of his blood, becoming communicants of the Word and Wisdom through his Incarnation and physical life. For he calls 'flesh and blood' everything to do with the holy secret of his dwelling [among us], and disclosed that teaching (consisting of ascetical, physical and theological elements) by which the soul is nourished and prepared for the contemplation of ultimate realities. This is probably what is meant by that expression.[13]

[5]16. And, again, 'My Father is greater than I' – the ungrateful creatures, those children of the Evil One, have used this expression, too! But I have come to believe that even from this phrase it can be shown that the Son is of one essence with the Father. I know that comparisons strictly refer to things that are of the same nature; for we say that this angel is greater than that, or this man more righteous than that, or this bird faster than that. If, then, comparisons are made of things in the same species; and the father is called 'greater' in comparison with the Son; then the Son is of the same essence as the Father.

17. There is another consideration bound up in those words. No wonder he who is the Logos and became flesh confessed that the Father is greater than himself! – for he was seen to be lesser in glory

than the angels, and lesser in form than other men. For it says, 'You have made him a little less than the angels' [Heb 2.7; Ps 8.6]; and again, 'He was made a little less than the angels' [Heb 2.9]; and 'We have seen him and he had neither form nor beauty, but his form was forsaken by all men' [cf. Is 53.2–3]. **18.** He endured all of these things out of great benevolence toward his handiwork, so as to rescue the lost sheep and restore it to the ninety-nine [cf. Lk 15.4]; and return in good health to his own country the man who 'went down from Jerusalem to Jericho, and thus fell among thieves' [cf. Lk 10.30–34].

Or perhaps the heretic will even scorn him for the manger for which he, being an infant, was nourished by the Word;[14] and bring up his poverty in that, as the son of a carpenter, he was not furnished with a cradle? The Son is less than the Father for this reason: he became a dead man for your sake, so as to deliver you from death and give you a share of heavenly life. It is as though someone were to accuse a doctor of enjoying the stench when he bends over a sickbed to heal those who are suffering!

[6] **19.** For your sake, he does not know the hour or day of judgement [cf. Mt 24.36]. Still, nothing is unknown to the true Wisdom, through whom 'all things were made' [Jn 1.3]; and no one at all is ever ignorant of what he has made. But he makes this dispensation for your weakness, so that those who are sinning would not fall into despair owing to the appointed time, as if insufficient time remained for repentance; and again so that those who have been long fighting against the opposing power would not abandon their posts owing to the length of time. For both groups, then, he makes the dispensation of assuming ignorance – for the one, cutting short the time for the good fight; for the other, regulating time for repentance due to their sins.

20. And even though, in the Gospels, he numbered himself among the ignorant for the sake, as I have said, of the weakness of the multitudes [cf. Mt 24.36]; still, in the Acts of the Apostles, when he was speaking as if to the perfect in private, he excluded himself when he said, 'It is not for you to know the times or hours which the Father has put in his own power' [Acts 1.7].

Let these words suffice for our purpose, though they are rather coarse. For now, the meaning of the expression must be scrutinised more precisely. We must knock at the door of knowledge, that perhaps we may rouse the Master of the house who gives spiritual bread to those who request it, since those to whom we are eager to be hospitable are friends and brethren [cf. Lk 11.5–10].

[7]21. The holy disciples of Our Saviour, once they had come to contemplation (as far as men may) and had been purified by the Word, yearn for the goal and desire to know ultimate blessedness.[15] This is the blessedness that Our Lord asserted that neither his angels, nor he himself, knew. For in saying 'day', he meant the complete and precise comprehension of God's purposes, and in saying 'hour', the contemplation of the One and Only – the understanding of which things he attributed to the Father only. So then I suppose that God is said to know concerning himself what is, and not to know what is not. God is said to know righteousness and wisdom, being justice itself and wisdom, but ignorant of injustice and impurity – for God who made us cannot be injustice and impurity. 22. If, then, God is said to know about himself what is, and not to know what is not; and our Lord is not the final object of desire,[16] in keeping with the purpose of the Incarnation and rudimentary doctrine;[17] then our Saviour does not know the goal and ultimate blessedness. 'Not even the angels know', he says [Mt 24.36]; that is, 'nor are their contemplations or the reasons for their service the final object of desire'. For even their knowledge is rudimentary by comparison with knowledge face to face [cf. 1 Cor 13.12].[18]

'Only the Father knows', he says – since the Father himself is the end and ultimate blessedness. For when we know God no longer in mirrors [cf. 1 Cor 13.12] or through any of the other intermediaries, but approach him as the One and Only, then we shall also see the final end. For they say that Christ's kingdom is the whole of material knowledge: but the kingdom of our God and Father is contemplation that is immaterial and, if one may say so, contemplation of unconcealed divinity itself.[19] 23. But Our Lord, too, is the end and the ultimate blessedness in consideration of the Word.[20] For what does he say in the Gospel? 'And I will resurrect him in the last day' [Jn 6.40], meaning by 'resurrection' the transformation from material knowledge to immaterial contemplation, and calling 'the last day' that knowledge beyond which there is no other.[21] Our mind has been resurrected and roused to the height of blessedness only when it shall contemplate the Word's being One and Only. For now, our thick mind has been linked to the earth and mixed with clay and cannot fix itself upon naked contemplation.[22] So, being directed by the beauty born with its body, it considers the works of its Maker and understands them in the meantime by their effects. Thus, having grown in strength little by little, it will be able even to approach the unconcealed divinity itself. **24.** It is in keeping with this understanding, I think, that the words were spoken, 'My Father is greater than I' [Jn 14.28] and 'It is not mine to give, but to them for whom it has been prepared by my Father' [Mt 20.23]. This is also Christ's giving the Kingdom to his God and Father [cf. 1 Cor 15.24]. For Christ is the first-fruit and not the end, according, as I have said, to rudimentary teaching, which contemplates Christ not in himself but, as it were, for us.

Again, since these things are truly so, when the disciples ask in the Acts of the Apostles, 'When will you restore the Kingdom to Israel?' – he says, 'It is not for you to know the times or hours which the Father has put under his own power' [Acts 1.6–7]. In other words, the knowledge of such a Kingdom is not for those who are chained by flesh and blood [cf. 1 Cor 15.50]. For the Father has put this contemplation under his own power – and by 'power', he means those who are under his power; and by 'his own', those in whom ignorance of things below has no part. **25.** As for 'times' and 'hours', please do not think of perceptible ones; but rather of certain intervals of knowledge produced by the intelligible Son. For that prayer of Our Master's must be brought to pass, since it was Jesus who prayed, 'Grant them that they may be one in Us, even as I and You are one, Father' [Jn 17.21]. For as God is one, he unifies all when he comes into each; and number is done away with by the presence of the Unity.

26. Now I have indeed put my hand to solving that passage for a second time. But if anyone can speak better or piously correct our words, then let him both speak and correct – and the Lord will repay him on our behalf! For no envy dwells in us. We did not undertake the investigation of these passages out of rivalry or vainglory, but rather for the benefit of the brethren, so that those earthen vessels containing the treasure of God [cf. 2 Cor 4.7] should not obviously be deceived by men with hearts of stone [cf. Ez 36.26] and uncircumcised men who have armed themselves with the arms of foolish wisdom [cf. Jer 4.4].

[8]**27.** Again, he was created, according to Solomon the Wise in the Proverbs – he says, 'For the Lord created me' [Prov 8.22]. He who leads us to the kingdom of heaven is also called 'the beginning of the evangelical ways' – not as one who became a creature in nature, but as one who became the 'way' according to the dispensation. In fact, 'coming to be' and 'being created' mean the same thing. And in the same way he became the 'way', so, too, he became the 'door',

the 'shepherd', the 'angel', the 'sheep', and again the 'high priest' and 'apostle', with the particular names being applied to particular considerations.[23]

28. Or, again, what would the heretic say concerning God who is insubordinate and yet was 'made a sin for us' [2 Cor 5.21]? For it is written, 'When he has subjected all things to him, then shall the Son himself be subject to the one who subjected all things to him' [1 Cor 15.28]. O man, do you not fear the God who for your sake is called no one's subject? For he made your subjection his own and calls himself 'insubordinate' because you are fighting against virtue.[24] So, too, he said that he was persecuted – for when Saul was hastening to Damascus, intent on imprisoning Christ's disciples [Acts 9.2], he says, 'Saul, Saul, why are you persecuting me?' [Acts 9.4]. And again, he describes himself as 'naked' – when one of the brethren is naked: for he says, 'I was naked, and you clothed me'; and when another was in prison, he says he was himself the one who had been locked away [Mt 25.36]. He himself took up our weaknesses and bore our infirmities [cf. Mt 8.17; Is 53.4]. But if he bore our sicknesses and sins, then insubordination is one of the weaknesses – and he bore it. So, then, the Lord made his own those difficulties that surround us by taking to himself our passions through communion with us.

[9]**29.** So, too, those who fight God seize on the verse, 'The Son can do nothing of himself' [Jn 5.19] in order to destroy those who listen to them. But to me even this passage attests chiefly that the Son is of the same nature as the Father. For if every rational creature with free will can do of itself what it wills and has equal inclination toward the good and the bad, whereas the Son can do nothing of himself, then the Son is no creature; and if no creature, then he is of one essence with the Father. And, again, none of the creatures can act like God does, but the Son himself makes such things as he sees the Father making. So, then, the Son is no creature. In other words, none of the creatures can do all that it wishes. But the Son 'has done whatever he desired in heaven and on earth' [Ps 134.6]. So, then, the Son is no creature. And, again, all creatures consist of opposites or admit of opposites. But the Son is righteousness itself and is immaterial.[25] So, then, the Son is no creature; and, if not, he is of one essence with the Father.

[10]**30.** This examination of the passages put forward is sufficient for us, having been carried out to the best of our ability. Now we shall proceed in our case against those who oppose the Holy Spirit,

abolishing their every haughtiness of thought which is exalted against the knowledge of God [cf. 2 Cor 10.5].

You say that the Holy Spirit is a creature. But every creature is its creator's slave. 'For all things are your slaves', he says [Ps 118.91]. If he is a slave, then he possesses holiness as an adjunct – but everything that possesses holiness as an adjunct admits of evil; whereas the Holy Spirit, being holy by essence, has been proclaimed 'the fount of holiness';[26] so, then, the Holy Spirit is no creature. But if he is no creature, he is of one essence with God.

But tell me – how can you call the one who frees you from slavery a slave? For he says, 'the law of the Spirit of life has freed you from the law of sin' [cf. Rom 8.2].

31. Nor will you dare to say his essence is changeable, once you consider the nature of the adverse power which fell, like lightning, from heaven [cf. Lk 10.18] and plunged from true life because it had holiness as an adjunct and its change resulted from its wicked will. Therefore on this account, having fallen from the One and repudiated its angelic dignity, it was called the Devil from its character. With his primitive and blessed state extinguished, this adverse power was enkindled.

32. If, then, he says that the Holy Spirit is a creature, he attributes limitation to his nature. How, then, do the verses stand that say 'the Spirit of the Lord has filled the whole world' [Wis 1.7], and 'Where shall I go from your Spirit' [Ps 138.7]?

But he does not even confess that he is simple in nature, it seems: for he calls him one in number. But not everything that is one in number is simple, as I have said.[27] But if the Holy Spirit is not simple, he is composed of essence and holiness, and as such is a composite being.[28] And who is so unintelligent as to say that the Holy Spirit is composite rather than simple and, by reason of this simplicity, of one essence with the Father and the Son?

[11]33. If it is now necessary to continue with the discourse and consider more important things, let us therefore chiefly contemplate the divine power of the Holy Spirit. We find that three creations are named in Scripture: first and foremost, the transition from non-existence to existence; second, the transformation from worse to better; third, the resurrection of the dead.[29] In them, you will find the Holy Spirit co-operating with the Father and the Son. For example, the coming into being of the heavens – and what does David say? 'By the Word of the Lord the heavens were established, and all their power by the Spirit of his mouth' [Ps 32.6]. Again, man

is created through baptism. 'For if anyone is in Christ, he is a new creature' [2 Cor 5.17]. And what does the Saviour say to his disciples? 'Go forth, teaching all nations and baptising them in the name of the Father and of the Son and of the Holy Spirit' [Mt 28.19]. Here again you see the Holy Spirit present with the Father and the Son. And what would you say about the resurrection of the dead, when we shall have departed and returned to our earth [cf. Ps 103.29]? For we are dust, and shall return to the dust [cf. Gen 3.19], but 'He will send the Holy Spirit and create us and renew the face of the earth [Phil 3.11]. What St Paul called the resurrection, David proclaimed as renewal.

34. Let us listen again to him who was snatched up to the third heaven [cf. 2 Cor 12.1]. What does he say? 'Do you not know that you are the temple of the Holy Spirit, who is in you?' [1 Cor 6.19]. But every temple is God's temple. If, then, we are the temple of the Holy Spirit, then the Holy Spirit is God. One may indeed say 'the temple of Solomon' –in the sense that Solomon built it. Even if we are temples of the Holy Spirit in that sense, the Holy Spirit is God: for 'God it is who created everything' [Heb 3.4]. But if it is in the sense that the Holy Spirit is worshipped by and dwells within us, then let us confess that he is God. For 'you shall worship the Lord your God and serve him alone' [Mt 4.10].

35. But if they reject the term 'God', let them learn what it is that the name signifies. He is called 'God' because he contemplates everything, or because he has established everything.[30] If, then, he is called 'God' because he contemplates or has established everything, and the Holy Spirit knows everything of God's, just as the spirit within us knows everything of ours [cf. 1 Cor 2.11], then the Holy Spirit is God. And again, if 'the sword of the Spirit is the Word of God' [Eph 6.17], the Holy Spirit is God. For the sword is his whose the Word is said to be. And if the Son is called the right hand of the Father (for 'the right hand of the Lord has worked power' [Ps 117.16] and 'your right hand, Lord, has slain the enemies' [Ex 15.6]), whereas the Holy Spirit is the finger of God – according to saying, 'If I cast out demons by the finger of God' [Lk 11.20], which in another Gospel reads, 'If I cast out demons by the Holy Spirit' [Mt 12.28] – then the Holy Spirit is of the same nature as the Father and the Son.

[12]**36.** Let such things as we have said about the venerable and Holy Trinity suffice for the moment – for it is not possible now to extend further the discourse about the Trinity. But, taking seeds

from our humility, cultivate for yourselves ripe corn, since we further require fruit from such things. For I have faith in God that through the purity of your life you will reap thirty, sixty and a hundredfold [cf. Mt 13.23]. For 'blessed are the pure in heart, for they shall see God' [Mt 5.8].

37. Brethren, do not consider the kingdom of heaven to be anything other than the true consideration of the things that are, which the Holy Scriptures call 'blessedness'.[31] For if 'the kingdom of heaven is within you' [Lk 17.21], and in the case of our inner man there is nothing with which contemplation could be united, then the kingdom of heaven would be contemplation. In fact, once we have been freed from this earthly body and put on an incorrupt and immortal body [cf. 2 Cor 5.2], then we shall see the archetypes of the things whose shadows we now see, as it were, in a mirror [cf. 1 Cor 13.12]. We shall see them, if indeed we direct our life toward righteousness and make provision for the right faith, apart from which no one shall see the Lord. For it says, 'Wisdom will not enter into a malicious soul, nor dwell in a body used by sins' [Wis 1.4].

38. Let no one protest by saying to me, 'You are philosophising to us about a bodiless and altogether immaterial being, though you are ignorant of the things at your feet!' For I deem it absurd if our senses are filled quite full with their proper food unhindered, while the mind alone is excluded from its accustomed activity. For just as the senses are befitting to sensible things, so too is the mind to mental things. But it must be said at the same time that God, who created us from the beginning, made the natural faculties so that they would not require teaching. For no one teaches sight how to perceive colours or shapes; or hearing how to perceive sounds and voices; or smelling how to perceive pleasant and unpleasant odours; or taste how to perceive tastes and flavours; nor touch how to perceive smooth and rough, or hot and cold, things. Nor indeed could anyone teach the mind to lay hold of mental things. And just as the senses, if they are ill, only require care and then they readily fulfil their accustomed activities, so too the mind – which is linked to the body and filled with bodily fantasies – needs faith and right conduct, which 'make its feet like the feet of the hart and steady it on high places' [Ps 17.34].

39. Even the wise Solomon gives the same counsel, when he once adduced for us the ant as an unashamed worker [cf. Prov 6.6] and thereby sketched for us the path of ascetic struggle; and else-where he enigmatically mentions the wise bee's waxen tool [cf. Prov

6.8] and thereby natural contemplation, to which he also blends a discourse about the Holy Trinity, if the Maker of beginnings is contemplated by analogy from the beauty of the creatures.

40. But giving thanks to the Father, Son, and Holy Spirit, let us make an end to the letter, since 'moderation in all things is best',[32] as the proverb says.

LETTERS
7, 8, 19 AND 20
(*CPG* 2437)

INTRODUCTION

Gabriel Bunge noted that the four letters translated below 'all have as their contents the same topic' – namely, Evagrius' response to Severa's proposal to travel from Jerusalem to Egypt, presumably for the purpose of visiting him.[1] From the first two letters, Evagrius' categorical opposition to the proposal is already clear. As he protests to Rufinus, 'I do not know what advantage will accrue to her from such an arduous trek across a long distance, though I can attest that she and those with her are capable of such sacrifices with the Lord's help' (7.2). Nevertheless, Evagrius commends Severa's 'love of learning' and rejoices at her 'progress' (20.1); it would therefore have been churlish of him to refuse to teach her. His second letter on the subject to Rufinus suggests that Evagrius seriously considered dedicating a treatise to Severa herself. In the event, he was unable to do so because the messengers were in haste to leave Egypt – so instead he sent 'with every good wish what we had previously said with the Lord's help', that is, a treatise he had already written for someone else (19.2).

An extremely strong case can be made for identifying the treatise that Evagrius sent to Severa as *To the virgin*, which also appears translated in the present collection.[2] It is known, for example, that Rufinus translated *To the virgin* into Latin, so he obviously had a copy at his disposal. In a Syriac manuscript of the letters, *To the virgin* is appended to the letter to Severa.[3] Furthermore, two passages in Evagrius' letter to Severa – where he mentions contemplating Christ the bridegroom and true knowledge – can be correlated with specific passages in *To the virgin*. This evidence is admittedly circumstantial, but it has the merit of offering a reasonable and specific conjecture and in nearly twenty years no case has been made against it.

These letters also shed some light on Evagrius as a spiritual counsellor. Severa, a deaconess and nun, apparently expressed to Melania her desire to visit Evagrius in Egypt; she may also have spoken with Rufinus about this plan. Both Rufinus and Melania wrote to Evagrius about Severa's plan. Evagrius replies to them both, and it is interesting that he assumes that Melania (rather than Rufinus) will bear this message to Severa. We find, then, a complicated pattern of monks and nuns conferring with each other. That Evagrius could play a central role in such edifying conversations is amply attested in other sources. For example, the *Coptic life* relates that pilgrims often came to Evagrius for spiritual counsel and that his steward was entrusted with funds to care for their needs.[4] Even though a (somewhat philistine) monk called Heros attacked Evagrius' teaching authority,[5] it is clear that many women and men sought out Evagrius' advice.

Source: Frankenberg (1912): 570–72; 572; 578; 578.

Translation: Bunge (1986): 220; 221; 232–33; 233–34.

TRANSLATION

Letter 7 (Evagrius to Rufinus)

1. I am not stretching out my soul to God like a righteous man in righteousness, since I am filled with my wicked thoughts. Again, I am not near to the Lord as the Creator, since for my part I do not understand the reasons of the corporeals and incorporeals, and of judgement and providence.[6] Again, I am not like one who stands in the presence of God – I who am unworthy! – since I am not yet competent to pray 'with uncovered head' [1 Cor 11.4] by my own authority, for I am carrying about the idols of this world; I even address them at the time of prayer.[7] I vow to withdraw in spirit from the world, but with my soul I make no petition to be turned away from [involvement] with other people: I knock on the door of every house and search out every city where perhaps I might find opportunity to buy for myself the wages of vainglory, as it were, for the satisfaction of this soul of mine that loves vanities.[8]

That is enough about your 'Lazarus', whom you said 'rests in the knowledge of Abraham's bosom' [cf. Lk 16.22].

2. I applauded the intention of the prudent deaconess Severa, but I did not approve of her doing it. I do not know what advantage will accrue to her from such an arduous trek across a long distance, but whatever she and those with her are lacking is supplied by my hands to preserve them in life by the power of the Lord. But I beg Your Holiness to hinder all those who have abandoned the world from taking to the road without necessity. For I would be surprised if, throughout the whole time, they did not drink of the waters of Gihon,[9] either in the thoughts of their minds or in actual deeds – but these things are foreign to the integrity of the prudent!

Letter 8 (Evagrius to Melania)

1. I will not win a crown through praise, nor do I wish to sow discord by reproach: praise makes for vainglory and again reproach makes for grief – and where there are vainglory and grief, there are all the other appetites as well. One who is deprived of his desires is distressed, whereas one who accomplishes his purpose gets for himself vainglory. It is for Paul to say, 'Conquer by the weapon of the right hand and the left' [2 Cor 6.7]; but this is for me to say, 'My sores are putrid and fester on account of my foolishness' [Ps 37.6], and again, 'Guard me from my iniquity, for it is great' [Ps 24.11].

These things are said by me in response to your holy letter. 2. As for you, teach your community and your sons that they should not travel on a long drawn out journey and that they should not go rashly into deserted places, for this is foreign to every soul that has withdrawn from the world.

3. Everyone who wishes to travel on the way of virtue should keep diligently from sin, not only by abstaining from the act, but from the very thought in his mind. The prohibition against sinning in action is from Moses, but the command concerning the thought is from the Saviour.[10] And I would be surprised if a woman who goes round and meets ten thousand people found it possible to perfect this discipline![11]

Letter 19 (Evagrius to Rufinus)

1. Your Holiness's letter comforted us and refreshed us from our many sufferings, in equal measure. Now 'the Lord grant' you 'to find

mercy with the Lord in that day' [Tim 2.18], because you were mindful of us lowly sinners who have nothing worthy of your love.

2. I very much wanted to give something profitable for her life to the prudent virgin, but the speed of those in haste did not permit it.[12] Nevertheless, we did convey with every good wish what we had previously said with the Lord's help: to pray unceasingly in her mind, to stifle her desire with the help of self-control and to restrain her anger with the help of meekness.[13] The Word of God was previously oppressed by these thoughts.[14] Abiding in us, He is perfected according to our power, and wishes to be seen in us through the hidden works of our virtues, and to reveal in us the hidden Father and Creator.

Letter 20 (Evagrius to the Deaconess Severa)

1. Your spiritual intention was reported to me – and I am surprised by your love of learning and rejoice at your progress. After you put your hand to the ploughshare, you have not turned back seeking this corrupted world and transitory things [cf. Lk 9.62]. Instead, 'you fight the good fight' so as to be 'crowned with the crown of righteousness' [cf. 2 Tim 4.7–8] and behold Christ the bridegroom,[15] whom you seek through good acts. For this is true seeking: when one seeks the Lord through action.

2. Now there is no one who works iniquity, yet seeks righteousness; no one who hates her companion, yet seeks love; no one who lies, yet seeks the truth. So now, this is seeking the Lord: to keep the commandments, with true faith and genuine knowledge.[16] 3. The model of these things is the writing we have sent to teach you;[17] it has expounded to you 'the strait and narrow path' [Mt 7.14] that nevertheless leads to the kingdom of heaven.

THE GREAT LETTER

(*CPG* 2438)

INTRODUCTION

The following letter is sometimes praised as containing a clear and forthright expression of Evagrius' mystical theology – a fair evaluation, since it discusses at some length what Evagrius expects will happen in the *eschaton*, and expresses his views of how the soul relates to the Trinity. At various points, the *Great letter* can be correlated to Evagrius' notoriously difficult *Gnostic chapters*. But the reader must not have inflated hopes: this is still a terse, elliptical and sometimes frustratingly opaque document. Evagrius is plainly aware that the letter may circulate broadly and so has reservations about expressing himself freely (cf. §17). Such forthrightness as can be found in the letter is justified in Evagrius' eyes by his knowledge of the recipient, who can be trusted to an uncommon degree. But this raises an important question: who was the intended recipient?

The letter is frequently identified as the 'Letter to Melania [sc., the Elder]'. But at three points in the letter, Evagrius addresses a *male* reader ('my dear sir' – or, in Syriac, *mary*: §§1, 32, 39). All the same, several scholars have claimed Melania as the addressee: Irénée Hausherr, working from Frankenberg's fragmentary text (in which the crucial word *mary* occurs but once), put it down to a 'distraction de copiste';[1] Nicole Moine points to the occurrence of 'Melanius' in the writings of Jerome and Paulinus – and we might add 'Melanion' in Palladius' – and suggests that the masculine form of the woman's name may have caused confusion;[2] Martin Parmentier echoes Hausherr in claiming 'that in a gnostic context names of women are often masculinised'.[3]

On the other hand, Gösta Vitestam has overturned the attempt to reduce the difference to a copyist's error by noting that it occurs three times in the complete letter. Vitestam has advanced the more plausible view that the letter was originally addressed to a man and was only assigned to Melania by a later tradition.[4] Gabriel Bunge also dissents from identifying Melania as the recipient, noting not only the implausibility of thrice mistranslating the Greek but also that 'the tone of the *Epistula ad Melaniam* is completely different from the authentic letters written to that great lady';[5] by comparing the forms of address that Evagrius uses in the *Great letter* to his other letters, Bunge advances a persuasive case that the original recipient was Rufinus.[6] At present, Bunge and Vitestam have made the undeniably stronger case *against* identifying the recipient as Melania.

It is as well to keep this small controversy in mind when reading the letter, because it highlights different approaches to Evagrius. For Parmentier, the traditional ascription of Melania as the recipient is to be maintained precisely because of the conviction that Evagrius is a 'gnostic' who would naturally expect masculinity and femininity to be sloughed off in the pursuit of esoteric salvation. For Bunge, traditions as basic as the recipient's identity are no more sacrosanct than are those that see in the *Great letter* a clear statement of Evagrius' heresy.

Sources: Frankenberg (1912): 610–19 (for §§1–32) and Vitestam (1964) (for §§17, 24, 25, 33–68). Regrettably, there is no critical edition that takes into account the witness of both manuscripts.

Translations: Parmentier (1985): 2–38; Bunge (1986): 303–28.

TRANSLATION

[1] 1. My dear sir,

You know that when those who are separated far from each other by a great distance (which many different necessities may occasionally bring about) want to know – or to make known to one another – those intentions and hidden secrets that are not for everyone and are not to be revealed to anyone except those who have a kindred mind, they do so through letters. And though they are far apart, they are near; though distant, they see and are seen; though silent, they speak and hear; though they seem to sleep, they keep vigil in that their intended actions are fulfilled; though sick, they flourish; though resting, they are active; I might even say, 'though dead, they live' – for a letter is able to relate not only what is, but also what has been and what shall be.

2. The mutual affection of the senses is visible in the way they all show their strength by compensating for their fellow-senses. Thus, the hand substitutes for the tongue; the eye, for the ear; the paper, for the soil of the heart that receives the intentions sown in it by the furrow of the lines. As for the rest – the many different benefits, significations, differences and strength that are found in them – now is not the time to speak concerning each and every one of them.

3. The one who can [read] these letters rejoices in them – and so, I would say, does one who cannot, when he is helped whenever necessary by one who can. The former benefits from what he sees, the latter from what he hears. But the benefit of hearing is not as great and stable as that of seeing; you know what a difference there is between them.[7]

4. In the light of all these things, who is able to give worthy thanks to the Giver of this gift? For this, I think, is greater than the multitude of his gifts: in it is shown more abundantly the might of the Giver's wisdom and love. It is evident, then, that one who is far from his friend becomes aware of his friend's intentions by the hand, finger, pen, ink and the rest of the things used for writing. One who is near has no need of all these things: either he uses his mouth, so that breath and word together tend to ear and heart, or else hand and finger alone tend to eye and heart. And indeed the one who is far from his friend and sees [the letter] is pleased by what he sees, whereas the one who is near is pleased by what he hears.

5. All these things done through letters are types for absolutely everything that is undertaken by those who are far from God, who through their contemptible deeds have created a rift between themselves and their Maker. Now God in his love has fashioned creation as an intermediary. It exists like a letter: through his power and his wisdom (that is, by his Son and his Spirit), he made known abroad his love for them so that they might be aware of it and drawn near.[8]

6. Through creation, they become aware not only of God the Father's love for them, but also of his power and wisdom. In reading a letter, one becomes aware through its beauty of the power and intelligence of the hand and finger that wrote it, as well as of the intention of the writer; likewise, one who contemplates creation with understanding becomes aware of the Creator's hand and finger, as well as

of his intention – that is, his love. 7. You may ask me, 'How can the hand and finger stand for the wisdom and power – or rather, the Son and the Spirit?' Listen to the Spirit of God, who says, 'The Lord's right hand has shown strength, and the Lord's right hand exalted me' [Ps 118.15]; and, 'Your right hand, Lord, is glorified in strength', etc. [Ex 15.6]. The 'right hand' and the 'power' are the Son. As for the Spirit, the Son says in his gospel, 'If it is by the Spirit of God that I cast out demons . . .' [Mt 12.28]; but according to another Evangelist, he says, 'by the finger of God' [Lk 11.20]; so the 'finger' and the 'wisdom' are the Spirit of God. It is thus evident that the hand and finger of God, and the power and wisdom of God, are the Son and Spirit of God. 8. All this ministry is through creation for those who are far from God, some of whom take pleasure in him by what they see and others, in what they hear.

But there are some who are so receptive because of their purity and good deeds and are so near to God that they do not need letters (that is, creation) to become aware of their Creator's intention, wisdom and power. They are ministered to by Word and the Spirit (that is, the hand and the finger) directly and not through the mediation of created things. 9. For example, one who speaks is not served by his word apart from his breath, nor is his breath comprehensible apart from his word;[9] one who gestures does not gesture with his hand and not his finger, nor with his finger and not his hand. As it says, 'Heaven was made by the Word of the Lord, and all its inhabitants by the Spirit of his mouth' [Ps 33.6]; and 'The heavens declare the glory of God and the firmament reveals the works of his hands' [Ps 19.1]; and 'Because they contemplated your heavens, the work of your fingers . . .' [Ps 8.3] – see, both 'Word' and 'Spirit', both 'hand' and 'finger'!

10. Do not ask, 'Why did you speak of *many* fingers, even though the Spirit is one?' Do not listen to me; instead, listen to Isaiah, who spoke of 'the Spirit of wisdom', 'the Spirit of understanding' and other spirits besides [cf. Is 11.2]. *Many* spirits, then? That is not what we should deduce from these words. You listened to him, so now listen to Paul, who says: 'There are many varieties of powers, but the Spirit at work is one' [1 Cor 12.4]. 11. Instead of creatures who minister by making known to those far off their Creator's intention, power and wisdom (insofar it is possible to do so though giving them form), his love, power and wisdom minister to those who are nearby and who, though creatures, are pure, rational and intelligible. They give form to their Creator's wisdom and power as clearly as mighty and ancient signs.

12. Just as the Wisdom and Power (that is, the Son and the Spirit) are signs by which the Father's love is known, in the same way rational beings are signs (as we have said) in which the Father's power and wisdom are known. The Son and the Spirit are signs of the Father by which he is known, and rational creation is a sign by which the Son and the Spirit are known (in keeping with the verse, 'in our image' [Gen 1.26]). The sign of intelligible and immaterial creation is visible and material creation, just as visible things are the types of invisible things. 13. Now we are the reasonable creation and (for reasons that it is not possible to explain here)[10] we are joined to this visible creation; so, with respect to visible things, we must eagerly advance by them toward, and come to understand, the things invisible. Yet we cannot accomplish this as long as we fall short of completely knowing the import of perceptible things. 14. Just as the affairs [written] in letters are hidden from those who do not know how to read, likewise one who fails to understand the visible creation also fails to be aware of the intelligible creation which is deposited and hidden in it, even as he stares at it. Thereafter, he begins to perceive the Power and Wisdom and to proclaim unceasingly the meaning of the incomprehensible Love that is administered by them, that is, the Power and Wisdom.

15. In short, the body by its actions reveals the soul that inhabits it, and in turn the soul by its movements proclaims the mind – which is its head; it is just the same with the mind – which is the body of the Spirit and the Word. Like the body with the soul, it reveals the one inhabiting it; its soul in turn reveals its mind – which is the Father. Now the mind through the mediation of the spirit acts in the body; in the same way, the Father through the mediation of his spirit acts in his body – which is the mind. 16. Now the mind's body does not know what the mind does, but the mind (that is, the body's mind) knows what the body has done, is doing and will do. This is because the mind is alone amongst all the creatures and orders in being the true form that is receptive of the knowledge of the Father, for it 'is being renewed in knowledge according to the image of its creator' [cf. Col 3.10]. 17. Now if letters, in service of those far away, can signify what has happened and what will happen, how much more can the Word and the Spirit know everything and signify everything to their body, the mind. I can truly say that many pathways full of various distinctions meet me here[11] – but I am unwilling to write them down for you because I am unable to entrust them to ink and paper and because of those who might in the future happen to come upon this letter. Furthermore, this paper is overburdened

with presumption and it is therefore unable to speak directly about everything.

18. It is clear that there are some things that ink and paper cannot relate – and likewise creation, which is like a letter, may be unable to convey its Author's complete intention (by which I mean, his nature) to those who are far away, since they are not all according to his image.[12] But the Word and the Spirit are signs of the Father: they know everything and make everything known, since they are not creatures but rather are the exact image and true radiance of the Father's essence. **19.** So every mind knows because the Word and Spirit make all known to it, for it is their true image and their likeness that is shown to it. In the same way, someone near his friend can make his every intention known through his word and breath – and if there is something that cannot be declared to his friend by word and breath,[13] it is not because he is unable to relate them, but because the listener is unequal to them all. **20.** The mind (qua *his* mind) is equal to everything, whereas the body does not even know its own nature and the soul knows its body's nature but not its own. If it knew its own nature, it would no longer be a soul but a mind. **21.** Yet the mind does not become aware of its own nature except through the Word and the Spirit, which are its soul. The body's nature is unknown except by the soul that inhabits it and the soul is unknown apart from the body;[14] likewise, the Son and Spirit are not known except through the mind that is their body. The mind's soul knows that mind forever, even without its body, since it has the same nature as that mind, i.e., the Father.

22. Now it will happen that the names and numbers of 'body', 'soul' and 'mind' will pass away since they will be raised to the order of the mind (as in, 'Grant them to be one in us, as you and I are one' [Jn 17.22]); likewise, it will happen that the names and numbers of 'Father', 'his Son', 'his Spirit' and 'his rational creation' – that is, 'his body' – will pass away (as in, 'God will be all in all' [1 Cor 15.28]).[15] **23.** But when it is said that names and numbers of rational creation and its Creator will pass away, that does not mean that the hypostases and names of the Father, Son and Spirit will be expunged. The mind's nature will be united to the nature of the Father in that it is his body [cf. 2 Pet 1.4]; likewise, the names 'soul' and 'body' will be absorbed into the hypostases of the Son and Spirit and the one nature, three persons of God and of his image will endlessly remain, as it was before the Incarnation and will be after the Incarnation, because of the concord of wills. **24.** Therefore there is number in body and soul and mind because of the variation of wills. Once the names and numbers that came upon the mind because of the movement have passed away, then the many names by which God is named will also pass away. Because rational beings actually are varied, God is necessarily addressed in a manner derived from providence – thus, the Judge because of offenders; the Avenger because of sinners; the Doctor because of the sick; he who raises the dead, because of the dead; he who repents and executes, on account of enmity and sin; and so forth.[16] **25.** It is not as though all these distinctions do not exist; rather, those who needed them do not exist. But the names and persons of the Son and the Spirit will not pass away, because there is no beginning and no ending to them: since they have not received them from an impermanent cause, they will not pass away. But when (and so long as) their Cause exists, they exist. They are unlike rational creation, whose Cause also is the Father: those [he caused] from grace, but these from the nature of his essence.[17]

26. As we said of the mind, it is one in nature, person and rank. Falling at some point from its former rank through its free will, it was called a soul. And it descended again and was named a body. But at some point there will be a time when the body, soul and mind – because of differences of their wills – will [become] this. Since their differences of will and movement will at some point pass away, it will rise to its former creation: its nature and person and name will be one, which God knows. The thing that rises in its nature is alone amongst all beings in that neither its place nor its name is known; and again the naked mind alone can say what its nature is.[18] **27.** Do not be surprised that I said concerning the unification of rational beings with God the Father that they will be one nature in three persons, without addition or alteration. If this visible sea (which is one in nature, colour and taste), when many rivers of different taste join it, not only is not changed to their qualities, but instead easily changes them completely to its own nature, colour and taste – how much more so the intelligible, infinite and immutable sea, that is, God the Father?[19] When like torrents to the sea the minds return to him, he completely changes them to his own nature, colour and taste: in his endless and inseparable unity, they will be one and no longer many, since they will be united and joined to him.[20]

28. In the mingling of rivers with the sea, no addition to its nature or change to its colour or taste is found; likewise there is, in the mingling of minds with the Father, no generation of doubled natures or quadrupled persons. The sea is one thing in nature, taste and colour before and after the rivers mingle with it; so, too, the divine nature is one in the three persons of Father, Son and Spirit before and after the minds mingle with it. **29.** We also see that, before the waters of the sea were gathered into one place and dry ground became visible, the rivers were one in it but afterwards they were separated from it [cf. Gen 1.9], being many and different because each and every one of them was differentiated by the taste of the earth in which it happened to be.[21] Likewise, before sin made a separation between the minds and God (in the same way that the land did between the sea and the rivers), they were one with him and undifferentiated. But when their sin became apparent, they separated themselves from him and estranged themselves from him in taste and colour, each and every one of them taking the taste of the body bound to it. Now when the land is removed from their midst, the rivers and sea will be one and undifferentiated. Likewise, when the sin between the minds and God is expunged, they will be one and not many. **30.** But although I said the rivers were formerly in the sea, do not therefore think that the rational beings were in the Father, as it were, eternally with him in their nature. Even if in his wisdom and creative power they were eternally with him, their creation was temporal.[22] Yet there is no end to them because of their union with him who has neither beginning nor ending.[23]

31. My thoughts were drawn to all these things when I was inclined to scrutinise the great gift of letters. And since by this great marvel I was gladdened and roused to the glory and grace of the one who gave it, I was inclined to set down these things for you, my friend, so that you might plait a garland of unending praise for him who makes praise his own. And let us petition him that, just as he has in his mercy counted us worthy to laud him for these small things, he will again in his grace – not through the mediation of any created thing, but through the mediation of his Son and his Spirit – count us worthy to delight in his unending love and to praise him for all he has done. Amen.

[2] **32.** Hear, then, what is the reason for this letter to your grace, and forgive us for dwelling a while on its cause.

I am certain, my dear sir, that you know there are some people who say that habit is a second nature. Now to me this expression seems not only unwise, it also heralds the lack of erudition and discernment of the people who use it. As an erudite man, you well know that, since the properties are not in their nature, it is as difficult for a camel to soar through the air like an eagle or a fish to frolic on dry land (and there are many other similar examples that would happen with difficulty!) as it is for a thing to be changed in its nature.

As for habit, just as an eagle can easily soar through the air or at need stand on the earth, and a fish makes its way readily from river to river, or river to sea, or sea to river, since this course is in their nature, likewise everything established by one habit is readily dissolved by another habit. This is because in its nature room is found for them both.

33. What I mean is that the matter is thus: I am in the habit of taking nourishment once a day;[24] but if I wanted to adopt a superior habit, I could take it every other day or, contrary to the habit, twice a day. As I said, one habit can dissolve another – since nature can be inclined this way and that. So, as for nature, it is *natural* to take nourishment at the appointed time, *supernatural* not to take any at all and *unnatural* to be constantly gluttonous; examples similar to all these [could be multiplied].[25] **34.** So a thing that is superior to habit or contrary to habit is unremarkable, since all these things happen according to nature. But a thing that is beyond nature or contrary to nature is remarkable indeed – and the remark appropriate to what is beyond nature is praise, whereas the remark for what is contrary to nature is reproof.

35. Now we must seek to know how many natures, ranks, combinations and dispositions there are;[26] how many movements each and every one has and what their opposites are; of their movements and their opposites, which of them are naturally set in motion at their appointed times from within apart from any created cause, which are built up (albeit by created causes in their nature), which creates an effect on its own nature when it happens to be constituted of elements – whether dry and warm, warm and moist, moist and cold, cold and dry – and one element becomes dominant or when the combination of all of them together is even; which of them, even if a cause sets them in motion, do not pass into action and which do not complete their action since the nature is not up to it; and whether any of them can be completely extirpated from the nature and, once extirpated, whether another can be planted in its place. **36.** Having threshed out all that, we will then understand what happens in nature, above nature and contrary to nature.

As I see it, unless one is first aware of all these distinctions, he will not take pains with what is above nature – even, I say, if he passes the course of his life according to nature. For who can depart from darkness if he has not seen the light, or abandon the husks [cf. Lk 15.16] if he has found no bread, and so forth? **37.** Now just as the blessed Moses made known the story of the perceptible creation to the sons of men (and you well know at what rank they are!), we pray that, by the help of God's grace, we likewise might be somehow able to speak about this visible body and its combinations, ranks, dispositions and movements.

38. Now then, as for the number of natures of created beings, only two are known: the perceptible and the intelligible. He whom we decline to approach (by reason of his concealment and grandeur) can be known – insofar as is possible – through this perceptible [nature], like the soul through the body. **39.** So let us begin, as best we can, with a word on the body's nature and properties. As a competent man, my dear sir, you know that this perceptible body has been composed from the four perceptible elements by the glorious Wisdom of God; and since it has its composition through them, it also has its life and death, its health and sickness through and from them – and none of this is apart from the providence of its Creator. **40.** It is like we said of the movements that conform to the combinations that are found in it.[27] The combinations are these: warmth and coldness, dryness and moisture. It is therefore impossible to live in dryness with no moisture and in warmth with no coldness. So when there is equilibrium of the combinations, then it is in health as its movements move in an orderly way; but when one of the combinations becomes dominant, it disrupts the whole order. Therefore these combinations are an inducement to equilibrium.

41. The ranks of the intelligible body are also these: life and death, health and sickness. Its dispositions are these: sitting and standing, walking and reclining, silent and garrulous. Its movements are these: hunger, sleep, lust, rage, fear, distress, enmity, sloth, disquiet, cunning, savagery, pride, mournfulness, lamentation and wickedness. The opposite movements are these: satisfaction, vigilance, loathing, serenity, fortitude, gladness, love, diligence, quiet, simplicity, meekness, humility, joy, consolation and goodness. Its senses are seeing, hearing, smelling, tasting and feeling. All of these properties – and whatever else may be like them that has not been noted – we have in common with wild animals, since the body has all that the wild animals have. **42.** There is no way to contemplate them all together constantly in the body. But when one of them is moved at its appointed time (whether it is by an internal or external cause), it effectively moves another, opposite effect from the body – even if [the latter] is mighty in the body, as can be seen at its own appointed time. Thus, when hunger is present, satisfaction is absent; likewise, sleep and vigilance, grief or fear and joy or fortitude, and so forth.

43. Yet you must know that these opposites are not completely removed. For hunger springs from satisfaction and grief from joy. The body cannot be without them, although it does not use them all simultaneously: it does not always keep vigil, nor does it always sleep; it does not always eat, nor does it always abstain. 44. This is so for all the aforementioned movements and their opposites, following the three ranks (by which I mean, following life, health, sickness) and six dispositions mentioned above. As for sleep and vigilance: those attached to vigilance and to health are separate from sleep and sickness, even if not entirely from all of them. In sleep, we observe that eating, vision, discernment, rage, distress and joy in effect are dormant – as with others like them. 45. But not all those that are dormant in sleep are dormant in sickness; instead, the movements are dormant according to how extensive and strong it is. On the other hand, all of them accompany health and vigilance, even if they do not all act simultaneously. Breathing, for instance, is always found, in vigilance and sleep, in health and in sickness, and in the body's every movement – for breathing is the body's life. Just as breathing is found in and with them all and they all accompany it, likewise death is separate from them all and terminates them all.

46. In accordance with what we said about the body's subjugation to the soul (since the latter is able to do everything like God, in whose image it is), it might be thought that even while the body lives certain of the movements we mentioned can be renounced. Again, it might be thought, as certain people say, that if it were perfectly in the likeness of God as it was created, it could even elevate it above all the movements; but since it renounced being the image of God and willingly became the image of animals [Rom 1.23], it is subjugated to all those movements of the body which it has in common with the beasts and wild animals. When it is beneath its nature by its actions, it is not possible for it to make its body above its nature by its movements. Fire cannot extinguish a fire, nor can water dry water; likewise, the soul that is in the body by its works not only cannot liberate the body from its own attributes, in fact it even lends to the body properties that do not belong to it – for pride, vainglory and avarice do not belong to the body.

47. Now when its movements follow, occurring in a natural and orderly way, they are a sign of some small portion of health for the soul; but when there are none, it is a sign of perfection.[28] Yet the body has no credit herein, since on its own it does nothing wonderful (that is, something beyond its nature); the soul does it. But, again,

the soul is not worthy of much remark, since it has not done anything worthy of much remark. Even if it made the body above its nature, all the same it remained in its own nature and what it has done in a natural way deserves neither remark nor credit. **48.** And this is not mine, but his who created the soul and who, knowing what the soul is able to do, said, 'But when you have done all this, say, "We are useless servants, we have only done what we were ordered to do"' [Lk 17.10]. It is obvious that the servant's master does not command what he cannot do. **49.** Again, it does not deserve remark, since it was not by itself and it remains in its own nature. Just as the body ascends from its nature through the health and strength of the soul, so, too, the soul ascends through the strength and wisdom of God according to his nature. **50.** What very much deserves remark is the providence of the Lord of All; what deserves remark is the fact that he made use of all these things (I mean, what is natural, unnatural and supernatural). Now it calls for remark and reproof when someone is found to act unnaturally, but neither reproof nor praise when he is acting naturally. As for acting supernaturally, this is not something he can do and therefore he deserves neither remark nor praise. He is merely far from being blameworthy, since even if he does many virtuous things, he is in the event acting in a natural way.

51. As the body cannot live without nourishment, likewise the soul cannot live without virtues; and as a single day's nourishment does not suffice the body for the rest of its days, likewise the virtues completed in a day do not suffice to keep us alive. Now if every day this perceptible and limited body needs such nourishment, how much more does the soul (which is not limited by people) need unlimited nourishment every hour? **52.** But why do I say that virtues are required by the soul like food by the body? Rather, aren't virtues required by it just as breathing by the body? The body can survive even for a few days without food, but not even for one hour without breathing.

53. Now I call for us neither to weary of cultivating virtues, nor to put our trust in accomplishments and forego cultivating them because we suppose the ones from the past are sufficient, nor expect thanks from anyone or from God because of what we have accomplished or are cultivating any more than we do for the food our body receives (after all, we do not expect thanks from anyone for something that we eat!). In fact, nothing we do because of our needs and on their account makes us praiseworthy: whether we do them is up to us and it is our loss if we do not. On the other hand, God has done everything – whether natural, supernatural or unnatural – for our sake and not his own, as he has no need of these things. Therefore he deserves praise for them all and it is impossible for him to be fittingly praised by the rational creatures. **54.** Everything he has done (as we have said) is natural, unnatural or supernatural: natural or unnatural for him, but supernatural for us. If a human does nothing above his nature and instead accomplishes virtues in keeping with nature, how much more is it the case that the one who is the Sum of All Goods will not do anything contrary to his nature?

55. There are three things impossible with God: first, a deficiency of his will or, second, of his creative power or, third, of his efficacy. For he does not wish anyone's death [cf. 2 Pet 3.9], nor can he create another essence that is eternal like him, nor commit a sin. And there is nothing that can be done beyond his nature. **56.** To his nature belongs this good, namely, that when we did not exist and when he had no need of us, without being asked he created us in his image and made us heirs to all that is his by nature and essence [cf. Rom 8.17; Gal 4.7]. What is unnatural (and yet natural)[29] to him is that he descended and endured everything that is ours because we departed from our own nature – that is, everything from conception to death. But it came upon him not as one whose actions deserved these punishments, but because of his natural love in freeing us from the curse and all that follows upon it (which we received because of our transgressions, but which he received without transgressing) – and he was able to blot them out from us.

57. It is unnatural that God should be 'born from a woman' [Gal 4.4]. Yet, because of his love for us and since his nature is not bound by or subjected to any law, God *was* born from a woman in keeping with his will (so that his being was not destroyed), to free us from the conception and birth of the curse and transgression and to bear us anew in a birth of blessing and righteousness. **58.** As for us, because we willingly corrupted our own nature, we arrived at this conception and birth that is enclosed by the curse. As for him, while being what he is, in his grace he received at his birth everything that follows from birth to death. Now these things are not only unnatural to him, but I would even say that they are unnatural to us, too. Because of the transgression we committed, we have willingly fallen into them – from which we are freed. But he willingly took them upon himself without transgression, since on our own we are unable to rise from them. We fell into them because we committed a transgression, but he not only did not dwell among them, but even raised us up because (as we have said) in his love he descended into them without transgression.

59. Now what is supernatural was for a person to be born from a woman without intercourse, for his mother's virginity remained intact.[30] What surpasses human nature was for a man to die voluntarily and, after his death, to rise voluntarily, without corruption and without assistance from others. God, who loves humans, became human, was voluntarily born without intercourse, died as he willed and voluntarily rose without corruption. For 'his right hand and his holy arm preserved him' [Ps 97.1], this God who became a man while still being God. 60. He is the leaven of divinity who, in his goodness, has hidden himself in the unleavened lump of humanity.[31] Not only did he not lose his own nature, taste and vitality, instead he drew the whole lump to all that is his. Just a little while and even leaven hidden in an unleavened lump is revealed; but after a time, even if the whole lump does not appear leavened, it actually is.

61. Likewise, Our Lord appeared as a human in our time, our world and our measure; but in his time, his world and his kingdom, even if the man does not seem to be God, he actually is. In this world, they were not two (God and man), but one (God for himself and simultaneously man for us); likewise, in his world, they are not two (God and man), but one God (God for himself who is God and man, since God became human) – for just as the former is man because of the latter, likewise the latter is God because of the former.[32] 62. Now when God became human, he lost not one of his natural attributes; but the man did not remain in all his natural attributes or in those surpassing his nature and instead lost that whereby causally he was a human. On the one hand, it belongs to human nature to be 'made in the image of God' [Gen 1.27]; on the other, it surpasses human nature for us to become in his likeness, as in 'I have come that they might have life and have it abundantly' [Jn 10.10] and again 'I was established in my kingdom and abundant glory was added to me' [Dan 4.36 (Theodotian)].

63. Rightly did the prophet, when he was amazed to see all that has been done, call him 'Wonder' [cf. Is 9.6] who did all these things from his love for the rational beings. Worthy of praise and amazement is this Wonder! For it is an unutterable wonder that the nature of the rational beings, which because of its creation and the beginning of its being and because of the mutability of its will is estranged from the divine nature (which in turn is uncreated and created all and is immutable), should be joined to the nature of its Creator and by his grace become one with him in all things without end. 64. Now, my dear, I tell you that, just as astonishment seized the prophet when he saw these things and cried 'Wonder!', wonder

likewise seizes me at all these things that happen to me along the way that I have taken. But I am kept from the goal that I began since I am bound by the mighty chains of loving those things that ceaselessly please me.[33] I fall short of fully completing what I began.

65. For my part, I say that this beginning doubtless occurs for the sake of that ending. Just as the journey of one seeking to arrive at the end of all torrents will arrive at the sea, likewise the one who seeks to arrive at the power of some created thing will arrive at the 'Wisdom full of diversity' [cf. Eph 3.10] who established it. **66.** Anyone who stands on the seashore is seized by amazement at its limitlessness, taste, colour and all it contains, and at how the rivers, torrents and streams that pour into it become limitless and undifferentiated in it, since they acquire all its properties. It is likewise for anyone who considers the end of the intellects: he will be greatly amazed and marvel as he beholds all these various different knowledges uniting themselves in the one uniquely real knowledge and beholds them all become this one without end.

67. Since just now, as the desired end suddenly came upon us, we have desisted from accomplishing our first goal, see what is treasured up for you and me and all who want it in the great treasury of all the stores of wisdom – Christ's bosom, on which John reposed at the Supper [Jn 13.23]. And it was shown to him who was the traitor, but this was disclosed to him at the Supper. So without the bosom and the Supper, the traitor would not be known. But consider that, as soon as he was made known, he departed and there was serenity [Jn 13.30].

68. It is not fitting for the good earth that has received seed to produce only what it received; instead, it should produce 'thirtyfold, sixtyfold, a hundredfold' [Mt 13.8, 23]. It is likewise with your competent mind: the seed that has been scattered in it should not remain alone, but take care that what was sown in you should bear much fruit, so that the Husbandman will be exceedingly glad and always entrust to you his seed. And the earth will be blessed and many poor cared for. And thus from the Husbandman and from the earth and from those who are cared for there will arise glory and hallelujahs to him who is the First Husbandman, to whom belong all the seeds of blessing for ever. Amen.

TREATISES

INTRODUCTION

Evagrius wrote a number of treatises and, though they are not as well known as some of his other writings, they are invaluable for understanding his work. With the greater scope of a sustained treatment, Evagrius makes connections that are only implicit in the chapters. This feature of the treatises can be particularly helpful in that Evagrius observed no restriction of subject in writing them, so it is possible to find in the treatises lengthy considerations of the full range of topics in the corpus. In the translations that follow, we find a general statement of the principles and motivations of the monastic life (*Causes*), a wide-ranging and intensive treatment of monastic psychology (*Thoughts*) and a briefer but still relatively extended discussion of prayer (*A word about prayer*). Thus, the themes that Evagrius explored in his treatises are co-extensive with his pedagogical division of Christianity into ascetical and ethical practice (*Causes*), knowledge of creation (*Thoughts*) and theology (*A word about prayer*).

Of the works here translated, *Thoughts* and *Causes* survive in Greek; *A word about prayer* comes down to us in Syriac – but we can be confident of its Evagrian provenance because, as the editor of the piece noted a long time ago, it contains an identifiable quotation from Evagrius' *Causes*. It bears pointing out that there are further treatises in both languages – for instance, in Greek: *To Evlogius* (*CPG* 2447) and *On the eight spirits of evil* (*CPG* 2451); in Syriac: *On the Cherubim* (*CPG* 2460) and *On the Seraphim* (*CPG* 2459 – a version of which also survives in Armenian).

In annotating these treatises, I have made an attempt to correlate them to other writings. But these notes are in no sense intended to be exhaustive. There are assuredly many other points of contact between the treatises and his other works, and (as I have already suggested) the rather more expansive format of the treatise allows Evagrius to draw connections that are not drawn when he writes in other genres. The reader is therefore encouraged to make connections between the teachings set forth in his treatises and the teachings set forth elsewhere: it may prove a worthwhile exercise for cultivating an Evagrian habit of thought.

THE CAUSES FOR
MONASTIC OBSERVANCES,
AND HOW THEY COMPARE
TO STILLNESS

(*CPG* 2441)

INTRODUCTION

The text here presented is in some ways quite basic: in it, Evagrius deals with primary concerns about how to lead a monastic life but does not treat of the higher mysteries of theology. The way the subjects are treated is deliberately accessible to novices. For example, the tone of *Causes* is very practical, as for instance when Evagrius comments rather diffidently on the need to sell one's handiwork. It is perhaps for this reason that *Causes*, though relatively widely available in modern translations, has received little scholarly attention. It does not speak to the issues for which many readers turn to Evagrius. This is a pity, as the treatise is hardly insignificant. Indeed, it is difficult to think of what could be more important than a lucid exposition by Evagrius of the foundations of monasticism.

Apart from this general importance, three features of this work are of special interest. The first is his emphasis on the importance of the cell in the monastic life.[1] Evagrius rarely allows himself to develop these themes at length (we might contrast his laconic observations about the cell to the far richer treatise by another desert father, Paul of Tamma),[2] but Evagrius' discussion here is all the more important for that. The second feature is Evagrius' emphasis at §9 on the use of a meditative, even imaginative, reflection on Judgement Day. This call to engage in a vivid, emotional meditation is at odds with the expectation that Evagrius' preferred form of spirituality was thoroughly free of imagery (if not outright hostile to imagery).[3] In this way, *Causes* 9 elucidates a much terser reference to remembering one's sins at *Prayer* 144; the coincidence of the theme in a basic and an advanced work thus suggests that such meditations are beneficial, even for accomplished practitioners. Finally, in this treatise more than in any other writing, Evagrius treats of stillness – or *hesychia* – a theme of tremendous significance in the Byzantine ascetic and spiritual tradition. The question of Evagrius' influence for that tradition is badly in need of further research and for any such research this treatise will surely be fundamental.

Source: No critical edition of the text is available, but two published versions are found in the *Philokalia* and in Migne. In addition, Migne also published a fragment, spuriously attributed to Athanasius, of *Causes* 1–8 (PG 28: 845–50); see Kirchmeyer (1958): 384 n. 4 and, more generally, Muyldermans (1932): 60–62. This translation is chiefly based upon the text reprinted by Migne (PG 40: 1251–64); at certain points I have followed the reading of the *Philokalia*, as indicated in the endnotes.

Translations: Palmer *et al.* (1979–): 1: 31–37; Bettiolo (1996): 165–83; Sinkewicz (2003): 4–11.

TRANSLATION

1. In Jeremiah, it is said, 'And you shall not take to yourself a wife in this place, for thus says the Lord concerning the sons and daughters who are born in this place: "They shall die a foul death"' [Jer 16.2–4]. Here is what the word reveals: that (according to the Apostle) 'the married man is concerned about things of this world, how he may please his wife', and he is divided; 'and the married woman is concerned about the things of this world, how she may please her husband' [1 Cor 7.33–34]. It is also clear that 'they shall die a foul death' was said by the prophet not just about the sons and daughters who come from a married life. It was also said about those sons and daughters who are begotten in the heart (that is, fleshly thoughts and desires) that they shall die in the foul and sickly and enfeebled arrogance of this world and not be prepared for heavenly and eternal life. 'But the unmarried', he says, 'is concerned about the things of the Lord, how he may please the Lord' [1 Cor 7.32] and will produce the ever blooming and deathless fruits of heavenly life.

2. Such is the monk, and it is fitting that the monk be thus: abstaining from a wife, having neither son nor daughter in the heart, as mentioned above. Not only that, but he should also be Christ's soldier, not material, not concerned, set apart from business considerations and actions – as the Apostle also said: 'No soldier embroils himself in the affairs of life, so that he may please the one to whom he signed on' [2 Tim 2.4]. Let the monk make progress in these things, especially as he is one who has given up all the things of this world, and hurries toward the beautiful and good trophies of stillness. How beautiful and good is asceticism for stillness, how truly beautiful and opportune! Its 'yoke is easy and its burden light' [cf. Mt 11.30]: the life is sweet, the struggle delightful.[4]

3. Do you wish, then, beloved, to take up the monastic life as it is, and hurry toward the trophies of stillness? Then abandon the cares of this world and the principalities and powers set over them! That is, be free from material things and from perturbations, set apart from every desire.[5] If you thus become a stranger to all that concerns them, you will be able to be still in happiness; yet if one does not withdraw from them, he will never be able to follow this way of life rightly.

Keep to meagre food that is cheap, not plentiful food that easily distracts. But if a thought of extravagant foods should arise (for instance, for the sake of hospitality), abandon it immediately; you should certainly not run to it! By it, the enemy lies in wait for you, to keep you away from stillness. You have the Lord Jesus rebuking Martha, a soul busy with such things, and saying, 'Why are you distracted and troubled about many things? There is need of one thing', he said, 'and it is to heed the divine word; after that everything follows with no toil.' And so he immediately went on, saying, 'For Mary has chosen the good portion, which shall not be taken from her' [cf. Lk 10.41–42].

You also have the example of the widow of Sarephtha, in whose home the prophet was hospitably received [3 Kgs 17.10–16]. Even though you only have bread, or water, with them you will be able to attain the reward of hospitality. And even if you do not have these things, but simply receive the stranger with a good disposition and give him a useful word, you will thus be able to procure the reward of hospitality. For it is said, 'Better a word than a gift' [Ecclus 12.16].[6]

4. About almsgiving, it behoves you to take care for such things as these: you should not desire to have wealth to give to the poor. For this, too, is a deception from the Evil One that often arouses vainglory and casts the mind into complicated business matters. You have the widow in the Gospel of whom the Lord Jesus bore witness, who surpassed the resolve and power of the wealthy when she left her two mites. 'For they', he said, 'out of their abundance cast into the treasury, but she put in her whole substance' [Mk 12.44].

Concerning clothes, you should not desire to have surplus clothes. Take thought only for what suffices for the exigencies of the body. Rather, cast your care on the Lord and he will take thought for you [Ps 54.23]. For he himself cares for us, it says [1 Pet 5.7]. If you need food or clothes, do not be ashamed to accept what others offer you, since that is a kind of pride. But if you yourself have a surplus of such things, give them to one in need. God would have his children care for each other in this way. Therefore the Apostle, too, when he wrote to the Corinthians about those in need, said, 'Your surplus for their need, so that their surplus may also be for your need, that there may be equality; as it is written, "The one with much does not abound, the one with little does not lack"' [2 Cor 8.14–15; Ex 16.18]. So when you have what you need for the moment, have no care for the future, whether for a single day, or a week, or a year, or months. For when tomorrow's time has come, the time itself will supply what you need. For your part, seek first the kingdom of heaven and the righteousness of God, since the Lord said, 'Seek first the kingdom of God and his righteousness, and all these things will be added to you' [Mt 6.33].

5. Do not have a boy, lest perchance the Enemy set in motion some scandal about you through the boy and stir up your sense of care so that you have a care for sumptuous foods.[7] For you will no longer be caring for yourself alone. And if as it were there comes the thought for bodily rest, think of what is better – I mean spiritual rest, since truly spiritual rest is better than bodily rest. Even if the thought enters your deliberation for the sake of the boy's welfare, do not obey it: this is not our responsibility. It belongs to others, namely, the holy fathers in communal life. Have a care for your own welfare, and protect the habit of stillness.

Be unwilling to live with material and encumbered men.[8] Either live alone, or with brethren who are not material and are likeminded with you. For one who lives with material and encumbered men will himself share completely in their encumbrance and be enslaved to human impositions, to empty chattering, and to all other dangers, to wrath, grief, madness for material things, fear, scandal. Do not be caught up in cares for parents or friendships with kinsmen. Instead, avoid even chance meetings with them, lest they carry you away from the stillness of your cell and involve you in their encumbrances. 'Leave the dead to bury their dead', said the Lord, 'but you come, follow me' [Mt 8.22].

But if even the cell in which you sit should be an encumbrance, flee it – do not spare a thought for it and do not slacken from love for it. Do and attempt everything that you may be able to be still and have respite[9] and become eager for the will of God and the struggle against the invisible ones. 6. If you are unable to be still readily in the parts where you live, fix your purpose on exile and stir up your thought for doing it. Become like a skilled businessman, examining everything with an eye to stillness and keeping only such still things as contribute to it. But I tell you, love exile, since it frees you from all encumbrances arising from that specific place and it makes the solitary free for the sake of stillness. Avoid spending time in the city, and steadfastly pass your time in the wilderness. 'For, behold,' says the saint, 'I have protracted my flight and dwelt in solitude' [Ps 54.8]. If possible, do not enter the city at all. You will find nothing there that is useful, helpful or beneficial for your way of life. Again, the saint says, 'I have seen lawlessness and iniquity in the city' [Ps 54.10].

Seek out places that are private and unencumbered, and do not be afraid of the noises of such places.[10] Even if you see apparitions of demons there, do not be dismayed nor flee from that stadium that will benefit us. Endure fearlessly, and you will behold the great things of God [cf. Acts 2.11], the aid, the solicitude and every other guarantee of deliverance. The blessed man says, 'I look for him who delivers me from faint-heartedness and from the tempest' [Ps 54.9]. Do not let the desire for roaming overcome your resolve, for 'roaming with desires undermines the incorrupt mind' [Wis 4.12]. There are therefore many temptations. Fear making a misstep, and sit in your cell.

7. If you have friends, avoid chance meetings with them, since you will be useful to them by putting off meeting them. But if you perceive that harm might come to you through them, do not so much as approach them: it is needful for you to have friends who are beneficial for, and likeminded with, your way of life. Flee, too, meeting evil and contentious people, and never live with such people. Instead, excuse yourself even from their wicked purposes, since they do not adhere to God, nor do they remain in him. Let your friends be peaceful people, spiritual brethren, and holy fathers. For the Lord was calling them by name when he spoke thus: 'My mother and brethren and fathers are those who do the will of my Father who is

in heaven' [Mt 12.50]. Do not dwell with people who are encumbered, and do not go to banquets with them, lest they draw you into their treacheries and lead you from the knowledge that is in keeping with stillness. That passion is among them, and they are truly harmful.

Let your desire be for the faithful of the earth, and the work of your heart be for imitating their mourning. For 'my eyes are on the faithful of the earth, that they may live with me' [Ps 100.6]. If one of those who walk in the love of God comes to you inviting you to eat with him, and you wish to go, then do – but return to your cell quickly. If possible, do not sleep anywhere else. In this way the grace of stillness will always abide with you and you will serve God in keeping with your purpose without embarrassment.

8. Do not be keen for good food and the treacheries of wantonness. As the Apostle said, 'the wanton woman is dead even as she lives' [1 Tim 5.6]. Do not fill your stomach with varied foods, so that you will not have a desire for them and conceive in yourself a desire for outsiders' tables. For it is said, 'Do not be deceived by a full stomach' [Prov 24.15]. If you find yourself being invited outside your cell frequently, excuse yourself. Frequently spending time outside your cell is harmful: it deprives you of grace, overshadows your care, quenches your desire.[11]

Consider with me the jar of wine that has long sat in the same place and has not been disturbed, how the wine is rendered clear, settled and fragrant. But if it is carried here and there, the wine is stirred up and gloomy and all at once it reveals the distasteful effect of the lees. So then compare yourself to the wine and benefit from the comparison: flee the conditions of the masses, lest your mind be cumbered and your habit of stillness be confounded.

Take care to work with your hands, and if possible do so day and night, to the end that you burden no one, but instead can make donations. This is in keeping with what the sacred Apostle Paul advised [cf. 1 Thess 2.9; 2 Thess 3.8; Eph 4.28]. Indeed, you can thereby overthrow the demon of despondency[12] and eliminate all the other desires of the enemy, since the demon of despondency lies in wait for laziness and 'is in desires', as it is said [Prov 13.4].

You will not avoid the sin of buying and selling. So whether you are buying or selling, suffer a little more than what is fair. Otherwise, impelled by eagerness for the sake of accuracy or out of greedy habits, you might fall into things dangerous to your soul's causes: arguments, false oaths, and going back on your words. In so doing, you would dishonour the honour of our profession and shame its worth. So, considering this, keep yourself from buying and selling. If you opt for what is best, and it is possible for you, cast this care of yours onto another one of the believers, so that being even-tempered you may have fair and happy hopes.[13]

9. So these are the useful things that the habit of stillness knows how to advise. Look, now I will set before you the meaning of the observations that follow it.

As for you, listen to me and do what I tell you. Sit in your cell and gather your mind. Recall the day of death. Next see the body's dying. Consider the event. Embrace the suffering. Reflect upon the vanity in this world. Have a care for fairness and zeal, so that you may always be able to remain in the same profession of stillness. And do not be weak. Remember, too, the state that now exists in Hell. Consider how the souls already there are, in what most bitter silence, or most terrible groaning, how great the fear and agony, what they have to look forward to – the unending pain, the unlimited spiritual tears – but also remember the day of resurrection and the proximity to God. Imagine that fearful and awesome judgement. Bring front and centre what has been set aside for sinners: shame before God and his Christ, angels, archangels, powers and all humans; all the forms of correction: the eternal fire, the worm that does not die [Mk 9.48], the underworld, the shadow, the gnashing of teeth [Mt 8.12] for all these things, the fears and the tortures. But also bring the good things that have been laid aside for the righteous: free approach to God the Father and his Christ, the angels, archangels, powers and every people; the kingdom and its gifts; the joy and the release.

Remember both of them to yourself. And groan, weep and put on the form of mourning for the judgment of sinners, fearing lest you yourself also be numbered among them. But rejoice, exult and be glad at the good things that have been set aside for the righteous. Exert yourself to enjoy the latter, but avoid the former. See to it that you do not forget these things, whether you happen to be in your cell or outside it somewhere, and be careful not to leave off remembering them. Thus, you will avoid sordid and dangerous thoughts through them.[14]

10. Let your fast equal your strength in the sight of the Lord. It will purify your iniquities and sins, magnify your soul, sanctify your purpose,[15] drive off the demons, and prepare you to be near God. Eat once per day, and do not desire a second meal, otherwise you will become extravagant and trouble your purpose.[16] In this way, you will be able to have a surplus for works of beneficence and you will also be able to put to death the body's passions. And if there

should be a meeting of the brethren and it is necessary that you should eat two or even three times, you should be neither embittered nor downcast.[17] Instead, rejoice – for you have been subject to necessity. And the second or third time you eat, give thanks to God since you have fulfilled the law of love and you will thereby have God as the steward of our life.

But there are also times when it happens that the body is sick, and eating two or three or many times is required, so let your thought be ready for it. It is not obligatory to persevere in the bodily sufferings of our way of life even in times of sickness. Instead, make a small concession so that, once you have returned quickly to health, there is once more exercise in the sufferings of our way of life. Now concerning abstinence from foods, the divine Word does not order us not to eat anything, but says, 'Lo, I have given you everything as herbs of the field; eat, asking no questions. And it is not what enters the mouth that defiles a man' [Gen 11.3; 1 Cor 10.25, 27; Mt 15.11]. So abstaining from food should be of our own resolve and the soul's labour.

11. Gladly bear sleeping on the ground and vigils and all other sufferings, looking toward the glory that will be revealed to you with all the saints.[18] 'For the present sufferings', he says, 'are not worthy to be compared with the future glory that will be revealed in us' [Rom 8.18]. But if you are disheartened, pray, as it is written [Jas 5.13] – pray with fear, reverence, effort, alertness and vigilance. It is necessary to pray thus, particularly on account of the malignant and indolent ones, that is, our invisible enemies who wish to abuse and threaten us at it. When they see us standing to pray, they are eager to stand near us and suggest to our mind things that it is not appropriate to ponder or consider at the time for prayer.[19] In this way, they lead our mind captive and make the petition and intercession of our prayer inactive and vain and useless. Prayer and petition and intercession become truly vain and useless when they are not brought to perfection in fear and reverence, with alertness and vigilance, as has already been said.[20] Since one comes before a human king to make a petition with fear and reverence and alertness, is it not all the more appropriate to stand likewise and similarly make one's petition and intercession before God the Lord of all and Christ, the King of kings and Power of powers?

So to God be the glory forever. Amen.

ON THOUGHTS

(*CPG* 2450)

INTRODUCTION

Evagrius is renowned for his penetrating psychological insight and he allows himself his broadest canvas for exploring these themes in this treatise. The focus of the work, however theoretically sophisticated it may be, is practical: with it, Evagrius seeks to instil in his readers an understanding of how to face, evaluate and respond to various thoughts. It may be significant that, in some manuscripts, the treatise bears the more specific title *On wicked thoughts*, because Evagrius is specially concerned to describe the process of temptations that come through thoughts. But this description is couched within an extensive consideration of basic psychological mechanisms. Since these concerns are found throughout his writings, *Thoughts* is, for our purposes, prerequisite for understanding the compressed and elliptical claims that Evagrius makes elsewhere. As regards his original readership, however, *Thoughts* should be regarded as a guidebook for the advanced. This is clear, for example, from the way that themes already announced in *Causes* are treated in far more detail when Evagrius returns to them in *Thoughts*. Evagrius' two treatises are related in a way comparable to trigonometry and calculus: in *Causes*, certain principles are announced and the reader, through practice, gains familiarity with their operations; in *Thoughts*, the principles already familiar from *Causes* are reconsidered within a broader framework that reveals *why* those operations function as they do, so that the reader, through practice, gains an even more intimate familiarity with their operations.

For the theoretical underpinning of the argument, Evagrius is chiefly indebted to the Stoics. He follows Zeno, for instance, in frequently using the middle form of the verb *typoô* (to be imprinted, or impressed, upon) to describe how the mind is affected by concepts or perceptions.[1] It is noteworthy that, for Evagrius, being thus imprinted upon in some way compromises the integrity of the person. He categorically exempts from this claim only those concepts or thoughts that come directly from God, which indicates that God is capable of acting upon the mind without disrupting it in any way. (This qualification to his psychological rule must be recalled when we read, in the *Great letter*, about the reconciliation of created minds to their Creator.)

Evagrius also considers in some detail the roles of memory, dreams and emotion in the ascetic life. In this way, he builds upon the theoretical foundation that he adapts from Stoic philosophical anthropology with the kind of practical considerations that have a bearing on monastic daily life. By incorporating such workaday features into the discussion, he is able to demonstrate how monastic introspection works as well as offer an account of why it works the way that it does. His aim in all of this is to promote pure prayer. It is therefore important when reading his *Prayer* to be aware of the principles set forth in *Thoughts*.

One particularly significant claim that Evagrius makes more clearly in this context than he does elsewhere is that emotions such as joy and sensations such as calmness are positively valuable as indicators of spiritual progress. For instance, at *Thoughts* 28, he distinguishes angelically inspired dreams from demonically inspired dreams by saying that the former 'have great calm of the soul, in-effable joy, the privation of perturbed thoughts by day, pure prayer, and some reasons of created things that slowly emerge from the Lord and reveal the wisdom of the Lord'. This ineffable joy is directly related to the feelings of joy that accompany pure prayer (see, e.g., *Prayer* 15, 23, 62, 93, 153). This positive valuation of emotion makes it clear that there is a vast difference between Evagrius' teaching of *apatheia* (translated in this collection as 'imperturbability') and apathy, or insensibility. It is worth dwelling on the point, if only briefly, because from as long ago as c.415, concern has been expressed about that term. Jerome, in his letter to Ctesiphon (*ep.* 133) objected to *apatheia* on the grounds that such a property is had only by God and by stones; he also connected it to sinlessness. Augustine similarly was anxious about *apatheia*, though in the end his own view was far more nuanced than Jerome's. Cassian never used the term himself, though he did provide an accurate Latin gloss of having this attribute as 'being free from all perturbations'.[2] This unease with the term in the Western tradition has been bequeathed to us, with the result that modern readers sometimes bring a level of anxiety to reading Evagrius' works that is not obviously warranted. As this treatise makes abundantly clear, there is no need to be anxious about Evagrian imperturbability as though it implied the extirpation of emotions.

Source: The text is translated from Géhin *et al.* (1998).

Translations: A French translation is available in Géhin's edition and a Latin translation appears with the text at PG 40: 1240–44 and 79: 1200–33; for an English translation, see Sinkewicz (2003): 136–82.

TRANSLATION

1. Of the demons who oppose the ascetic struggle, the first to arise for battle are those devoted to the appetites of gluttony, those who suggest avarice to us and those who lure us toward human glory;[3] all the others march after them, taking up in turn those who have been wounded by them. It is not possible to fall into the hands of the spirit of evil unless one has already fallen under gluttony. Nor can the irascible part be stirred up unless one is fighting over food or wealth or glory. Indeed, it is not possible to flee the demon of grief if one loses or cannot obtain all these things. Nor can anyone who has not discomfited avarice, which is 'the root of all evils' [1 Tim 6.10], evade pride, which is the Devil's firstborn — since indeed 'poverty humbles a man' [Prov 10.4], according to Solomon the wise.

To speak to the point, no one can fall to a demon unless he has been wounded by these demons on the front line. For this reason the Devil presented these three thoughts to the Saviour: first, bidding him to turn stones to bread; second, offering the whole universe if he would bow and worship him; third, saying that if he obeyed he would be glorified, suffering nothing from such a fall. But Our Lord, showing himself superior to these things, ordered the Devil to get behind him [cf. Mt 4.1–10], thus teaching us that it is not possible to repel the Devil unless one despises these three thoughts.

2. All the demonic thoughts import concepts of perceptible things into the soul. The mind, being imprinted on by them, bears about in itself the shapes of these things and from the thing recognises at length the demon that has drawn near. Thus, if the face of one who

has wronged or dishonoured me should appear in my thinking, the thought of grudge-bearing is proven to be approaching. Or again, if a recollection of wealth or glory should appear, what is afflicting us will be clearly recognised from the thing. It is likewise for the other thoughts: you will find who is present and suggesting them from the thing. But I do not mean that all memories of such things result from demons. After all, when one sets it in motion, the mind itself naturally brings up appearances of created things. I refer only to such memories as unnaturally draw along one's irascibility or desire. Through the disorder caused by these powers, the mind commits adultery and fights in its thinking so that it is unable to take up the appearance of God the law-giver,[4] whereas this luminosity appears to the governing faculty at the time of prayer after the suppression of all concepts of things.[5]

3. One cannot divest oneself of impassioned memories without taking care for one's irascibility and desire, by consuming the former with fasting and vigils and sleeping on the ground and calming down the latter by being long-suffering, free from grudges and charitable with alms.[6] From these two passions arise nearly all the demonic thoughts who bring the mind 'to ruin and destruction' [1 Tim 6.9]. It is impossible for one to overcome these passions without completely scorning food and wealth and glory – and even his own body since there are those who often try to strike it. So it is altogether necessary to imitate those who, being in danger on the sea on account of the force of the winds and swelling waves, throw their tackle overboard.

But in this case exacting attention is necessary lest, in throwing our tackle overboard, we make a spectacle before other people – for then we will have our reward in full and a second shipwreck more dangerous than the first will follow as the demon of vainglory stirs up unfavourable winds.[7] So to instruct the pilot (that is, the mind), Our Lord said in the Gospels, 'Pay attention in your almsgiving not to do it before other people so as to make a spectacle for them; if not, you have no reward from your Father who is in heaven' [Mt 6.1]. And again, he said, 'When you pray, do not be like the hypocrites, who love to pray in front of the synagogues and market-places that they may be seen by other people; amen, I tell you, they have their reward in full' [Mt 6.5]. And he said again, 'When you fast, do not put on a sombre face like the hypocrites, for they darken their faces that they may be seen by other people to be fasting; amen, I tell you, they have their reward in full' [Mt 6.16].

So in this case it is necessary to pay attention to the physician of souls: how he heals the irascibility through alms, purifies the mind through prayer and again palliates the desire through fasting. From these practices, 'the new man' arises 'being renewed according to the image of his Maker' in whom, through holy imperturbability, 'there is no male and female' and, through a single faith and love, 'there is no Greek and Jew, circumcision and uncircumcision, barbarian, Scythian, slave and free, but Christ is all in all' [Col 3.10–11].[8]

4. How the demons imprint on and shape our governing faculty by appearances in dreams must also be explored. Such things typically result in the mind either through the eyes for one who sees something or the ears for one who hears something; or from some kind of perception; or else from a memory that, rather than making an impression on the governing faculty, instead sets in motion what it has obtained through the body. So then the demons seem to me to imprint on the governing faculty by setting memory in motion, since the organ of perception[9] rests in sleep and is inactive.

Again, how they set the memory in motion must be explored. Is it perhaps through the passions? Clearly so, from the fact that those who are pure and imperturbable never suffer such an incident.[10] But there is also a certain simple movement of the memory that happens either from us or from the holy powers and, in keeping with it, in our dreams we meet the saints and converse with them and entertain them within our homes. Again, attention must be paid to the fact that, quite apart from the body, the memory can set in motion the false images that the soul receives from the body.[11] This is obvious from the fact that we often suffer this even in our dreams when the body is at rest. Now just as it is possible to remember water with thirst and without thirst, it is likewise possible to remember gold with greediness and without greediness; so, too, with other things. It is a token of their ability to work evils that the mind finds such different kinds of appearances. At the same time, this too must be known: the demons also use external things to fabricate an appearance, such as with the sound of waves for sailors.

5. When our irascibility has been set unnaturally in motion, it strongly contributes to the aim of the demons and becomes extremely useful for all their wicked schemes. Thereafter none of them fails to stir up the mind by night and day. But when they see it bound to meekness, they find some just pretexts for loosening that bond so that the mind, having become keener, may be used for their beastly thoughts. It is therefore necessary never to provoke it,

whether for just or unjust causes, and not to give an evil sword to those who suggest it – which is something that I know many people often do and get worked up more than is necessary for small pretexts.[12] Tell me, what is it that you cast yourself so readily into a quarrel for [cf. Prov 25.8], if indeed you scorn food and wealth and glory? Why are you feeding the dog while claiming you have nothing?[13] If it barks and attacks people, it is quite clear that you have goods inside and want to guard them.

As for me, I am persuaded that such a person is far from pure prayer, as I know that irascibility destroys such prayer. For the rest, I am stunned that such a person has forgotten the saints – such as David, who cried out, 'Leave off anger and renounce irascibility' [Ps 36.8], and the Preacher who proclaims, 'Put away irascibility from your heart and drive evil from your flesh' [Eccl 11.10], and the Apostle who bids us 'in every place lift up hands without anger and disputes' [1 Tim 2.8]. What do we not learn from the ancient and mystical custom of people who drive the dogs out of their houses at the time of prayer? This enigmatically shows that irascibility should not be present in those who pray. Here again: 'The wine of dragons is their anger' [Dt 32.33] – and Nazarites abstained from wine [cf. Num 6.3]. Also, a pagan sage proclaimed that the gall-bladder and loin are inedible for the gods; but I do not think he knew what he was saying, since I reckon that the former is the symbol of anger and the latter, of irrational desire.[14]

6. I think it is redundant to write concerning the fact that one ought not to be anxious about clothing or food, since Our Saviour himself forbade this in the Gospels: 'Do not be anxious in your soul about what you will eat, or what you will drink, or what you will wear' [Mt 6.25, 31]. This is obviously the part of heathens and un-believers who set aside the Master's providence and deny the Creator. But it is utterly foreign to Christians, once they have believed that even 'the two sparrows that are bought for a copper' [Mt 10.29] are under the stewardship of the holy angels. However, the demons' custom is to launch thoughts of anxiety after they have launched impure thoughts, with the result that Jesus will 'turn aside on account of the crowd' [Jn 5.13] of concepts in the area of thinking and the word, having been 'choked out by the thorns' of care, will be fruitless [cf. Mt 13.22].

So having set aside the thoughts that come from anxiety, let us be satisfied with what is available and cast our anxiety on the Lord [cf. Ps 54.23; 1 Pet 5.7]; adopting a poor way of living and dressing, let us strip off the fathers of vainglory. But if someone reckons he will be disgraced by a poor way of dressing, let him look to St Paul who awaited a crown of justice 'in cold and nakedness' [2 Cor 9.24]. And since the Apostle called this world a 'theatre' and a 'stadium' [1 Cor 4.9; 9.24], let us see if it is possible to 'run toward the prize of the high calling of Christ' [Phil 3.14], or to fight against the 'powers and authorities and rulers of this world of darkness' [Eph 6.12], whilst clothed in thoughts of anxiety. For my part, I do not know. I have, however, learnt from observing perceptible things: clearly, an athlete dressed this way will be impeded by his tunic and will easily be dragged round by it; likewise the mind, by its thoughts of anxiety[15] – as indeed the word is truthful which says that the mind is resolutely attached to its treasure: 'For where your treasure is', he says, 'there will your heart be also' [Mt 6.21].

7. Of the thoughts, some wound and others are wounded; the evil thoughts wound the good ones, and again they are wounded by the good thoughts. So then the Holy Spirit attends to the thought that is established first, and either condemns or accepts us on account of it. What I mean is this: I have some thought of hospitality and I have it from the Lord; but it is wounded when the Tempter approaches and suggests that I be hospitable for the sake of glory.[16] And again: I have the thought of hospitality for the sake of being made known to people; but this, too, is wounded when it is outrun by the better thought which instead steers our virtue toward the Lord and forces us not to do these things for the sake of other people.[17] If then we ultimately abide with the first thoughts in our actions, even though we have been tempted by the second ones, we will only have the reward of the thoughts established first. Being human and having to fight the demons, we are not always strong enough to retain the right thought unscathed. On the other hand, since we have the seeds of virtues, we are not always strong enough to keep the wicked thought from being tested. But if one of the wounding thoughts endures, it is established in the place of the one it wounded and ultimately it is according to that thought that we will be moved to act.

8. We have learnt the difference between angelic, human and demonic thoughts, after much observation.[18] Firstly, the angelic thoughts thoroughly investigate the natures of things and trace out their spiritual reasons; thus: Why was gold created and strewn like gravel in the lower parts of the earth, and why is it found only with much effort and difficulty? And [they investigate] how, once it has been discovered, it is washed in water and committed to the fire and thus put into the hands of the craftsmen who made the lamp-stand, the censer, the thurible and the vessels of the Tabernacle

[cf. Ex 25.31; 1 Macc 1.21–23]. By the grace of Our Saviour, the King of Babylon no longer drinks from those vessels [Dan 5.1–5], but Cleopas bears a heart burning with these mysteries [cf. Lk 24.32].[19] Now the demonic thought neither knows nor understands these things, but shamelessly suggests only the possession of perceptible gold and foretells the delight and glory that will come from it. And the human thought neither desires to possess gold, nor thoroughly investigates what gold is a symbol of, but simply introduces into one's thinking the simple form of gold, as distinct from the passion of greediness.

The same analysis can be carried out on other things, if it is mystically practised according to this rule.

9. There is a demon called 'Wanderer'[20] who, coming near the brethren chiefly around dawn, leads the mind around from city to city, from village to village and from house to house. By making supposedly simple encounters, then encountering acquaintances and talking at length, the mind thus corrupts its own status by these meetings and gradually becomes further from the knowledge of God and even forgetful of virtue and of its own profession. So it is needful for the anchorite to observe whence this demon begins and where he leaves off – for not by accident nor by chance does he make this long trip. Instead, he does these things wishing to corrupt the anchorite's status, so that the mind, incited by these things and inebriated by the many encounters, will fall more readily to the demon of impurity or of wrath or of grief, who particularly ruin the radiance of its status.

But if we have as our purpose to understand clearly the demon's villainy, let us neither address him quickly nor disclose the things that are happening, such as how he fabricates these encounters in our thinking and in what manner he drives the mind by degrees toward death. If we disclose those things, he will flee from us (for he will not endure being seen to do these things) and we will ultimately know none of the things we had wanted to learn. Instead, let us allow him a day or two to perform his little act so that, having learnt his deception quite precisely, we can with reason put him to flight by refuting him thereafter.

Now since it sometimes transpires at the time of temptation that the mind, being turbid,[21] does not know precisely what is happening, do this after the demon's withdrawal: sit down and remind yourself of the particular things that have befallen you (whence you departed, where you were going, in what place you were apprehended by the spirit of impurity or of wrath or of grief – again, how the things that happened, happened). Study these things and commit them to memory so that you will be able to refute him when he approaches and point out his hiding-place and that in the end you will not follow him.

And if you want to drive him mad, challenge him as soon as he appears and with a reasonable word demonstrate the first place where he tried to enter, and the second, and the third. He will be deeply angry since he cannot bear the shame. Take as proof that you have addressed him in a timely fashion, the fact that the thought flees from you; for it is impossible that he should remain once he has been openly challenged. A very deep sleep follows upon this demon being defeated, as does mortification along with a great chilling of the eyelids, unlimited yawns and shoulders that are heavy and numb — all of which the Holy Spirit thaws by eager prayer.[22]

10. Hatred for the demons contributes greatly to our salvation and is convenient for working at virtue, though we are not strong enough by ourselves to rear it up like a good child. This is because the pleasure-loving spirits corrupt virtue and call the soul back to friendship and habit. But the Physician of souls heals this friendship — or rather, this inoperable gangrene — through abandonment.[23] For he allows us to suffer some terror from those spirits by night and day, so that the soul hastens back to its original hatred, having been taught by the Lord to say with David, 'I have hated them with a perfect hatred, they have become enemies to me' [Ps 138.22]. For the one who never sins in action or in thinking hates the enemies with a perfect hatred: and this is a sign of the greatest and foremost imperturbability.

11. Why is it even necessary to speak about the demon who makes the soul insensitive? For my part, I am afraid even to write about this — how the soul is transported from its proper status at the time of his coming and gives up the fear of God and reverence; how it does not think that sin is a sin, nor reckon that transgression is a transgression; how it recalls chastisement and eternal judgement simply as words, and actually 'laughs at the fire-bearing earthquake' [Job 41.21]; and how it supposedly acknowledges God, but does not know what he has ordered. When it is moved to sin, you beat your breast but it remains insensitive; you reason from the Scriptures but it is totally calloused and does not listen; you expose it to the censure that comes from other people, but it thinks nothing of the shame among the brethren; it has no understanding, like a pig who closes its eyes and breaks through its fence.

Persisting thoughts of vainglory summon this demon, whom 'if the days were not shortened, no flesh at all would survive' [Mt 24.22]. It is also the part of those who rarely approach their brethren – and the cause of this is self-evident, for he is put to flight by the misfortunes of others who are oppressed by illnesses or who lie in prisons or who are overtaken by sudden death. This is because the soul is gradually pricked and comes to feel compassion as the callousness worked up by this demon is done away with. But we lack these [opportunities] owing to the desert and to the dearth of sick people among us. In the Gospels, the Lord ordered us to look after the sick and watch over those in prison chiefly to put to flight this demon, when he said, 'I was sick and you watched over me, in prison and you came to me' [Mt 25.36].

What is more, it must be known that if one of the anchorites, falling to this demon, does not accept impure thoughts or abandon his home out of despondency, he has received the moderation and endurance that come down from the heavens and is blessed in such imperturbability. But as many as resolve to dwell with seculars, even though they profess piety – let them beware of this demon! As for me, I am ashamed before men to say or write anything more about it.

12. All the demons teach the soul to love pleasure, except for the demon of grief,[24] who does not try to do this. Instead, he even destroys the thoughts of those who draw near, cutting off and drying up every pleasure of the soul by grief, as indeed 'the bones of the grieving man are dried up' [Prov 17.22].[25] But if he fights fairly, he will render the anchorite approved. For he will persuade the anchorite to approach none of the things of this world and to avoid every pleasure. If, however, he is resolutely attached, he sires thoughts who advise the soul to slip away from itself or forces it to flee to a faraway place – which is what St Job thought about and suffered when he was tormented by this demon. 'If only', he said, 'I could lay hands on myself or at least make another do it for me!'[26] [Job 30.24].

Now this demon's symbol is the viper, that beast whose secretion destroys the poison of other beasts when given to people in the proper dosage, but when taken straight destroys even the animal itself.[27] Paul gave over the transgressor in Corinth to this demon, and so he wrote again quickly, saying to the Corinthians: 'Confirm your love toward him, otherwise such a man would be overwhelmed by too great a grief' [1 Cor 5.5; 2 Cor 2.7–8]. But he knew that this spirit that afflicts people can become a patron for good repentance. And that is why St John the Baptist called those who were goaded by this demon and fled to God a 'brood of vipers', saying, 'Who warned you to flee from the coming wrath? Therefore make fruit worthy of repentance, and do not presume to say to yourselves, "We have Abraham for our father" – for I tell you that God is able to raise up children for Abraham from these stones' [Mt 3.7–9]. So then everyone who has, in imitation of Abraham, come out from his land and from his kinsman [cf. Gen 12.1] has become mightier than this demon.

13. If one has conquered irascibility, he has conquered the demons; but if one is enslaved to it, he is altogether a stranger to the monastic life and foreign to the ways of Our Saviour, as indeed the Lord is said to 'teach the meek his ways' [Ps 24.9]. And so the mind of the anchorites becomes difficult to capture when it flees into the plain of meekness, for the demons fear hardly any of the virtues as they fear meekness. The great Moses himself possessed this and was called 'meek beyond all other men' [Num 12.3]; and St David declared that it is worthy of being remembered by God, when he said, 'Remember, Lord, David and all his meekness' [Ps 131.1]. Our Saviour also bade us be imitators of this meekness, saying, 'Learn of me, for I am meek and lowly in heart, and you shall find rest unto your souls' [Mt 11.29].[28] Now if someone abstains from food and drink, but irritates his irascibility with wicked thoughts, he is like a ship sailing the open sea that has a demon for its pilot. So it is necessary, as far as possible, to pay attention to this dog of ours and to teach it only to destroy wolves and never to eat lambs, showing all meekness to everyone.

14. Alone among the thoughts, that of vainglory has a surfeit of material, embraces nearly the entire inhabited world and opens the doors to all the demons, like a wicked man betraying a city.[29] Furthermore, it particularly humbles the mind of the anchorite by filling up the mind with words and things, ruining the prayers by which the anchorite strives to heal the wounds of his soul.

All the demons, once they have been defeated, join in exaggerating the thought of vainglory,[30] and again through it they all have an entrance into the soul, thus truly making 'the last state worse than the first' [Mt 12.45]. From this thought is also born that of pride, which cast 'the seal of the likeness and crown of fairness' [Ez 28.12] down from heaven to earth. 'But turn from this place and do not delay', lest we betray our living to others and our life to the merciless [cf. Prov 9.18; 5.9]. Now what puts this demon to flight is intense prayer and doing or saying nothing that would contribute toward accursed glory.

15. When the anchorites' mind attains a bit of imperturbability, then taking the horse of vainglory it rushes straight to the cities and fills itself with the undiluted praise that comes from its glory. Then by God's dispensation the spirit of impurity encounters it and closes it up in one of his pig-sties, teaching it never to do so much as get out of bed before it has perfect health and not to imitate the disarray of those sick folk who, though still bearing in themselves the remnants of infirmity, take to roads and to the baths untimely and relapse into their diseases.[31] Therefore, keeping seated, let us attend rather to ourselves so that, progressing in virtue, we may become disinclined toward vice;[32] being renewed in knowledge, we may take hold of the fullness of diversified contemplations; again, being elevated by prayer, we may see the clearer light of Our Saviour.[33]

16. I am unable to write about all the villainies of the demons, and ashamed to catalogue their ruses, fearing for the simpler of those who eventually come upon this book.[34] Still, listen about the villainy of the spirit of impurity: when one has obtained imperturbability of the concupiscible part and the shameful thoughts begin at last to cool, it is precisely then that he introduces men and women cavorting with each other and makes the anchorite a spectator of shameful things and shapes. But this is not one of the temptations that lasts for long, since short prayer and a strict regimen, with vigils and exercises of spiritual contemplations, will drive him away like 'a waterless cloud' [Jude 12]. Sometimes he even lays hold of the bodies, stoking in them an irrational heat.[35] And this wicked one fashions myriad other devices which it is not necessary to publicise or commit to writing.

Now the seething heat of irascibility is extremely useful against these thoughts of the demon, which is chiefly what he fears when it is stirred up against the thoughts and destroying his concepts. Hence, the passage, 'Be angry and sin not' [Ps 4.5] – a useful medicine to apply to the soul faced with temptations! But the demon of anger also imitates this demon and feigns certain parents or friends or kinsmen being abused by worthless people and sets the anchorite's irascibility in motion so as to address some wicked word or do some wicked thing to the apparitions in his thinking. One must be attentive to such things and immediately tear such idols out of one's mind, lest by dwelling on them one become a 'smoking fire-brand'

[Is 7.4] at the time of prayer. Irascible people, particularly those who are readily inflamed with anger, fall to these temptations – and such people are far from pure prayer and the knowledge of Christ our Saviour.

17. The Lord gives one the concepts of this age as sheep to a good shepherd, 'and', it says, 'he gave the age to his heart' [Eccl 3.11], having yoked to him irascibility and concupiscence to assist him. This is so that, by irascibility, he may put to flight the concepts that are of wolves and, by concupiscence, he may show his love for the sheep, even though he is often battered by the wind and the rain. With these things, he has given a pasture where he may tend the sheep, 'a green place', 'water of refreshment', a 'harp', a 'cither', a 'rod' and a 'staff', so that from this flock he may nourish and dress himself and 'gather the mountain provender' [Ps 22.2; 56.9; 107.3; 22.4; Prov 27.25]. 'For who', it says, 'shepherds a flock and does not drink of its milk?' [1 Cor 9.7].

It is therefore necessary that the anchorite guard this flock by night and day, lest one of the concepts be caught by wild beasts or fall prey to thieves. If such a thing should happen 'in the dale', he must snatch it 'from the mouth of the lion and the bear' [cf. 1 Kgs 17.34–37]. Now the concept concerning a brother is caught by wild beasts if it is pastured in us with hatred; that concerning a woman, if it is reared in us with shameful desire; that concerning silver and gold, if it is corralled with greediness; the concepts of spiritual graces, if they are grazed in one's thinking with vainglory; and it happens likewise for the other concepts that are stolen by the passions.

It is necessary to watch out for these things not only during the day, but also to keep guard at night by keeping vigil, since it also happens that one who has shameful and wicked appearances loses his property – and this is what was said by St Jacob: 'I have not brought you a sheep that has been caught by wild beasts; for my part, I have repaid the thefts by day and the thefts by night, and I was burnt by the heat of the day and the cold of the night, and sleep was put far away from my eyes' [Gen 31.39–40]. If, then, despondency also comes over us from the toil, let us have recourse to the rock of knowledge for a while and busy ourselves with the harp, plucking the chords of knowledge with the virtues; then once more let us graze the sheep on Mount Sinai, so that the God of our fathers may call us (even us!) from out of the bush [cf. Ex 3.1–6] and grace us (even us!) with the reasons of 'signs and wonders' [cf. Ex 7.9; 11.9–10].

18. Of the impure demons, some tempt a person like a person, but others trouble the person like an irrational animal. Now the first, when they draw near, put in us concepts of vainglory or pride or jealousy or accusation, which concern none of the irrational beings. The second, when they approach, set the irascibility or concupiscence in unnatural motion – and these passions are common to us and to irrational animals, even though they are covered over by our rational nature.[36] So the Holy Spirit says to those who succumb to human thoughts, 'I have said, "You are gods and all sons of the Most High; but you will die as men and fall like one of the mighty"' [Ps 81.6–7]; and to those who are moved irrationally, he says, 'Do not be as the horse or the mule, who have no understanding – with bit and bridle you must restrain their jaws or they will not draw near you' [Ps 31.9]. If 'the soul that sins will die' [Ez 18.4, 20], it is quite obvious that people who die as people will be buried by humans, but those who perish or fall like animals will be eaten by vultures or crows, whose young either 'cry out to the Lord' [cf. Ps 146.9] or else 'sully themselves on blood' [cf. Job 39.30]. Let anyone who has ears to hear, hear!

19. When one of the enemies draws near to wound you and you want 'to turn his sword', as it is written, 'against his own heart' [Ps 36.15], then do as I tell you. Analyse within yourself the thought that has been sent by him against you: which is it; of how many things is it composed; and which among them chiefly afflicts the mind? What I mean is this. Let us suppose the thought of avarice is sent by him. Analyse this into the mind that received it, the concept of gold, the gold as such, and the avaricious passion; finally, ask which of these is the sin. Is it the mind and, if so, how? For the mind is the icon of God. Is it the concept of gold, then? Who in his right mind would say that? So is the gold as such a sin? Then why was it created? It follows, then, that the cause of the sin is the fourth, which is neither a thing that subsists in essence, nor a concept of a thing, nor yet a bodiless mind; instead, it is a certain misanthropic pleasure born from self-determination which forces the mind to use God's creations badly and which the law of God has been entrusted to excise. Now as you scrutinise these things, the thought will be dissolved in this contemplation and thus destroyed; the demonic [thought] will flee from you as your thinking is raised on high by this knowledge.

Now if you wish to use his sword but you want first to bring him down with your sling, then you, too, should take a stone from your shepherd's satchel and consider this contemplation:[37] how is it that the angels and demons draw near to our universe, but we do not draw near to theirs? For we are unable to make angels closer to God, and we cannot opt to make demons more impure. And how is it that the Morning Star, who rises before dawn, was cast down to the earth [cf. Is 14.12] and 'he regards the sea as a box of unguent, the pit of the abyss as his prisoner, and makes the abyss boil like a pot' [Job 41.23–24]? For he troubles everything by his evil and wishes to rule over all. The contemplation of these things seriously injures the demon and puts his entire encampment to flight. But this happens only for those who are slightly purified and to some extent see the meaning of created beings; as for the impure, they do not know the contemplation of these things, and even if they learnt it from others and chanted it they would not be heard, owing to the profusion of dust clouds and clamour raised in battle by the passions. For it is absolutely necessary to quieten the encampment of the foreigners so that Goliath alone goes to meet our David.

Let us make similar use of this analysis and idea of battle against all the impure thoughts.

20. Let us consider the reason why certain of the impure thoughts are rapidly put to flight. Why does this happen? Is it because of the unlikelihood of the thing (the matter being difficult to provide), or was the enemy powerless owing to the presence in us of imperturbability? Thus: if one of the anchorites, being tormented by a demon, considers in his heart being entrusted with the spiritual government of the capitol city, he clearly will not imagine this thought for long and the cause for it is patent from what we have been saying. But if it should be any city at random and he still thinks thus, he is blessed with imperturbability.[38] Upon inspection, this technique will likewise be proven for other thoughts. It is necessary to know these things for our zeal and energy, so that we may know whether we have crossed the Jordan and are near the 'City of Palms' [cf. Dt 34.3] or whether we still dwell in the desert and are struck by foreigners.

21. The demon of avarice seems to me particularly diversified and clever in deceit. Often restricted by extreme renunciation, he quickly impersonates a steward who cares for the poor, by generously receiving guests who are not yet present; by ministering to the needy; by keeping watch over the civic prisons and supposedly ransoming those who are going to be sold; by associating with wealthy women and pointing out who should be well treated; again, by bidding others who have a heavy purse to renounce it. Having thus beguiled the soul by degrees, he brings to it thoughts of avarice

and hands it over to the demon of vainglory, who introduces a throng of people praising the Lord for these acts of stewardship and even some people who speak a little amongst themselves of the priesthood. Finally, he foretells the death of the current priest and adds that one who has done so much ought not to flee.[39]

Thus the miserable mind, bound by these thoughts, attacks those people who have not accepted the idea and readily grants gifts to those who have accepted it, praising their good sense. As for those who rebel, he gives them over to the judges and demands that they be expelled from the city. Now as these thoughts are present and twisting around inside him, at once the demon of pride appears, giving the impression of continuous lightning bolts in the air of the cell and sending in winged dragons besides, thus bringing about a total loss of wits. But we, having prayed for the destruction of these thoughts, live in poverty with thanksgiving – for 'we brought nothing into this world and clearly we are not able to take anything out; so we are content with having food and clothing' [1 Tim 6.7–8], remembering that Paul said, 'avarice is the root of all vices' [1 Tim 6.10].

22. All the impure thoughts that endure in us through the passions make the mind descend 'to ruin and destruction' [1 Tim 6.9]. Just as the concept of bread endures in one who is hungry because of the hunger, and the concept of water endures in the one who is thirsty because of the thirst, so, too, the concepts of wealth and possessions endure because of greediness, and the concepts of food and the shameful thoughts born from food endure because of the passions. And it is likewise evident in the case of the thoughts of vainglory and other concepts. It is not possible for the mind choked by such images to stand before God and win the 'crown of righteousness' [2 Tim 4.8]. Drawn down by these thoughts, that thrice-wretched soul in the Gospels declined the invitation to the meal of the knowledge of God [cf. Mt 22.2–7]; and again the one bound hand and foot and cast into outer darkness by these thoughts had a garment woven from them, which the one who invited him declared was unworthy of such weddings. For the wedding garment is the imperturbability of a rational soul who has renounced worldly desires. The reason why enduring concepts of physical things destroy knowledge will be discussed in the chapters *On prayer*.[40]

23. Let no anchorite take up the anchoritic life out of wrath or pride or grief, nor let him flee the brethren while tormented by such thoughts. From such passions arise distractions of the mind, when the heart moves from this concept to another and from that one to

yet another, and from that one to still another, falling by degrees into a pit of forgetfulness. We have known many of the brethren caught up in this shipwreck, whom the others retrieved with tears and prayer to a life that befits humans. But some, who had embraced forgetfulness irretrievably, were no longer able to return to their former state and to this day we behold with downcast spirits the shipwreck of our brethren.

This passion happens chiefly as a result of thoughts of pride. When someone in this state takes up the anchoritic life, first he sees the air in his cell aflame and lightning flashing on the walls at night. Then there are the sounds of some in pursuit and some being pursued, and the impression of horse-drawn chariots in the air, and the whole house filled with Ethiopians and chaos. At length, he falls to mental distraction due to overwhelming cowardice, becomes insecure and forgets his human state out of fear.[41] So it is necessary to take up the anchoritic life with much humility and meekness and to encourage his soul with spiritual words and say to it the words of St David: 'Bless the Lord, my soul, and forget not all the benefits of Him who is benevolent to all your iniquities and heals all your disease, who saves your life from destruction and crowns you with mercy and kindness' [Ps 102.2–4]. Say this and similar things to that soul, like a mother at a festival who constantly looks after her child, lest any malefactor abscond with him.[42] But always and especially call that soul to the Lord with intense prayer.

24. Not all of the demons tempt us simultaneously, nor do they put thoughts in us at the same time, for it is not in the nature of the mind to accept two concepts of perceptible things at the same moment. As we said in chapter 17, no impure thought occurs to us apart from something perceptible.[43] Even if our mind in its extremely rapid movement joins ideas to each other, it is not necessary on that basis to reckon that they are all formed at the same time. The potter's wheel does such a thing, too, when by the great rapidity of its motion it joins to each other two pebbles fastened at diametrically opposed ends of the wheel.

It is also possible for you to form in yourself your father's face, then see whether another face appears whilst the former remains or whether the second face arises after the first has vanished. Now if it were possible to receive both the concept of gold and of one who had wronged us, then it would of course happen that we fall to the demon of avarice and of grudge-bearing at the same moment. But this is impossible because, as I said, the mind is not able to receive both the concept of gold and the concept of the one who had wronged us at the same moment. So it is necessary in moments of temptation to try to move one's mind from an impure thought to a different concept and from that to yet another, and thus to flee that evil taskmaster.[44] If the mind clings to the thing and does not move on, it is plunged into the passion and at length it is at risk of progressing toward enacting the sin, and such a mind really needs much purification and fasting and prayer.

25. Many people have contemplated things in their natures and, from their contemplations, offered a demonstration; my demonstration is first and foremost my reader's heart – particularly if it is intelligent and experienced in monastic life. I have mentioned this on account of the physical object that is now proposed for our contemplation and is being established by the reader on the basis of what has transpired in his thinking.

Let us begin with a word on how the mind by its nature receives concepts of all perceptible things and by them receives an impression through this bodily organ of perception. Now the mind necessarily receives an icon of the sort that corresponds to the shape of the thing, and because they retain the same shape these perceptions are called 'likenesses'. So just as the mind receives concepts of all perceptible things, likewise it receives them from its own organ of perception – for this, too, is perceptible – except of course for its own countenance.[45] (Never having contemplated this, the mind is incapable of forming it within itself.) With this schema,[46] our mind does everything: in its thinking, it sits, it walks, it gives, it takes. It does and says what it wants at the speed of the concepts. Taking the schema of its own body, it stretches forth its hands to receive something it is being given; then, speedily putting off that one and taking the schema of a neighbour, as it were, it gives something from its own hands. The mind could not act without such shapes, since it is incorporeal and bereft of all movements of that sort.

It is therefore necessary for the anchorite to guard his own mind at the time of temptations. For, as soon as the demon presents himself, he will seize the schema of his own body and engage inside himself in a fight with a brother or copulate with a woman. In the Gospels, Christ named a man an adulterer who has already committed adultery in his heart with a neighbour's wife [Mt 5.28]. But apart from the aforementioned schema, the mind could not commit adultery here, since it is incorporeal and unable to approach something perceptible without such concepts – and these are transgressions. So pay attention to yourself in regard to how the mind puts on the shape of its own body without the face, but expresses in thought its neighbour completely since it has seen and conceived of that person completely.[47] But it is impossible to see how these things come to be during temptations and are completed so quickly in one's thinking, without the Lord rebuking the wind and the sea, making a great calm and leading the sailor to the land to which he was hastening [cf. Mt 8.26].

Is it therefore necessary for the anchorite to attend to himself 'lest a lawless word be hidden in his heart' [Dt 15.9]? For it will be that at the time of temptations, when the demon presents himself, the mind will seize the schema of its own body. Moved by this contemplation, we have also provided an explanation of the rationale of the impure thought. For the demonic thought is an imperfect icon of the perceptible person fabricated in one's thinking, with which a mind moved to passion says or does something lawless in secret by successively forming idols for itself.[48]

26. If one of the anchorites wishes to acquire the knowledge of discernment from the Lord, first let him eagerly fulfil the commandments in hand leaving out nothing and thus, at the time of prayer, 'let him ask' knowledge 'of God who gives to everyone simply and does not chide: let him ask doubting nothing' and not casting about on the waves of disbelief, 'and it will be given him' [Jas 1.5–6]. It is not possible for one who is negligent of the things he already knows to acquire knowledge of many things more, so that he should not be accountable for many sins more for having many transgressions. And it is a blessing to be subject to the knowledge of God, for it is truly dangerous not to do the things commanded by it but a blessing if one does all that is learnt from it. The mind wanders when it is perturbed and becomes unrestrained when it looks over the materials that make for pleasures.[49] But it ceases straying when it becomes imperturbable and encounters the incorporeal ones who fulfil its spiritual desires.

So it is not possible to obtain knowledge without having made the first, second and third renunciations. Now the first renunciation is the voluntary abandonment of worldly things for the sake of the knowledge of God. The second is the riddance of vice that comes by the grace of Christ our Saviour and human zeal. The third renunciation is separation from ignorance of those things that by their nature appear to people according to the level of their state.[50]

27. So those who undertake the anchoritic life are tempted by the demons during the day and fall to diversified thoughts, and again during the night in sleeping they combat winged asps and are encircled by wild carnivores and hemmed in by serpents and thrown down

the precipice of lofty mountains. Sometimes even when they waken they are encircled again by the same beasts and see their cell filled with fire and smoke. And when they do not succumb to these appearances or give in to fear, again they see at once demons turning themselves into women who are shamefully degenerate and want to cavort disgracefully. They think up all these things because they want to trouble the irascibility or concupiscence so as to wage war on the anchorites, for the irascibility is quite keenly tempted in the day after it has been wrecked by night and concupiscence easily follows after impure thoughts after it has been set in motion by apparitions in sleep.

The demons send these apparitions on the anchorites, as I said, preparing the way for the following day or wishing to humiliate as much as possible those who were being wrecked first by night. The angry and irascible of the brethren are more likely to fall to frightening apparitions, and those who have consumed too much bread and water are more likely to fall to shameful apparitions. So then it is necessary for anchorites 'to fast and pray that they not enter into temptation' [cf. Mt 26.41] and 'guard the heart with all protection' [Prov 4.23], putting irascibility to rest by meekness and psalms, and quenching concupiscence with hunger and thirst. Mercy and doing good work well together against such apparitions. Solomon the wise clearly teaches this in Proverbs, saying,

> If you sit, you will have no fear; if you lie down, you will sleep sweetly and you will not fear the sudden terror nor forthcoming attacks from the impious – for the Lord will be upon all your ways and will stay your foot so that you do not waver. Do not abstain from doing good to the needy when your hand can offer assistance; do not say, 'Go and come later, and I will give you something tomorrow', for you do not know what the day will bring [Prov 3.24–28].

28. When the demons are unable to stir up irascibility or concupiscence by night, then they weave a dream of vainglory and make the soul descend into a pit of thoughts. To put it briefly, their dreams are of this kind: someone often sees himself censuring the demons and healing certain bodily infirmities, or wearing the shepherd's cloak and shepherding a flock.[51] Upon waking, he immediately acquires an apparition of the priesthood and then all day long thinks about the concerns of the priesthood; or, as if the graces of healing were about to be given to him, he foresees the signs that will be

performed and imagines the people who will be healed, the honours from the brethren, the presents brought by outsiders, and many people drawing near from Egypt and abroad who were driven to him by his reputation.

Often they cast anchorites into inconsolable grief by depicting for them certain of their kin being sick or in danger by land or sea. Sometimes through dreams they predict the shipwrecks of the monastic life to the brethren themselves, thus casting from the high ladders those who had climbed them and again making them blind men who feel their way along the walls.[52] And they talk up myriad wonders, availing themselves of the sound of wind for the arrival of demons or wild beasts or telling tales to pass the hours for praying the offices. It is necessary not to pay attention to them, but challenge them with a sober thought when they do these things to cheat and mislead the soul. Dreams from angels are not of that kind. Rather, they have great calm of the soul, ineffable joy, the removal of perturbed thoughts by day, pure prayer, and some meanings of created things that slowly emerge from the Lord and reveal the wisdom of the Lord.

29. If one of the anchorites should be untroubled by frightening or impure appearances among those that come during sleep, but is instead angered that they are shamefully near him, and strikes them; again, if he should be unaroused when for the sake of healing women's bodies – for the demons also show this – he touches them, and rather counsels some of them about moderation, then he is truly blessed in such imperturbability. For the soul that has by God's aid rightly pursued ascetic struggle and been loosened from the body will be in those places of knowledge where the feathers of imperturbability will give it rest and whence it will at length also receive the wings of that Holy Dove, and take flight through the contemplation of all ages, and be at rest in the knowledge of the venerable Trinity [cf. Ps 54.7].[53]

30. Of the impure thoughts, some are contemplated on the path of virtue and others alongside the path. How many of those that oppose doing God's commands pass their time 'alongside the path'! And again, they are all 'contemplated on the path' that, without pleading that God's commands not be done, suggest that the commandments (when they are done) should be done as a sight for other people – thus corrupting our aim or the manner in which it is necessary to do the commandments. Now it is necessary that one who does the commandment does it for the Lord and accomplishes it gladly, as it says 'let the one who shows mercy do so in gladness'

[Rom 12.8]. What is the use in stripping myself of the thought of greediness by gift giving, and that of gluttony by self-control, if I then dress myself in other thoughts like vainglory or griping? At the time of prayer, I will surely experience from those thoughts what also happened to me upon the first thoughts – an overwhelming of the light that illuminates the mind at the time of prayer. The blessed David also wrote about these thoughts: 'In the way in which I went they laid a snare for me' [Ps 141.4]; and again, 'They stretched out ropes as a snare for my feet; for me they placed stumbling-blocks that have the track' [Ps 139.6], where 'have' seems to me to mean 'be near' the track.[54]

31. Against the demonic thought there are three opposing thoughts that cut it off if it endures in our thinking. They are the angelic thought, the thought that is influenced by our resolve for the better, and the thought given by human nature in keeping with which even pagans are moved to love their own children and honour their parents. But against the good thought there are only two opposing thoughts. They are the demonic thought and the thought that devolves from our resolve for the worse. No thought is evil from nature; for we were not evil from the beginning, as indeed the Lord sowed good seed in his own field [cf. Mt 13.24].[55] Even if we are capable of something, it is not the case that we certainly have the power of it, since though we are able not to be we do not have the power of non-being (after all, powers are qualities and non-being is not a quality).[56] Now there was a time when there was no vice, and there will be a time when there will not be. [But there was no time when there was no virtue, and there will not be a time when there will not be.] For the seeds of virtue are indestructible. The rich man in the Gospels who was condemned to Hell but still pitied his brothers persuades me of this [cf. Lk 16.19–31], for having pity is the fairest seed of virtue.[57]

32. If someone aims at pure prayer and bringing God a mind without thoughts, let him master his irascibility and watch over the thoughts that come from it, by which I mean those arising from suspicion, hatred and grudge-bearing. It is especially those thoughts that blind the mind and corrupt its heavenly status. That is also what St Paul exhorts us, when he says: 'Lift up to the Lord holy hands without anger and disputes' [cf. 1 Tim 2.8]. But an evil custom dogs the renunciants' steps and they fight with their own people, frequently even going to court, for the sake of wealth or possessions that ought to be furnished to the poor. In our view, these people are

the demons' playthings and they make the path of the monastic life even narrower for themselves by igniting their irritability for the sake of wealth and then striving to extinguish it with possessions. It is as if someone were to prick his eyes with a pin so that he could apply eye-salve![58] Our Lord ordered us to sell our belongings and give to the poor [cf. Mt 19.21] – but not with fights and lawsuits. 'The Lord's slave ought not to fight' [cf. 2 Tim 2.4], but should give even his cloak to the one who wants to sue him for his tunic and turn the other cheek to the one who strikes him on the right [cf. Mt 5.39–40]. He should ultimately be eager, not for how he might return to take back his wealth, but for how he might not die by falling to thoughts of grudge-bearing, as indeed 'the paths of grudge-bearers lead to death', according to Solomon the wise [Prov 12.28]. In sum, let everyone who holds fast to such wealth know that he has snatched food and shelter from the blind, the lame and the leprous and that he owes the Lord an explanation on Judgement Day.

33. There are some impure demons who always sit down beside those who are reading and try to snatch their mind, frequently even taking their pretexts from the sacred scriptures themselves and finishing off with wicked thoughts. Sometimes they force them to yawn more than normal and bring on a very deep sleep that is quite different from normal sleep. Although some of the brethren have imagined that this is due to some inexplicable natural reaction, I myself have observed it many times and have learnt the following.[59]

They touch the eyelids and the whole head, cooling it with their own body (for the demons' bodies are very cool and somewhat like ice), so that we even feel as though our head is being pulled with a shrill noise by a cupping-glass.[60] They do this so as to draw off the heat stored up in the skull for themselves. At length, the eyelids are so slack from moisture and coolness that they slide over the pupils of the eyes. In fact, I have often found in touching my face that my eyelids were frozen like ice, my entire face lifeless and shuddering. Natural sleep, however, by its nature warms the body and makes the faces of healthy people fresh and bright, as experience itself teaches; whereas they prompt unnatural and protracted yawns and, shrinking themselves, they touch the inside of the mouth. Though I myself have not understood this even to this day, still I have often experienced it; but I have heard from St Macarius, who told me about it and gave the example that those who yawn sign themselves over the mouth, in keeping with an ancient and ineffable tradition.[61] We suffer all these things from not being soberly attentive in our reading and not remembering that we are reading the sacred words of the Living God.

34. Now since there is a sequence of demons when the first is weak in battle and incapable of setting his favoured passion in motion, we have found out the following from closely observing them. When the thoughts of some passion are infrequent for a long time, and suddenly there is the desire for and motion of it even though we have given no pretext for it through negligence, then we know that a demon harsher than the first has followed and kept the place of the one who fled, filling it with his own wickedness.[62] Now this one understands our soul very well, attacking it much more fiercely than usual and digressing from the thoughts of yesterday and the day before, even though no pretence has come from outside.

When the mind beholds such things, let it flee to the Lord. Receiving the 'helmet of salvation' and donning 'the breastplate of righteousness', drawing 'the sword of the Spirit' and raising 'the shield of faith' [cf. Eph 6.14–17], let the mind say with tears as it gazes up to its heavenly home, 'Lord' Christ, 'the power of my salvation' [Ps 139.8], 'incline your ear to me, hasten to deliver me, be for me a protecting God and a place of refuge for saving me' [Ps 30.3]. Let it polish its sword particularly with fasting and vigils. For seven whole days, it will be afflicted in battle, by 'the Evil One's flaming darts' [Eph 6.16]. But after the seventh day, it will know that the demon has by degrees become like the one he succeeded and ultimately it will remain for a whole year, being struck more often than striking, until the one who succeeds him arrives, if indeed like Job we 'fall to them for a prescribed time and our houses are pillaged by the lawless' [cf. Job 12.5].

35. When the demon of gluttony is powerless to corrupt the self-control that has been imprinted (even though he tries much and often), he casts the mind into a desire for stricter asceticism. Afterwards, he brings in evidence those men with Daniel, their life of poverty and their grains [cf. Dan 1.12, 16 *Theodotion*]; he calls to mind certain other anchorites who have always lived thus, or have begun to do so, and forces one to imitate them. Thus, someone pursuing an immoderate abstinence will fail even in a moderate one, as the body is no match owing to its usual feebleness. As this demon truly 'blesses with the mouth and curses with the heart' [cf. Ps 61.5], I reckon it is right not to obey him and not to keep away from bread, oil and water.[63] The brethren have learnt from experience that this is a very fine diet when not eaten to satiety and only once a day.

I would be surprised if anyone who ate to satiety were able to receive the crown of imperturbability. By imperturbability, I do not mean what hinders sins in action – for I call that 'abstinence' – but rather what circumcises the impassioned thoughts in one's thinking, which St Paul called 'the spiritual circumcision of the hidden Jew' [cf. Rom 2.29]. If someone is discouraged by the things that have been said, let him recall that 'vessel of election', the Apostle, finishing the course 'in hunger and thirst' [cf. Acts 9.15; 2 Tim 4.7; 2 Col 11.2]. Furthermore, the demon of despondency imitates this person, suggesting to those who endure a stricter withdrawal and calling him to emulate John the Baptist and Anthony the chief of the anchorites. The result is that, unable to bear the lengthy and inhuman withdrawal, he flees in shame, abandoning his place, and at last the demon vaunts, saying, 'I have prevailed over him' [Ps 12.5].

36. The impure thoughts receive much material for their growth and stretch out toward many things;[64] indeed, they traverse great seas in a person's thinking and do not decline to make long journeys for the sake of the great ardour of the passion [cf. Mt 25.13]. But those thoughts that to some extent are being purified are rather more straitened than these thoughts, in that they are not able to stretch out toward many things because of the weakening of the passion. They are therefore set in motion rather unnaturally and, according to Solomon the wise, 'they roam outside for some time' [Prov 7.12]. Since they are no longer receiving straw, they gather cornhusks to make their illicit bricks [cf. Ex 5.7–12]. So it is necessary to 'guard the heart with all protection' [Prov 4.23], so that it may be saved 'like a roe from the nets' and 'like a bird from the snares' [Prov 6.5]. It is easier to purify an impure soul than it is to restore to health someone who had been purified but was wounded again. The demon of grief would not allow it, but at the time of prayer would always pounce on the pupils of a person's eye and bring along an idol of the sin.[65]

37. The demons do not know our hearts as some people reckon: God alone, 'who knows people's mind' [Job 7.20] and 'fashioned their hearts one by one' [Ps 32.15], knows the heart [cf. Acts 1.24; 15.8]. They, on the other hand, know many of the things that are in the heart from a word being uttered and comparable bodily movements.[66] For my part, I wanted to specify them clearly, but our holy priest forbade me, stating that publishing such things and putting them in the ears of the impure is inappropriate – 'as indeed', he said, 'one who has intercourse with a menstruating woman is guilty before

the law' [cf. Lev 15.19–24].[67] [He would let me say] only that they know the things hidden in our heart from the aforementioned signs and from them they take their point of departure against us.

So then, we often prove ourselves uncharitably disposed toward certain people when we speak evil of them. Thus we fall to the demon of grudge-bearing and against those people we instantly take the evil thoughts that arose in us before we had noticed. It is quite right that the Holy Spirit reproaches us, saying, 'Sitting, you have spoken against your brother and placed before your mother's son a stumbling-block' [Ps 49.20], opened the door to thoughts of grudge-bearing and troubled your mind at the time of prayer by always imagining your enemy's face and deifying it – for certainly what the mind beholds at prayer is worthy to be confessed as God![68] Let us flee, my brethren, the disease of slander; let us never remember ill of anyone; let us not change our countenance at the memory of a neighbour. For the wicked demons thoroughly pore over our every appearance and leave nothing of ours without scrutinising it – not how we lie down, sit down, stand up; not a word, a departure, a glance – they work through them all, they set them all in motion, all day long they are focused on deceits against us so that, at the time of prayer, they can falsely accuse the humble mind and quench its blessed light. You also see what St Paul says to Titus [Titus 2.8]: 'In your teaching, [show] incorruptibility, sound reason that is irreproachable, so that an adversary may be ashamed, having nothing mean to say about us.' Blessed David also prayed, saying, 'Deliver me from men's false accusations' [Ps 118.134] – using the word 'men' for 'demons' on account of the rational part of their nature, just as the Saviour in the Gospels also said the Enemy was a 'man' who sowed within us the weeds of vice [cf. Mt 13.25].[69]

38. It is Christ who, through the contemplation of all ages, raises the rational nature that had been put to death by vice – but it is his Father who, through the knowledge of himself, raises the soul that has died the death of Christ. This is what the Apostle meant in the verse, 'If we die with Christ, we believe that we will also live with him' [Rom 6.8].[70]

39. When the mind, having taken off the old man, clothes itself with the one from grace [cf. Col 3.9–10], then at the time of prayer it will see its own state resemble sapphire or sky-blue – which Scripture also calls 'the place of God', seen on Mt Sinai by the elders [cf. Ex 24.9–11].[71]

40. The mind could not see the place of God in itself, unless it had become loftier than all [concepts][72] from things. But it would not become loftier, unless it had put off the passions that bind it to perceptible things through concepts. It will put aside the passions through the virtues; it will put aside the bare thoughts through contemplation; it will even put aside contemplation itself, when there appears to it that light at the time of prayer which sets in relief the place of God.[73]

41. Of concepts, some imprint and shape our governing faculty, and others only provide knowledge without imprinting or shaping the mind. For example, the verse 'in the beginning was the Word and the Word was with God' {Jn 1.1} puts a concept in the heart, but it does not imprint or shape it. Another: the words 'taking bread' shape the mind, and again 'he broke [it]' imprint the mind [cf. Mt 26.26];[74] and the verse 'I saw the Lord seated upon an lofty and exalted throne' {Is 6.1} imprints the mind – apart from the words 'I saw the Lord'. Even if the saying seems to imprint the mind, the meaning in fact does not. With a prophetic eye, he saw the rational nature elevated through ascetic struggle and receiving in itself the knowledge of God, since God is said to be 'seated' where he is known and therefore the pure mind is called 'God's throne'. Likewise, it is said 'a throne of dishonour is the *woman*' – in the place of *soul* – 'who hates justice' [cf. Prov 11.16 LXX], for the dishonour of the soul is vice and ignorance.

Thus, the concept of God is found, not amongst the concepts that imprint the mind, but amongst those concepts that do not imprint it. Therefore it is necessary for the one who prays to separate himself altogether from the concepts that imprint the mind. And you should inquire whether it is the same for the incorporeals and their meanings as it is for the corporeals and their meanings, and whether the mind will be imprinted in one way when it sees a mind and disposed another way when it sees that mind's meaning.[75] From this we know how spiritual knowledge moves the mind from the thoughts that imprint on it and establish it, unimprinted, near God – since the concept of God is not amongst the concepts that imprint on the mind (for God is not a body), but amongst those that do not imprint on it.[76] Once more, of contemplations that do not imprint on the mind, some signify the being of the incorporeals, others signify their reasons. In fact, it is *not* the case that incorporeals are the same as the corporeals. As for the corporeals, some imprint the mind and others do not. But here, neither concept imprints the mind.[77]

42. The demonic thoughts blind the soul's left eye, which is directed toward contemplation of created things;[78] but those concepts that imprint on and shape our governing faculty darken the right eye, which at the time of prayer contemplates the blessed light of the Holy Trinity and through which the Bride ravishes the Bridegroom in the Song of Songs [cf. Song 4.9].[79]

43. Aspirant for pure prayer, guard your irascibility; lover of moderation, control your stomach! Do not give your stomach bread to satiety and restrict its water. Be vigilant in prayer and keep grudge-bearing far from you. May the reasons of the Holy Spirit not abandon you, and knock on the door of Scripture with the hands of virtues. Then imperturbability of heart will arise for you and in prayer you will see your mind like a star.

Appendices[80]

1. Of the demons opposed to ascetic struggle, three are foremost. The whole encampment of the rest follows after them. They are the first to rise for battle and through impure thoughts they call souls toward vice; they are the thoughts entrusted with the appetites of gluttony, who suggest to us avarice and who call us toward human glory.

2. Of the demons opposed to ascetic struggle, those who are entrusted with the appetites of gluttony, who suggest to us avarice and who call us toward human glory are the first to rise for battle and, through impure thoughts, they call souls toward vice.

3. The demons are armed by wicked ascetic practices and, once armed, they treat those who have armed them harshly.

A WORD
ABOUT PRAYER

(CPG 2453)

INTRODUCTION

In two Syriac manuscripts formerly in the collection of the British Museum, William Wright identified a brief work by Evagrius entitled 'His *memre* on prayer'.[1] These texts were subsequently edited by Irénée Hausherr, translated into Latin and published as the first section of his *De doctrina spirituali Christianorum orientalium*. The authenticity of the work has not been questioned and any inchoate doubts can be settled by noting that the first chapter has been excerpted from *Causes* 11. (The ultimate provenance of the other two chapters has not been determined.) However, it is possible that the form in which we find the material is owed to a later compiler rather than to Evagrius himself. In this respect, we might compare *A word about prayer* to *Definitions*, *Excerpts* and *Aphorisms*, translated below: *Definitions* was certainly compiled at a later date, and it may be that the other two are likewise the works of a later hand. But even if *A word about prayer* is a later production, the content is entirely consistent with Evagrius' other writings and we therefore have no reason to suppose that it is pseudonymous.

Source: Hausherr (1933): 149–52 (with Latin translation).

117

TRANSLATION

1. Now if you are distressed, pray – but pray with fear and reverence, effort, alertness, vigilance, particularly on account of our invisible enemies who are perverse in their habits and given over to vice and who are accustomed to abuse us at this time. When they see us standing to pray, they also eagerly stand near us and suggest to our mind things that it is unseemly to ponder or consider at the time for prayer. In this way, they lead our mind captive and make the petition and intercession of our prayer idle and foul and worthless.[2]

2. Let us be eager to attain to the discipline[3] in this the brief span of our life, since habit maintains the vigour of nature. Make it your habit to pray frequently throughout the day, and offer hymns of praise to God in vigils by night as well; let your tongue never say a word before it prays.[4] When you go out the door of your cell, make the sign of the cross on your forehead and confess God within your mind. Having thus taken up arms, then indeed walk along, sealed by the cross and with your heart's confession. When you return again to your cell, make many and frequent offerings to your Lord.[5]

By the same token that a building established on a firmly packed foundation will not crumble quickly even if many tempests buffet it, neither will we be overthrown quickly if we gird up the discipline of our deeds with constant prayer every day of our lives [cf. Mt 7.24–25; Eph 6.13–17]. We see soldiers hanging on their houses the implements of warfare – swords and spears, bucklers and breastplates – to reveal their occupation; as for us, God gives us arms not made from gold and silver, brass and iron, but rather from good will and steadfast faith. So hang these arms on the walls of your cell and on your bed and on your table. And when you are making ready to break bread and drink the cup, do not eat or drink unless you have first sealed them and made the sign of the cross over them. If you do this in faith, no harm from the Devil will befall you.

3. Whether you stand or bow or genuflect while praying, eagerly raise your mind to God so that you may reach your true city. Struggle with your thoughts so that you may pray with your cares laid to rest. This is the great struggle: averting your gaze from these earthly things and from every blow. When you strive to pray in your petitions, the thought of fornication vexes you; if you struggle against it, the desire for money or thought of wrath rushes upon you; and when you make peace, you will glow with anger within[6] – and as long as you are weary, the powers of the Evil One harass you all the more.

Therefore, my child, you must not be remiss. Instead, steel your soul for the battle against evils and beseech God that he grant you victory. For you cannot be victorious by yourself, since the fight against evil thoughts is too difficult for you alone. Therefore it is essential for us to invoke God and persevere in prayer, seeing that it is he alone who is able to calm our mind.

NOTES ON
SCRIPTURE

INTRODUCTION

Scripture commanded a great deal of Evagrius' attention. In the *Coptic life*, we read that during his years in Kellia he spent a third of his nights in studying Scripture. It is clear from his great *Collection of responses* (*Antirrheticus* – *CPG* 2434) (Frankenberg (1912): 472–544) that there was a practical motivation behind this: Evagrius committed to memory vast amounts of Scripture to be cited at will against demonic temptation. But his appropriation of Scripture did not end there. References to Scripture are woven throughout all classes of his writings. Indeed, it is the measure of the gnostic that he or she (for instance, in the cases of Melania and Syncletica) has a profound understanding of Scripture.[1] As for the theological heights of Evagrius' writings, the extent to which he relies on Scripture has not been adequately appreciated. This oversight is perhaps due to the persistent habit of thinking of Evagrius as someone who was more interested in exploiting and contorting the sacred writings, than in expositing them. This leads us to one of the most important reasons for taking Evagrius' comments on Scripture seriously: by noting when he shifts from using Pauline language to using Johannine language, for example, one can discern textures within his works that were previously overlooked and that may very well be indispensable for a sympathetic and responsible reconstruction of his worldview.[2] One of the most promising developments in the recent study of Evagrius has been the opening up of this possibility for using Evagrius' comments on Scripture as scaffolding (so to speak) for making sense of the way he structures his chapters. We

121

are therefore deeply fortunate in the number and variety of Evagrius' comments and notes on Scripture that are available to us.

From the number of scholia (or 'notes' on particular verses) that come down to us, it is clear that Evagrius spent a great deal of his time in commenting upon Scripture. The nature of his comments is variable, but they are typically very brief. Indeed, at a few points he specifically states that, in deference to the regulations that govern scholia, he will have to pass over some interesting points that he could otherwise make.[3] Typically, Evagrius is interested in the 'spiritual meaning' of the text that he is annotating – typically, but not exclusively – and this meaning is frequently Christocentric. Our attention is naturally drawn to notes in which Evagrius follows Origen in metaphysical matters (as when, e.g., he links the situation of each person to God's providential ordering of creation).[4] But this should not lead us to lose sight of the philological and historical concerns that Evagrius also demonstrates in his notes (as when, e.g., he comments on variant readings of the Greek at Job 30.24, or on the impossibility that the solar eclipse described at Lk 23.44–47 could have occurred naturally).[5]

As regards the texts here translated, most of them are from the Greek. *Notes on Ecclesiastes* is translated from a critical edition that has been disentangled from the catena (or 'chain') of notes on Ecclesiastes by various Greek fathers; *Notes on Job* is translated from a critical edition of the catena on Job, based on my collation of Evagrian texts from that edition. *Notes on Luke* is not based on a critical edition, but it is important to include it nevertheless, because it is by no means the case that Evagrius was interested only in annotating the Old Testament. For the same reason, it seemed good to include *On the 'Our Father'* – though that decision was also motivated by the fact that *On the 'Our Father'* is preserved in Coptic and it is worth calling attention to the largely untouched question of how Evagrius' writings were received in the Coptic tradition.

NOTES ON JOB

(*CPG* 2458B)

INTRODUCTION

In his seminal study of Evagriana, Hans Urs von Balthasar noted the existence of numerous scholia by Evagrius that were dispersed among patristic catenae on various books of the Bible. What follows is a translation of one such set of scholia, namely, Evagrius' *Notes on Job*.[1] No critical edition of the *Notes* as such has appeared. The present translation is based on my collation from *Die älteren griechischen Katenen zum buch Hiob*, edited by Ursula and Dieter Hagedorn (whose enumeration of the scholia I have included in the endnotes for ease of reference),[2] and Patrick Young's *Catena Graecorum patrum in beatum Iob*,[3] whose variants I have included as scholia 8 *bis* and 10 *bis*.

This collation on occasion departs from the Hagedorns' attribution, but every such instance is noted and defended. In all cases, such a departure will be based on manuscript attribution and in most cases the attribution is attested in several manuscripts. This has resulted in forty scholia. It should be noted, however, that approximately thirty more could be defensibly called 'Evagrian' – some of which are unattributed, others of which are attributed to multiple authors, and still others of which might be described as attesting to the influence of Evagrius' views.[4] The similarity between these thirty scholia and the forty translated below is such that one wants to proceed cautiously in dealing with this material. It is not impossible that some of the thirty scholia might go back to Evagrius himself.

The decision to incorporate sch. 1 *on Job* 1.5 calls for special comment. That scholion, which is also known as 'On the divine names', is attributed in some manuscripts to Origen, and Robert Devreesse has made a generally accepted argument that the scholion is, in fact,

Origen's.[5] Devreesse's attribution is based on a comparison of the scholion to Origen's *Selecta in Ps* 2.4 (PG 12:1104) and a conjectured scribal error that resulted in the cipher for Origen's name being transformed into the cipher for Evagrius'. Although Devreesse thinks that the comparison of 'On the divine names' with Origen's remarks on Ps 2.4 makes the attribution of the former to Origen secure, it should be noted that the differences between the two are at least as striking as their similarities. Of the ten names mentioned in 'On the divine names', only three are found in Origen's *Selecta*; Origen mentions differences between the Hebrew characters used in old manuscripts and contemporary Hebrew characters, but never spells the Tetragrammaton – whereas 'On the divine names' features the spelling twice in close succession; Origen does not refer to Ex 28.36 in the *Selecta*. The similarities are therefore inadequate evidence for Origen's authorship of 'On the divine names'. Furthermore, the oldest manuscript evidence unambiguously ascribes the scholion to Evagrius. (It was this evidence that Devreesse conjectured an antecedent scribal error to account for.) But even though Devreesse's case is inconclusive, his observation about the passage from Origen is not to be dismissed out of hand. The prudent course appears to be to accept the manuscript attribution, while acknowledging the evidence adduced by Devreesse, and thus affirming that Evagrius was indebted for at least some of his information to Origen's *Selecta in Psalmos*.

Sources: Hagedorn (1994–2004); Iunius (1637) – the specific sources for each scholion are given in the footnotes.

Translation: Previously untranslated.

TRANSLATION

1.5: 'For Job said, "Lest my children have thought wicked things in their minds before God."'
   1. About the Hebrew designation for the Lord, these things should be said – God is named by the Hebrews with ten names. Of these, one is called Adonai, that is, 'Lord'. Another is Ia, which was also translated into Greek as 'Lord'. Besides these, another is the four letters which are never pronounced by the Hebrews, but which by stretching the language is called 'Adonai' by them and 'Lord' by us.

And they say this was written on the gold plate that was upon the brow of the High Priest, in accordance with what was said in the Law: 'the imprint of a signet, *Holiness by the Lord*, יהוה' [Ex 28.36]. The rest of the names are these: El, Eloheim, Adon, Sabaoth, Shaddai, Iaie, Eserie and the three written before, of which the four letters are written with these characters: *yodh, he, vov, he*: ייהוה: GOD.[6]

1.6: 'And behold, the Angels of God came'
2. These are the angels who manage the earthly realm and have knowledge of all the things on the earth.[7]

1.9: 'Does Job revere the Lord for nought?'
3. For nought the one who for the sake of neither punishments nor promises [fears the Lord].[8]

3 *bis*. One who serves God for the sake of neither punishments nor promises is a true human.[9]

1.21: 'And naked shall I return thither.'
4. Job, since he is righteous, will go forth naked of wickedness and sin.[10]

5. Never, then, does he call the first creation that frames humans from the earth, naked of all wickedness, 'the womb'. That is, 'Naked I was fashioned from the earth, one unencumbered and even immaterial, *and naked shall I return thither.*' Where? To the place free from sorrow.[11]

1.21: 'The Lord has given, the Lord has taken away.'
6. Let the one who has possessions in a righteous way say, 'The Lord has given.'[12]

2.1: 'And the Devil came in the midst of them.'
7. Truly is the Devil now said to be in the midst of the angels as someone who, by his request, has broken through their care for Job.[13]

2.2: 'I am here having passed through beneath heaven and walked about in the universe.'
8. Therefore the Devil did not walk about with Job, because one who has a 'citizenship in the heavens' [Phil 3.20] is not 'beneath heaven'. So the Devil lies when he claims to have worked everywhere, since he does not lay hold on the friends of God.[14]

8 *bis*. Therefore he did not walk about with Job because Job was not beneath heaven, having a 'citizenship in the heavens' [Phil 3.20]. So the Evil One lies when he says that all people tempted by him

have been subjected to him. And so he is confuted at once – for how have you trampled on all people, as you claim, though you were unable to overcome Job who is but one man?[15]

8.21: 'He shall fill the true mouth with laughter.'
   9. Instead of this, 'He shall fill the intellect with knowledge.'[16]

10.1a: 'For thus I am baffled, suffering in my soul.'
   10. 'For my soul does not suffer with my body.'[17]
   10 *bis*. 'For my soul does not suffer with my body' – since the latter has indeed been pummelled by blows, but the soul has not succumbed to evils.[18]

10.2: 'And I shall say to the Lord, "Do not teach me to be impious".'
   11. Instead of 'Do not teach me to be impious', 'Remove impious thoughts from me'. For the Lord teaches no one to be impious.[19]

10.13a: 'I know that, having these things in yourself, you can do all things.'
   12. 'Having these things in yourself': which things? Life, mercy and visitation.[20]
   13. Truly, [these are] the creative, providential and judging faculties.[21]

11.6: 'Then he will announce to you the strength of wisdom, since it is double those which are against you.'
   14. He has called 'double' that of his wisdom which is conceivable and that which is not; or, not only in his perceptible works but also in his intelligible ones is his wisdom contemplated.[22]

12.10: 'Is not the soul of everything that lives in his hand, and the spirit of every man?'
   15. 'The souls of the righteous are in the hand of God' [Wis 3.1].[23]

12.11: 'For the ear discerns words, and the palate tastes bread.'
   16. For just as we have received the palate for the discernment of foods, likewise the mind unto the knowledge of God.[24]
   17. The mind discerns mental things and perception, perceptible things.[25]

13.1: 'Behold, these things my eye has contemplated and my ear has heard.'

18. 'By both experience and teaching I have received these things.'[26]

13.14: '. . . taking my flesh with my teeth'.
19. I shall declare my perturbations with my mouth.[27]

16.13: 'Those who were not afraid of hitting my kidneys, spilled my guts on the ground.'
20. He means the appetitive faculty, then the courageous part – which are, as it were, the body of the inner man [cf. Eph 3.16].[28]

16.16: 'My belly is parched from wailing.'
21. Henceforth you can say that the mind is looking upon ascetic struggle and contemplation.[29]

25.3: 'Let no one think there is respite for thieves.'
22. Duration of life or omission of punishment.[30]

28.14: 'The abyss said, "It is not in me"; and the sea said, "It is not with me".'
23. Those below the earth would say, 'Wisdom *is not in us*'; and those on the earth [would say], 'Wisdom *is not with us*'.[31]

28.23–24: 'The Lord . . . gazed upon everything beneath heaven, seeing all the things in the earth which he made.'
24. I reckon he says this about Christ.[32]

29.15: 'I was an eye for the blind, a foot for the lame.'
25. He was the eye for mental guidance, and the foot for ethical guidance.[33]

29.16: 'And I found out the plight which I did not know.'
26. This should be said to those who precipitously make known declarations and hand down judgements.[34]

30.24: 'If only I could put hands on myself through and through, or ask another to do this for me.'
27. 'Putting hands on' is not given in the Tetraselides,[35] or by the Septuagint, or by the rest whose renderings we have compared. But it can be left to one side ethically, according to an old convention. This is because some grief or shame or some other passion would provoke these thoughts for the imperfect.[36]

31.5: 'If I have walked with scorners . . .'
28. From this we understand that it is necessary to flee scorners.[37]

31.18: 'Since from my youth I have reared them as a father and from their mother's womb I have guided them.'
29. Before they laid hold of wickedness, he led the youth into virtue. Thus the passage, 'from the womb I have guided' someone, is true.[38]

34.21: 'For he is one who beholds men's deeds.'
30. For providence goes before each one and the deeds of each.[39]

34.32: 'Beside myself, I see; you show me.'
31. 'If I have gone out of myself', he says, 'in knowing the truth, you show me it.'[40]

34.32: 'If I have wrought injustice, I will do it no longer.'
32. 'Show, then,' [Elius] says, 'O Job, if I say these things unjustly, and I desist.'[41]

40.8: 'Or have you done away with my judgement? Do you suppose I have done otherwise with you that you might appear righteous?'
33. Here he reveals the cause of abandonment.[42]

40.16: 'Behold, now, his strength is in his loins.'
34. What he is saying here in an honourable way is fornication and every shameful pleasure.[43]

40.25: 'Will you draw out the dragon with a fishing-hook?'
35. I think the aforementioned sea-monster [cf. Job 25.12] and the dragon here are one and the same, since the Hebrew 'Leviathan' encompasses both, while other dragons are not so named by the Hebrews, but have the common name of their species. Indeed, the name of dragon, going back to the chief of the enemy forces, is peculiarly called Leviathan just as though it were its owner's proper appellation.[44]

41.13: 'His breath, live coals; and a flame goes out from his mouth.'
36. From which go forth 'flaming darts' [cf. Eph 6.16].[45]

41.20–21: 'The bronze bow would not wound him, with him sling-stones are turned into grass; darts are counted as stubble.'
37. None of these things wounds Satan, but self-control and love abolish him.[46]

42.5: 'With the hearing of the ear I heard of you beforehand, but now my eye has beheld you.'

38. With the temptation he has learned more precisely the reasons of what has come to be.[47]

43.10: 'He remitted them their sin.'

39. From this we understand that the prayer of the righteous abolishes sins.[48]

42.17: 'And his friends came to him: Eliphaz, king of the Thaimans, the sons of Esau; Baldad, tyrant of the Sauchai; and Sophar, king of the Minai.'

40. Eliphaz' son was Sophar, and Amalek was born to him by a concubine. So Eliphaz and Sophar became students of Isaac and Jacob, and Amalek of Esau [cf. Gen 36.11–12].[49]

NOTES ON
ECCLESIASTES

(*CPG* 2458e)

INTRODUCTION

Ecclesiastes is by tradition a problematic book. The Rabbis, for example, repeatedly expressed concern about whether it was to be received into the canon, citing the problem of inconsistency within its teachings: 'The Sages wished to hide the Book of Ecclesiastes, because its words are self-contradictory.'[1] The Beth Shammai rejected its authority – to hold the book did not necessitate washing one's hands, because it was not a holy book – and, as has been noted in a recent translation of the *Aboth d'Rabbi Nathan*, Ecclesiastes was subject to fierce criticism as a heretical book.[2] One major problem is clearly evinced in the potentially cynical outlook expressed throughout the book. The eponymous Preacher's rallying cry – 'all is vanity' – could readily undermine confidence that moral actions will in the fullness of time meet with their just reward. For this reason, it is all the more striking that when Evagrius turns to comment upon Ecclesiastes, he shows no predilection at all for making otherworldly remarks that disparage creation, life or matter (as one might expect an ascetic scholiast to do). To the contrary, he subtly modifies the rather pessimistic outlook of the Preacher by glossing the vanity of all things to which he refers as meaning nothing more than that they are vain by comparison with the knowledge of God (see sch. 2 on Eccl 1.2).

This recasting of the Preacher's method is fundamental for Evagrius' project of reading the text's sundry denunciations as inducements to contemplate the meaning (or indeed *meanings* – the *logoi*) of what happens in life. Thus, on Evagrius' reading, Ecclesiastes stands out as a call to order aright one's understanding of what matters. It is therefore not surprising that in the *Scholia on Ecclesiastes*, Evagrius is chiefly concerned with the second grade of the Christian life: natural contemplation. Such an undertaking presupposes ascetic struggle – and means that, in passages like sch. 15 on Eccl 3.10–13, Evagrius can look back on the struggle and make illuminating remarks about it. But Evagrius also points the way forward by making allusions to theology proper (e.g., sch. 52 on Eccl 6.10–12). In other words, Ecclesiastes is well suited for those who have progressed in ascetic practice to the point of gaining knowledge of God's creation; Evagrius' notes are thus directed chiefly to the 'gnostic' Christian.

Source: Géhin (1993).

Translations: Apart from the French translation by Géhin (1993), no other translations are known to me.

TRANSLATION

1.1: 'The words of the Preacher, the son of David, king of Israel in Jerusalem.'

1. The church [*ecclesia*] of pure souls is the true knowledge of the ages and worlds, and of judgement and providence concerning them. So the Preacher [*Ecclesiastes*] is Christ, who brings this knowledge into being – or rather, the Preacher is the one who purifies souls by ethical considerations and leads them into natural contemplation.

1.2: '"Vanity of vanities", says the Preacher, "vanity of vanities, all is vanity."'

2. To those who are entering the church of the mind and are wondering at the contemplation of the created things, the Word says, 'You must not think that these things are the final goal that has been stored up for you by the promises – for they are all vanity of vanities in comparison with the knowledge of God himself. For just as medicines are vain after one's health has been completely restored, so, too, the meanings of the ages and worlds are vain after one has knowledge of the Holy Trinity.'[3]

1.11: 'There is no memory of the first things.'

3. If there is no memory of the first things, how is it that David says, 'I remembered days of old' [Ps 124.5] and 'I remembered ages of years' [Ps 76.6]? Perhaps we become forgetful of these things when our rational nature touches upon the Holy Trinity – for then 'God shall be all in all' [cf. 1 Cor 15.28]. For if the concepts of things that are in the intellect lead the mind to remember the things, and if the mind that is contemplating God is separated from all concepts, then the mind that is touching upon the Holy Trinity will forget everything that is created.

1.13: 'For God gave the sons of men a wicked business that they should be busy with it.'

4. What he means by 'wicked' is 'difficult to bear', rather than 'opposed to the good' – for God gives no one that! Being the source of goodness, he is not the cause of evils. Or else 'gave' here means 'permitted', in keeping with the rationale of abandonment.[4]

1.15: 'The crooked thing cannot be adorned anew; the lack cannot be numbered.'

5. What he means by 'the crooked thing' is 'the impure intellect', as in 'the crooked heart devises evils' [Prov 6.14]. And in Proverbs, wisdom is called an adornment, when it says, 'wisdom is an adornment for the youth' [Prov 20.29]. 'Wisdom will not enter into a soul that works evils' [Wis 1.4]. But he did not say it cannot be adorned; instead, he said it cannot be adorned *anew* – for one is *adorned* by a right life, but *adorned anew* by the wisdom of God. So, then, a crooked intellect can be adorned; but it cannot be adorned anew unless through the virtues it purifies itself and makes itself a vessel fit for the Master [cf. 2 Tim 2.21].

6. God's number that numbers the saints indicates a definite spiritual rank; for he 'numbers the host of stars and gives them all their names', it says [Ps 146.4]. By this number, the Lord bade Moses to number the children of Israel [cf. Num 1.2]. And what did David say about men who crawl and are enslaved to pleasures? 'Here are creeping things of whom there is no number' [Ps 13.25]. In Proverbs, Solomon said about evil, 'Many has she wounded and vanquished, and innumerable are the ones she has slain' [Prov 7.26]. So, then, the 'lack' mentioned here, together with those slain, and the creeping things, are all referring to the same state of being out of harmony with the spiritual number.

Even if David said that of God's understanding there is no number [cf. Ps 146.5], he did not write it as though God's understanding is undeserving of a number; he wrote it because God's understanding by its very nature does not admit of being subject to a number. After all, the word 'invisible' has two senses: first, that which by its very nature cannot be seen (like God); and second, that which by its very nature can be seen, but is in fact not seen (like iron that is hidden in the depths by the water). Likewise, 'innumerable' has two senses: first, that which by its very nature cannot be numbered; and second, that which is in fact not numbered for some reason.

2.6: 'I made myself pools of water, to water from them the thicket-bearing wood.'
   7. This is inverted. Here is the correct reading of the verse: 'to water from them the wood-bearing thicket'.[5]

2.10: 'And I did not withhold from my eyes all that they desired; nor did I restrain my heart from any joy.'
   8. The soul seeks wisdom not by reason, but by purity. For he says, 'Not everyone who says to me, "Lord, Lord," will enter into the kingdom of heaven, but the one who does the will of my Father' [Mt 7.21]. So we receive wisdom in proportion to our standing, if indeed by the measure with which we measure it will be measured back unto us [cf. Mt 7.2]. Thus, the mental desire is the imperturbability of the rational soul that quaffs holy wisdom. So the one who makes himself fit for all knowledge takes on board nothing from his eyes – and by 'all knowledge', I mean such knowledge as is meet for a soul linked to flesh and blood.
   9. Only the one who commits no sin at all does not restrain his heart from any spiritual joy.

2.11: 'And, lo, all was vanity and the resolve of a breath.'
   10. The 'breath', or 'spirit',[6] to which he refers is the soul, since resolve is a kind of movement of the mind. Thus, David said, 'Into your hands I commit my spirit' [Ps 30.6]; and Stephen, 'Lord Jesus, receive my spirit' [Acts 7.59]; and in *Reigns*, 'David did not sadden the spirit of Amnon, his son' [2 Kgs (= 2 Sam) 13.21].

2.14: 'The wise man's eyes are in his head.'
   11. If 'Christ is the head of everyone' [1 Cor 11.3], and the wise man is someone, then the wise man's head is Christ. But Christ is our wisdom – for 'wisdom is begotten of God for us' [1 Cor 1.30] –

so wisdom is therefore the wise man's head, in which he has the eyes of the intellect through which he contemplates the meanings of the created things.

2.22: 'Thus it happens to a man in all his labour and in the resolve of his heart, by which he labours upon the earth.'
12. Here it is shown that the resolve of the spirit is the resolve of the heart.

2.25: 'For who shall eat and drink in the absence of [God]?'
13. Who, then, will be able apart from Christ to eat his body (which is the symbol of virtues) and drink his blood (which is the symbol of knowledge)?[7]

2.26: 'And to the sinner he has given business to add and to heap up [wealth], so that he may give [it] to him who is good before God; for this is vanity and the resolve of a breeze.'
14. This is like the Proverb that says, 'The one who augments his wealth by interest and usury gathers it for the one who pities the poor' [Prov 28.8]; and 'The envious one strives to be rich, and does not know that the merciful one will rule over him' [Prov 28.22]. So, in keeping with the scholia here presented, we ought to be content. Apart from this, it must be known that he declares 'vanity' to be the assemblage of sins, not that he received a good teacher from God.

3.10–13: 'I have seen the business which God has given the sons of man to be busy with. Everything that he has made is beautiful in its time; he has also given the age to their hearts, in such a way that man cannot discover the work that God has worked from the beginning even unto the end. I have recognised that there is no good for them except to rejoice and do good in one's life. As for everyone who eats and drinks and sees good from all his toil – this is a gift from God.'
15. I have seen, he says, perceptible things busy the intelligence of man, which God has given to men before their purification to be busy with them.[8] Their beauty, he says, is temporal and not eternal. For after purification, the pure person no longer regards perceptible things as merely busying his mind, but as having been placed in him for spiritual contemplation. For it is one thing for sensible things to make an impression on the mind as it perceives them sensibly through its sense, and another for the mind to arrange the meanings that are in sensible things by contemplating them. But this know-

ledge only follows for the pure, whilst thinking about perceptible things follows for the impure as well as for the pure.

Thus, he said that the latter, temporal business has been given by God. For God, in his providential care for the impassioned soul, gave it perceptions and perceptible things so that, by busying itself with them and considering them, it might flee the thoughts that would be inspired in it by the enemies. But, he says, he also gave them the age, that is, the meanings of the age – for this is the 'kingdom of heaven' which the Lord says we have within us [cf. Lk 17.21], which is not found by men when it is hidden by sins. Therefore I have recognized, he says, that it is not for good things, but for the reasons of the things, that the rational nature naturally rejoices and does good. For nothing provides the mind with food and drink as do virtue and the knowledge of God.

16. We do good through the timely use of the things God has given us; thus shall everything be good 'in its time' and, 'lo, all things [shall be] very good' [cf. Gen 1.31].

3.14: 'I have recognised that everything that God made will exist forever. It is impossible to add to it, and it is impossible to subtract from it. And God made them so that they should be in awe in his presence.'

17. If 'everything that God made will exist forever' and God did not make vice, then vice will not exist forever.

18. It is impossible to subtract from the 'many-splendoured wisdom' [cf. Eph 3.10],[9] and impossible to add to it. For God made it, he says, so that men who strive for wisdom would cease from vice: for 'by the fear of God shall everyone turn from evil' [Prov 15.27].

3.15: 'That which has already been created, is; and that which is going to be created, has already been created; and God seeks out that which has followed.'

19. If 'those who are persecuted for the kingdom of heaven' are blessed, 'for theirs is the kingdom of heaven' [Mt 5.10], and the meanings of the ages that have been and will be created are the kingdom of heaven – then those who are persecuted will be blessed, since they have known the contemplation of what has been created.[10] For God is said to seek out the one he has illuminated by knowledge, and not to seek out the one he has not illuminated by knowledge. As David said, 'I have wandered like a lost sheep: seek out your servant, for I have not forgotten your commandments' [Ps 118.176]; and he was also persecuted: 'many are they who have sorely persecuted me and oppressed me; but I have not turned away from your testimonies' [Ps 118.157].

3.18: 'Then I said in my heart about the prattling of the sons of men: "God will judge them and will show that they are beasts."'

20. Now what he calls 'the prattling of man' is man's life, if indeed for every vain word we shall give an account on the Day of Judgement [cf. Mt 12.36] when both the pure and the impure are made manifest.

3.19–22: 'And indeed for them, what befalls the sons of men and what befalls the beast are one and the same for them: as is the death of the one, so is the death of the other, and there is one spirit for all of them. And what more does the man have than the beast does? Nothing – for all is vanity. All tend to one destination, all were taken out of the dust and all shall return to the dust. And who knows whether the spirit of the sons of men goes up? And who knows whether the spirit of the beast goes down to the earth? And I saw that there was no good except that a man rejoices in his works, for such is his lot. For who shall bring him to see what shall arise after him?'

21. He calls 'what befalls them' that which commonly happens to all men in this world, whether they are just or unjust – such as life, death, sickness, health, richness, poverty; loss of limbs, of spouses, of children, of property – on the basis of which it is impossible to discern the just from the unjust before the Judgement. He says that their common properties are being taken out of the dust, returning again to the dust and having one soul by nature (though not by number):[11] 'For', he says, 'there is one spirit for all of them.'

Now what he calls a 'beast' is the man who was made in honour and who does not understand, but who has been compared to a mindless beast because of its irrational pleasures and because he became like a beast. But it is not through what they do that the just and the unjust will be distinguished before the Judgement, in that many of the unjust have converted to righteousness and been lifted up, whereas many of the just have fallen from virtue and been humbled.

'What have I found among them that is remarkable?' Here, he says, 'Nothing.' For all is vanity – apart from spiritual rejoicing, which naturally arises from man's actions and virtues. For one who has lost this rejoicing will not come here again to do things conducive to possessing it.[12]

22. Furthermore, the irrational soul is called a spirit.

4.1: 'And I turned about and saw all the oppressions that happen under the sun; and, lo, the tears of the oppressed, and there is no one to comfort them – there is might in the hands of those who oppress them, and there is no one to comfort them.'

23. By 'oppressions' he means those who are opposed to us – for he says, 'stand surety for the good of your servant; let not the proud oppress me' [Ps 118.122]; and again, about Christ the Saviour, he says, 'he will humble the oppressor and endure as long as the sun' [Ps 71.4–5]. Those who were being oppressed before Christ were people for whom there was no comforter like the one who said, 'I comfort you, I who am in chains, to carry on in a manner worthy of the calling by which you were called, with all humility and meekness, with generosity, supporting one another in love' [Eph 4.1–2].

4.2: 'And I ranked the dead, who had already fallen, above the living who are alive till now – and above them both the one who has not yet been born, who has not seen the wicked work that is done beneath the sun.'

24. And I ranked those who have already fallen in Christ and been delivered from their oppressors, above those who lived in evil and persist in it even until now. The good one is the one who has separated himself from evil without need of death and has not been in evil, who has not known the oppressors' evil strife waged against those who are under the sun.

4.4: 'And I saw all the toil and all the strength of the creature – that it is from one man's jealousy for another – and this, too, is vanity and the resolve of a breeze.'

25. 'I saw', he says, 'every vice and the Evil One who is strong in it.' For it is the Evil One whom he calls 'one who is strong' amongst the impious and who oppresses the poor, as well as 'creature' – since 'he has been created to be derided by the angels' of God [Job 40.19; 41.25]. And I saw all the jealousy that he had toward people, which is vain but emboldens his heart. For it is necessary that God shall wholly be 'all in all' [cf. 1 Cor 15.28] and that the prayer said by Jesus shall be fulfilled: 'Grant them that they may be one with us, just as you and I are one, Father' [cf. Jn 17.21–22].[13]

4.5: 'The senseless man crosses his arms and devours his own flesh.'

26. If the arms are the symbol of ascetic work, everyone who does not work righteousness folds his arms – and that, he says, is why such a person devours his own flesh, filling himself with the sins that spring from the flesh.

4.6: 'Better a full hand with repose, than two full hands with toil and the resolve of a breeze.'

27. 'The resolve of a breeze' seems to me to be like impassioned spiritual will.[14] For this reason, a good hand of virtue is preferred to two hands of vice and ignorance and the resolve of a breeze. Likewise is the passage, 'Better a little for the just man than the great riches of the sinner' [Ps 36.16]; and 'better to receive a little with righteousness than much produce with injustice' [Prov 15.29]. This verse is like those: 'I have chosen rejection in God's house rather than dwelling in the tents of the wicked' [Ps 83.10 LXX]; and 'better to live under the corner of the roof than share the house with a railing woman' [Prov 25.24]. And this verse also follows on from the others: 'Better hospitality with beans for the sake of friendship and kindness than laying on beef with enmity' [Prov 15.17]. It is as if one were to say, 'Better to learn a single spiritual contemplation than numerous contemplations of foolish wisdom.'

4.8: 'He is one and there is no other, and there is no son or brother for him, and there is no end to all his work, and his eye is not satisfied with wealth. For whom do I toil and deny my soul good things? For this is vanity and wicked business.'

28. If someone has no brother, then he has not received the spirit of adoption [cf. Rom 8.15]; and if someone is not a father, then he is wicked – for, he says, 'There will be no offspring for the wicked' [Prov 24.20]. It is appropriate that one who denies his soul the knowledge of God would be unable to have his fill of vice.

I am speaking here of 'father' and 'brother' in keeping with the intention of Scripture. For I am not unaware that the propositions advanced here are not rightly applied to perceptible brethren and fathers. But if someone also wants to grasp the plain sense of the verses, he will categorically denounce the wealthy who have no children and those who are keen to obtain for themselves a surplus of possessions, particularly if they should also be unapproachable by their friends. The words written here certainly apply to such men.

4.11: 'And if two lie together, it is warm for them; but how can one man warm himself?'

29. Without the Lord there is no one who can become ardent in spirit, 'for the Lord is spirit' [2 Cor 3.17].

4.12: 'And even if one alone is overpowered, two can withstand him, and a cord of three strands is not broken quickly.'

30. I reckon that the one who is overpowered is the Evil One, against whom stand the two – a man and an angel of God – so that, once the Devil has been conquered, the man is worthy of the knowledge of God and becomes a cord of three strands which is not broken quickly. This is also clearly taught by the patriarch Jacob, who blessed Joseph's children, saying, 'May my angel, who delivered me from every evil, bless these children' [Gen 48.16]. Similar to this is what we find from David: 'The angel of the Lord will encamp round about those who fear him and will deliver them' [Ps 33.8].

31. The cord of three strands is the imperturbable mind full of spiritual knowledge, or the wise mind that has the angel of God as a companion. But it is good not to say, 'it will not be broken', and instead to say, 'it will not be broken *easily*'. For rational nature is subject to change.

4.13: 'Better a poor and wise child than an elderly and senseless king who does not yet know how to be attentive.'

32. The one who has guarded the instruction of his youth [cf. Prov 2.17] is a child; the one who has departed from the instruction of his youth and forgot the divine covenant and aged in vice is elderly. The first is Christ's; the second, the Evil One's.

4.14: 'For out of the prison-house he shall depart to reign, or he may have been born poor in his kingdom.'

33. The perceptible universe is a prison-house, in which 'each is bound by the chains of his own sins' [Prov 5.22].

4.17: 'Watch your step when you enter into the house of God, and draw near to listen; better your sacrifice than the gift of the senseless, for they do not know that they do evil.'

34. 'They do not know how they are stumbling', being ignorant because they transgress the law.

5.1–2: 'Do not be hasty with your mouth and do not let your heart be quick to utter a word in the presence of God: for God is in heaven, and you are on the earth: therefore let your words be few. For a dream comes in the abundance of temptation and the voice of a fool in the abundance of words.'

35. 'We do not know what we ought to pray for' [Rom 8.26]. Or perhaps he did not mean to say this, but instead ordered us not to speak of God impudently.[15] For it is not possible, when one is among perceptible things and takes concepts from them, to discourse without error about God, who is among intelligible things and flees every perception. Therefore he said, 'Let your words be few', that is, truthful and prudent. The word 'few' seems to me to signify something like the verses 'Better a little for the just man than the great riches of the sinner' [Ps 36.16] and 'better to receive a little with righteousness' [Prov 15.29].

To those who have not observed it, he says, 'a dream comes in the abundance of temptation and the voice of a fool in the abundance of words'. By 'dream', he means the demon who attacks sleeping souls with a multitude of temptations and deeply troubles the soul, about whom Job said to the Lord, 'you have frightened me with dreams and terrified me by visions' [Job 7.14]. And David, avoiding this enemy, called out to the Lord, saying, 'Enlighten my eyes lest I sleep unto death, lest my enemy say of me, "I have overcome him"' [Ps 12.4–5]. And in the Proverbs, 'Do not give sleep to your eyes, nor slumber to your eyelids, so that you may be saved like a roe from the noose and like a bird from the trap' [Prov 6.4]. He also called it 'the voice of the senseless', which stands near with lying words and deceives the soul; the verse 'from the voice of the reproachful and the shouter' [Ps 43.17] is the same. This verse can also be associated with the voice of the senseless: 'sin is not lacking from prolixity' [Prov 10.19]. The Saviour, too, in the Gospels ordered the man to keep vigil and pray that he might not enter into temptation [cf. Mt 26.41]. For sleep is the rational soul's ignorance and vice, so that Paul too awakens those who are thus sleeping, saying, 'Wake up, sleeper, and rise from the dead, and Christ shall shine on you' [Eph 5.14].

5.3–4: 'If then you make a vow to God, do not delay in fulfilling it: for there is no will among the senseless, so for your part fulfil such things as you have vowed. Better that you should not vow than that you should vow and not fulfil it.'

36. Of good gifts, some are given to God from the soul, but others from the body, and still others from what is outside the body. Now from the soul we give him right belief and true doctrines, righteousness and courage and temperance; from the body, abstinence and virginity and monogamy;[16] from what is outside the body, sons and daughters and servants and riches and possessions.

Let us consider, then, the words 'promising' and 'delaying' – for perhaps 'delay' does not imply a long interval of time, but a simple denial of one's promise. For it appears that only after many years did Jacob render unto God the tithes that he had promised to give him when he marched toward Mesopotamia [cf. Gen 28.6, 22], and Anna presented Samuel to God after a long time [cf. 1 Sam 1.21–25].

So much for gifts that are outside the body; but in what sense shall we think of the gifts of the soul and of the body? I reckon that one who has promised right belief and says that One of the Trinity is a creature, is thus delaying; that one who professes the confession that all things have come to be from God and reintroduces chance into the discussion,[17] is thus delaying; and likewise as regards other doctrines. As for the virtues, the one who promises justice and is unjust, delays in rendering his vow; and again the one who professes temperance and is wicked, is thus delaying. As for the gifts of the body, the one who promises abstinence and partakes of varied foods, is thus delaying; and the one who professes virginity (or else monogamy) and marries (or else re-marries), delays in rendering his vow.

In what way it is 'better that you should not vow than that you should vow and not fulfil it', we shall explain with recourse to the passage from the Gospel that says a servant who does not know and does not perform will receive few [beatings], whereas a servant who does know and does not perform will receive many [cf. Lk 12.47–48].

5.5: 'Do not let your mouth make your body sin, and do not say in the presence of God, "It is ignorance", lest God be angered by your voice and destroy the works of your hands: for in a multitude of dreams and vanities and many words . . .'

37. Man, he says, is in a multitude of wicked dreams and vanities and lying words, once his words have been destroyed by abandonment from God, which will befall him owing to his own lawlessness.

5.7–11: 'If you see in the country the oppression of the poor and the withdrawal of justice and righteousness, do not be surprised at it: for one of high rank watches over another of high rank, and those on high over others. And the abundance of the earth is for all, the king is for the cultivated field. One who loves silver will not be satisfied with silver; so, too, one who loves his property in its multitude. This, too, is vanity. In the multitude of goodness are those multiplied who partake of goodness, and what strength does one get from it? Chiefly, seeing it with his eyes. But the servant's sleep is sweet, whether he eats much or little; but there is no allowance for sleeping to the one who satisfies himself with being rich.'

38. If, he says, you see among men some who are oppressed, some being unjustly treated in judgement and some being just, do not be

surprised that these things happen, as if there were no providence.[18] Know, rather, that God watches over all things through Christ and he for his part, knowing everything upon the earth, exercises providence for them through the mediation of the holy angels. For God is king over the universe which he made. He sends affliction upon those who prefer the desire and vanity of this life to the knowledge of Christ. But to those who live and serve in goodness and courage and justice, he gives knowledge of God and sweet repose, whether they know few things of those here below or many of their meanings, from partial knowledge and partial prophecies. Such an end awaits them; but as for those who fill themselves with vice, the worm born of that vice will not allow them repose.

Moses showed that the Lord has entrusted this world to angels when he said, 'When the Most High separated the nations, as he dispersed the children of Adam, he set the boundaries of the nations in accordance with the number of the angels of God' [Dt 32.8]. Our Lord himself also called the world a field, when he said in the Gospels, 'The world is the field' [Mt 13.38]. By 'the abundance of the earth', he means the knowledge of the things on the earth, if indeed the meek are blessed, 'for they shall inherit the earth' [Mt 5.5]. For what else is the inheritance of the rational nature than the knowledge of God? And he calls the angels 'those of high rank', since they partake of the Lord Most High; for, he says, 'The Lord is most high above all the nations' [Ps 112.4].

5.12: 'Sickness is what I have seen beneath the sun: wealth being guarded by its owner to his harm.'

39. The multitude of vice is now revealed under the word 'wealth', and this vice is meant by the term 'sickness'. Therefore everyone who guards this wealth for himself does not know the wisdom of God, nor does he incline his heart to intelligence, nor yet does he convey it to his son through instruction; for he has neither received the words of God's law, nor hidden them in his heart.

5.13: 'And this wealth will be lost in wicked business; and he begot a son, and there is nothing in his hand.'

40. The wicked business is ignorance, with punishment that separates the impure from spiritual contemplation.

5.14–15: 'Just as he came naked from his mother's womb, he shall turn and depart as he came, and he shall retain nothing from his labour that he can carry in his hand. This, again, is wicked sickness – for just as he came, so too shall he go.'

41. Job also said, 'Naked I came from my mother's womb, and naked shall I go forth' [Job 1.21]; and this person, 'shall turn and depart naked, just as he came from his mother's womb'. But Job, since he is righteous, goes forth naked of vice and wickedness;[19] but this person will depart from here with the same ignorance that accompanied him into the world.

5.17–19: 'Lo, I have seen what is good, what is fair: to eat and drink, and to see goodness in all one's toil with which one toils under the sun the number of the days of his life, which God has given him – this is his part. After all, everyone to whom God has given wealth and resources and whom God empowers to eat and take his part and be glad in his toil – this is a gift from God. For he will not much remember the days of his life, since God busies him with the gladness of his heart.'

42. The knowledge of God is called the mind's food and drink and goodness and part and wealth and resources and gladness and godly business and light and life and gift – and the Holy Spirit gives many other names to knowledge that are impossible to list now, since it is prohibited by the principle of writing notes on Scripture.

43. As distinct from those who receive the wealth of wisdom and knowledge, but do not keep it, it says 'and [God] empowers him'. For even Judas the traitor had mental wealth and spiritual resources, but he had no power over them, since for the sake of profit he betrayed the wisdom and truth of God.

44. When one receives spiritual knowledge from God, rarely does he remember this world and the perceptible life, for his heart is always occupied with contemplation.

45. Godly business is true knowledge that separates the purified soul from perceptible things.

6.1–3: 'There is an evil that I have seen under the sun, and it is great for people: there is a man to whom God gives wealth and resources and glory, and there is nothing lacking of all his soul desires – yet God does not empower him to devour it, but a stranger will devour these things. And surely this is vanity and a wicked sickness. Even though a man should have a hundred offspring and live many years and the days of his age be multitude, if his soul does not fill itself with goodness and he has no tomb, I say that one stillborn is better than he. For in vanity the stillborn child has gone and into shadow he has departed, and his name will be received in the shadow; he has not seen the sun, nor known anything – but his rest is better than that other man's. Even if he has lived cycles of millennia and has not known goodness, do they not all go to the same place?'[20]

46. In this chapter, he speaks of those who have been counted worthy of imperturbability and knowledge but have fallen again owing to the Devil's envy. The second chapter concerns the long life of an impure man who has many children and has not known God. The stillborn is considered more honourable than he is, and after death he shall have the same lot as one stillborn.

47. The one who destroys the accumulated wealth of all knowledge and all wisdom is the Evil One, whom he calls a 'stranger' and a foreigner to the knowledge of God. For the verb 'to devour' refers to food, but also to destruction: thus, 'If you are willing and listen to me, you shall eat the good things of the land; but if you are not willing and do not listen to me, the sword will eat you up' – instead of 'destroy you' – 'for the mouth of the Lord has spoken it' [Is 1.19–20]. This is also the stranger whose arrival persuaded David to sacrifice the poor man's lamb, and so Nathan the Prophet also called him 'a stranger' [cf. 2 Sam 12.1–4].

6.7: 'All a man's toil is for his mouth, and still his soul is not satisfied.'

48. All a man's vice stays in his heart, and he does not say, 'From his fullness we have all received' [Jn 1.16].

6.8: 'For what more does the wise man have than the fool? By contrast, it is the poor man who knows how to conduct his life.'

49. [It is the poor man] who says, 'I am the life' [cf. Jn 11.25].

6.9: 'A good spectacle for the eyes is above one who roams in soul, for even this is vanity and the resolve of a breeze.'

50. The one who follows after the knowledge of God is better than the one who follows after the soul's desires; or, better the knowledge of God than corruptible pleasure. According to Symmachus, it is better to look toward the future than to enjoy the present.[21]

51. It is not proper to attribute vanity and wicked business and the resolve of a breeze to everything in the chapter. They should instead be attributed to blameworthy things, but not to praiseworthy things. I say this because he did not charge the whole chapter altogether with vanity and business and the resolve of a breeze; in it there are also praiseworthy things. For the vain one is not the poor person who conducts his life, but rather the one who has lived for thousand year cycles but never contemplated goodness: again, vanity is not the good spectacle of the eyes, but the conduct of the soul.

6.10–12: 'If something has been, its name has already been called; and it is known what man is; and he is unable to contend with one mightier than he is. For many are the words which increase vanity. What advantage is there for a man? For who knows what is good for a man during his life, the number of the life of the days of his vanity? For he has passed them in a shadow; and who will tell a man what will happen under the sun after him – and how will he be who tells him?'

52. Concerning names, some correspond to bodily nature but some to bodiless nature. The names of bodily nature designate the quality of each thing, which is composed of dimension, colour and shape; but the names of bodiless natures show the standing of each rational being – whether it is praiseworthy or blameworthy. Whereas the first names are simply applied to things, the second names are not, for they depend upon choice. For it belongs to self-determination to flow[22] either toward justice, and be counted worthy of the knowledge that makes of it an angel, archangel, throne or principality [cf. Col 1.16]; or else toward vice, and be filled with the ignorance that makes of it a demon, Satan, or other ruler of this world which lies in shadows [cf. Eph 6.12].

If then, he says, what came to be at the time of the world's creation took a name designating its standing, man also took a name appropriate to his standing.[23] Therefore, he says, let no one say, 'For what reason was I joined to this body, and why was I not made an angel? Is there then no partiality with God [cf. Rom 2.11], or were we not made beings who are self-determined?' – for such words as these multiply vanity. And how will what has been made say to its maker, 'Why have you made me thus?' Or how will he respond to God [cf. Rom 9.20]? But let the creature make an end to such words, and do what contributes to virtue and knowledge such as is found in this age of shadows, thinking all the while that everything is vanity and shadow and that the things of this life, after we depart from it, are covered over by forgetfulness.

7.1: 'A good name is better than good oil, and the day of death better than the day of birth.'

53. Names by their own nature are neither good nor wicked; they are made up of different letters, and no letter is either good or wicked. It is when they are applied to good things that they are called 'good', or to wicked things that they are called 'wicked'. Here, then, 'a good name' designates a good thing – and Solomon called none of the created things good, except for virtue and the knowledge of God.

In some cases, what is good by nature is said to be good (e.g., virtue); in other cases, things like gold and silver are said to be good. Thus, even the rich man had good things in his life, 'and Lazarus conversely had bad things' [cf. Lk 16.25]. That the word 'oil' is used in place of 'delights' is clear when David says of men, 'from the fruit of their grain and wine and oil they have been satisfied' [Ps 4.8].

54. If the good death that the righteous die in Christ naturally loosens the soul from vice and ignorance, then conversely the birth opposite to such a death links the soul to vice and ignorance. For this reason, such a death is more honourable than such a birth.

7.2: 'Better to go to the house of mourning than to the house of merriment; for that is the end of all men, and the living man will give good to his heart.'

55. The end of man is blessedness. If the Lord blesses mourning in the Gospels (for he said, 'Blessed are those who mourn, for they shall be comforted' [Mt 5.4]), then Solomon rightly says that the end of man is mourning, which fills those who live in it with spiritual goods.

7.3–7: 'Better anger than laughter, for the heart will rejoice in the face's sadness. The heart of the wise is in the house of mourning, and the heart of fools in the house of rejoicing. Better to hear the reproof of a wise man than for a man to hear the songs of fools. For like the sound of thorns under the pot is the sound of the fools' songs: this, too, is vanity. For oppression wearies the wise man and destroys the strength of his heart.'

56. When anger, struggling for virtues, spars with the demons, it is mighty and praiseworthy; but when it contends with other people for perishable things, it is blameworthy. So what he is saying here is this: the fool takes pleasure in vice and laughs and rejoices in it, nor does he give up shameful songs and laughter that destroy his soul like fire under thorns; but the righteous man is angry and indignant against such passions and he judges mourning to be more honourable than such rejoicing and the reproof of a wise man more honourable than such songs. And he calls such a life 'vanity' and 'oppression', for it easily abuses the heart of the wise man and wearies his strength for virtues.

7.8: 'Better the last of the words than the first.'

57. Better, he says, the one who accomplishes the law than the one who hears the law [cf. Rom 2.13; Jas 1.22]. For the first words are called words of instruction, and the last words are called words of deeds, if indeed words are said to be good words for the sake of good deeds.

7.9: 'Do not hasten to be angry in your spirit, for anger rests in the bosom of fools.'

58. It should be noted that here he clearly calls the soul 'the bosom' – for one would not say that anger rests in the perceptible bosom.

7.10: 'Do not say, "How does it happen that former days were better than these days?" – for it is not in wisdom that you have enquired concerning this.'

59. If 'the fear of the Lord adds days' [Prov 10.27], it is down to us to enjoy the good or better days of knowledge. It is not the wise who reckon that the first fruits of knowledge are given to those who are elders according to their age; and it is not because one is old that one deserves honour. After all, vice is exceedingly ancient, but does not deserve honour on account of its age, if indeed 'it is not the immensely aged who are wise, nor the old men who know judgement' [Job 32.9].

7.11–12: 'Wisdom with an inheritance is good, and it is useful to those who contemplate the sun; for in its shadow, wisdom is like the shadow of silver, and the advantage of the knowledge of wisdom will give life to him who has it.'

60. Just as those who contemplate the sun have some advantage over those who had contemplated it but do so no longer, so those who have wisdom and the power over it – for this is what 'with an inheritance' means – have something more than those who had it but lost it due to their own iniquity. For anyone who has first possessed wisdom, then lost it, had the shadow of wisdom, not wisdom as such; and so he is like one who has kept the shadow of silver, but has no silver as such. For it is the nature of wisdom to give life through knowledge to the one who possesses her, not when she is taken by him, but when she abides with him.[24]

7.15: 'There is a just man being destroyed in his justice, and there is an impious man abiding in his vice.'

61. Abandonment for the sake of being tested is also called 'destruction', as with Job: 'I was destroyed and I became a stranger' [Job 6.18].

62. 'But very nearly', said David, 'were my feet overthrown, very nearly did my steps slip: for, contemplating the peace of sinners, I was jealous of the iniquitous' [Ps 72.2–3].

7.16–18: 'Do not become overly just, nor needlessly wise, lest you should be dumbstruck; do not be overly impious, nor become hardened, lest you should die in a time not your own. It is good for you to hold fast to this, and not to remove your hand from it, for the one who fears God will accomplish everything.'

63. Let not, he says, an impious thought stay long in your heart, lest your soul should die in its impiety. The men of Sodom and Gomorrah died in a time not their own. And if this moment is the time for reform, then those who die at this time and are separated from the Life who says, 'I am the life' [Jn 11.25], do not die at the appropriate time.

64. It is good for you to hold fast to not being overly just, and indeed not to soil your heart with impiety, for you will be delivered from all evil if you fear God.

8.2: 'Watch the king's mouth.'

65. Now by 'mouth' he means word or law.

8.12–13: 'For indeed I know that it will be good for those who fear God, and it will not be good for the impious, and in this shadow he will not lengthen his days who does not show fear in the presence of God.'

66. Now by 'good' he means the knowledge of God.

8.14: 'There is vanity that is done on the earth: that there are righteous people to whom it happens like the work of the impious, and that there are impious persons to whom it happens like the work of the righteous. I said, this too is vanity.'

67. It is vanity, he says, which happens on the earth, that there are righteous who fall into troubles as though they were impious, and that there are impious who enjoy good things as though they were righteous. And about them the prophet said to the Lord, 'Yea, I will speak to you of judgements: why does the way of the impious prosper?' [Jer 12.1] And David said, 'But very nearly were my feet overthrown, very nearly did my steps slip: for, contemplating the peace of sinners, I was jealous of the iniquitous' [Ps 72.2–3].

9.1: 'For I gave all of this to my heart, and my heart looked at all this.'

68. One leads things into his heart when he is disposed to examine them and, after this, the heart knows the things. This is why it says, 'I went around, and my heart, to know' [Eccl 7.25]. For the one who leads a thing into his heart by scrutinising it also 'goes around' it and the heart in turn knows it. But know this: not everything that one goes around is therefore known by the heart – for we scrutinise many things, but understand few.[25]

9.10: 'For there is no work, no thought, no knowledge, and no wisdom in hell, where you are going.'
69. If there is no thought in hell, how does the rich man exhort Abraham to send Lazarus to him [cf. Lk 16.19–25]?

9.12: 'And not even man knows his time.'
70. Man does not know that his time is the moment for reform; for 'time' indicates 'proper time'.

11.9: 'And march, blameless, in the paths of your heart and in the vision of your eyes.'
71. . . . in ascetic struggle and in contemplation.

11.10: 'And remove anger from your heart and put away wickedness from your flesh.'
72. From this we know that the irascible part is joined to the heart, and the concupiscible part to the flesh.
73. Now by 'wickedness' he means luxury and gluttony.

ON THE 'OUR FATHER'

(*CPG* 2461)

INTRODUCTION

Evagrius' *On the 'Our Father'* is somewhat unusual in that it is only preserved in Coptic (in the Bohairic dialect) and in Arabic.[1] Although there is a long and distinguished scholarly tradition of research into Evagrius' reception among Greeks and Syrians, the question of how Evagrius' works were received by later generations of Egyptians has been rarely, if ever, posed, and never answered. In 1963, Muyldermans published a list of seven references to Evagrius; three are found in Coptic literary sources (which include quotations attributed to him) and four in documentary texts (which attest to the circulation of his works among Coptic readers).[2] Muyldermans curiously neglected to mention the extensive account of Evagrius' life that is found in Coptic.[3] Subsequent research has brought additional Coptic translations to light.[4] We are not yet in a position to determine from these scattered references what sort of reputation Evagrius had in Egypt in the generations after his death, but the preliminary evidence suggests that he was valued as a spiritual author. Since the Second Origenist Controversy raged outside the bounds of the Coptic Church, and since Evagrius was a teacher vastly respected by other Oriental Orthodox Christians, the question of how the Copts received Evagrius' works in the centuries immediately after his death should be regarded as still open.

The text translated attests to another facet of Evagrius' reception by the Egyptians. What we have here is taken from a lengthy catena of Coptic authors on Gospel, edited by Paul de Lagarde in 1886. This fortuitous discovery might indicate that Coptic sources can be as promising as the various Greek catenae that have yielded up precious scholia on Job, Psalms and other books. The authorship is reasonably secure on the basis of comparing the contents with other writings by Evagrius, as has been shown in a study by Bunge,[5] and remarks by Hausherr.[6]

Source: de Lagarde (1886): 13.

Translations: Bunge (1987): 59–61 (complete German translation); Hausherr (1960): 83–84 (partial French translation).

TRANSLATION[7]

The holy Abba Evagrius commented upon the prayer which is in the gospel according to Matthew: 'Our Father who art in heaven . . .'.

Many have spoken about this holy prayer, and those who did so were greater than we. We, too, in adding to their purpose and their teaching, shall speak to your charity by the grace that is in every word of this holy prayer. It is well suited to lead man to his first nature,[8] if we but give it all our attention.

> *Our Father who art in heaven . . .*

This word is for those who can enter with boldness[9] into the presence of God, as a son draws near to his father's bosom.

> *. . . hallowed be thy name . . .*

That is, may thy name be hallowed among us in that, because of our good deeds, we are glorified by the nations who say, 'Behold, the true servants of God!'

> *. . . thy kingdom come . . .*

The kingdom of God is the Holy Spirit; we pray that he will descend upon us.

> *. . . thy will be done on earth as it is in heaven.*

The will of God is the salvation of every rational soul. We pray that what is done by the mental powers in heaven, may also happen on earth.[10]

Give us this day our daily bread . . .

Our daily bread is the inheritance of God; here, we pray that he give us today this pledge, that is, that in this age its kindness and its longing become visible in us.

. . . and forgive us our trespasses . . .

The forgiveness of sins means the release from passion and the strengthening of the soul against sin, and that we are gentle to one another, as this word teaches it, which comes to this.[11]

. . . as we forgive one another.

Forgiving our debtors means that we do not remember bad thoughts against those who are angry against us.

And lead us not into temptation . . .

That is, that we may not surrender ourselves to temptation, apart from God's will.

. . . but deliver us from the Evil One.

That is, that if it pleases God to lead us in temptation, he should give us strength not to fall to it and not return to it.

For thine is the power . . .

That is, the Son.

. . . and the kingdom . . .

That is, the Holy Spirit.

forever and ever. Amen.

NOTES ON LUKE

(*CPG* 2458F)

INTRODUCTION

Attention was first drawn to the survival of the following notes by Fabricius-Harles's *Bibliotheca graeca*, in commenting upon the work of Balthasar Corderius.[1] On the basis of an exemplar from Cardinal Bessarion's library, Corderius had produced a Latin translation of patristic scholia on Luke; his avowed intention of bringing out a bilingual edition was, however, not realised.[2] (In fact, the Greek text was not published for another two centuries, when Angelo Mai published Nicetas' *Catenae on Luke*.)[3] Finding in the manuscript two notes attributed to 'Evagrius', Corderius ascribed them to Evagrius Scholasticus and speculated that they were extracted from some now lost work.[4] He never made it clear precisely why he thought the scholia derived from the historian, and Fabricius rightly queried this attribution. But although Fabricius was surely correct to claim instead that they had been written by Evagrius Ponticus, he advanced no argument for this claim.

Another hundred years passed before the case was taken up by Balthasar, who made a preliminary argument in favour of Evagrius Ponticus' authorship of at least some of them, based first and foremost on the striking parallel between sch. 1 on Luke and several scholia on the Psalms.[5] We are able to advance further evidence in support of this claim on the basis of a distinctive phrase found three times in sch. 1 (*epechein logon* – 'to play the role of' or 'to correspond to'), which can be found in Evagrius' *Notes on Proverbs* (sch. 5, 72, 203) and *Gnostikos* 3. Balthasar was not persuaded, however, of the authenticity of sch. 5 and 6, chiefly on the grounds that they lack characteristically Evagrian vocabulary and that the style features unusually long sentences. He also queried the authenticity of sch. 4, claiming again that it is stylistically atypical. Counter to this, it should be noted that Balthasar accepted the authenticity of sch. 1 even though it also demonstrates unusually long sentences. Furthermore, one is always justified in asking whether it makes sense to suppose that a Greek text would have been attributed wrongly to Evagrius in the manuscript tradition. As we see from the *Definitions*, Evagrius' name bore a stigma as early as the mid-seventh century, so it is difficult to imagine that a text not belonging to Evagrius would be attributed to him in the Greek manuscript tradition (as may very well have happened on multiple occasions in the Syriac tradition); it is far easier to imagine Evagrius' sayings preserved anonymously. But this is hypothetical. The transmission of his notes on Scripture clearly demonstrates that he was regarded as a valuable expounder of scripture.

Balthasar does make a valuable point that we should consider, however, in noting that these scholia are unusually long. It will be recalled that, in commenting on Ecclesiastes 5.17–19, Evagrius remarked that 'the Holy Spirit gives many other names to knowledge that are impossible to list now, since it is prohibited by the principle of writing notes on Scripture' (sch. 42). Even though some of his notes are rather long, we have nothing to compare to the length of these comments. It may well be the case that what Nicetas preserved was not originally intended by Evagrius as scholia; perhaps they were extracted from sermons or the like.

Beyond the similarities with other works by Evagrius which Balthasar noted, other evidence supports his conclusion. In the first scholion, on the parable of the Good Samaritan, the schema of angels, demons and humans is typical of Evagrius, as is the interpretation of the two denarii as 'virtue and theological contemplation'. Similarly, Evagrius' remarks in sch. 4 about Joseph – that he 'was instructed in the divine laws so that he withdrew from all pleasures and other passions' – and his explanation of 'divine subjects of instruction' as the Master's *logika hyperchonta* ('rational possessions'), are deeply consistent with his conventional manner of expression and his conceptual scheme. Perhaps the most unexpected feature that emerges from the notes is Evagrius' knowledge of astronomy and the Jewish calendar, as revealed in sch. 6. But as we have seen in the *Scholia on Job*, Evagrius demonstrates there an informed awareness of Hebrew etymology and alludes to consulting the text in the original. So his claim that an eclipse is impossible on the Passover is not entirely unprecedented.

In Mai's publication, the comments on Luke 19.4 and 19.11–17 appear after the catena. But for this translation, the comments have been re-organised so that they follow the narrative of Luke's gospel.

Source: Mai (1825–38): 9: 675–76, 688, 713–16, 721–22.

Translations: Although Corderius provides Latin translations for parts of sch. 1 and 7, this work has not previously been translated into a modern language.

TRANSLATION[6]

10.25–37: *The parable of the good Samaritan*

1. Moses led man out from sinning in deed, but his successor Jesus cut off the second one, that is, sin in thought.[7] Likewise, then, the priest did not heal the man half-dead, but the Samaritan did, who did not say with the word of the prophet, 'There is no dressing, oil, or bandages to apply' [Is 1.6 LXX]. That he came providentially[8] is clear from the fact that he had such oil and bandages – for he brought these things along for many wounded men. So the angels hold fast to the word of the living [cf. Phil 2.16], but demons, the word of the dead, and men, the word of the ailing. The physician came for the latter; for the sake of his other deeds, he is also called the 'saviour'. Now if a rational nature is said to be sickly, he is called its 'physician'; if a sheep, he is called its 'shepherd'. And of humans, he is called the 'King'.[9]

Now there are three things: the physician, the medicine and the patient. And if someone takes the medicine but is not healed, then he has not been healed either by the doctor's orders, or the medicines' impotence, or his own lack of discipline. But the physician of souls gives orders appropriately, and his commands are appropriate to the passions – so then the sickly man remains unhealed due to his own lack of discipline. For the physicians have written how each of his limbs must be healed, but the Saviour [has prescribed] a panacea in the passage where he said, 'You shall love your neighbour', and firstly, 'You shall love the Lord your God' – through which it is possible thereby to keep all the other commandments.[10]

And if there are two denarii [Lk 10.35], they are virtue and theological contemplation, that is to say, faith and works, the love of God and the love of one's neighbour. And it is necessary to see that the law orders us to do such things as must be observed out of love.

As in the case of tribute [cf. Rom 13.7], so with love; therefore it is said, 'Owe no one anything, except love' [Rom 13.8]. Whatever one does of one's own resolve – virginity or ascetic withdrawal – is by way of a gift.[11] It is as with hospitality: hospitality is not offered out of love; if it were, it would not be hospitality. For we have simply done what we are required to do [Lk 17.10].[12]

12.58: 'When you go to the judge with your adversary, as you are in the way, take care to be delivered from him; otherwise, he may take you before the judge, and the judge deliver you to the officer, and the officer throw you into prison.'
2. And one is well inclined toward his adversary by doing the opposite of the wicked things that the Devil suggests.

19.4: 'And he ran before, and climbed up into a sycamore tree to see him: for he was to pass that way.'
3. The sycamore designates conversion, and the crowd, passions. So the one who separates from them and is exalted by humility [cf. Lk 14.11; 18.14] sees Jesus and is seen by him, welcomes the one who 'tabernacled' beside him [cf. Jn 1.14], receives salvation, and becomes a son of Abraham.

19.11–27: *The parable of the servants who are made rulers over ten cities, or five*
4. Some of those who complete their task have from the Saviour the reward of having authority over ten cities or five, and will be proclaimed as lords of these cities at the resurrection of the dead; but some have considered this promise in a lowly, earthly way, reckoning that they will be entrusted with governorship and sovereignty for having lived well and pursued a Christ-like way of life. So they thought to rule and reign, supposing, as it were, the prizes of virtue to be a bodily reward in the Jerusalem below which is being built up from precious stones [cf. 1 Pet 2.5]. For a lust for ruling and having authority still held them while they pursued their life here below, even as they gave themselves over to serving their neighbours without arrogance, with an eye to the word spoken by Christ, 'Everyone who humbles himself will be exalted' [Lk 18.14]. But in not rejecting from their soul the passion of love for power and glory, they long to be revealed as governors or leaders and generals at the resurrection of the dead. It is necessary to lead them from this lowly, earthly assumption. So it must be asked what these cities are, and how they are, and where they might be, over which the King and

Saviour wishes to give power to those who carry out his charges to the utmost.

We reckon, therefore, that these cities closely resemble the heavenly Jerusalem that is the city of the living God, about which in the Psalms it is said by those who approach it, 'Just as we have heard, so too we see in the city of the Lord of powers' [Ps 47.9]. For there are those who even while in human life hear about the city above, the conduct in it and such things as are accomplished for its sake in a godly and holy way, and who approach it. And finding the things that they had learned here in word being accomplished there in deed, comparing what they have heard to the things they have seen, they say, 'What we have heard, that we also see. For truly this is the city of the King of All, the Son of God, who is the Lord (so to speak) of all military powers.' And this city is not established by chance, but by the one who has brought all created things into being, so that it is said, 'God established it forever' [Ps 47.9]. In agreement with these things, he wrote about the hope of the saints when he said, 'He was looking forward to the city with foundations, whose architect and builder is God' [Heb 11.10].

Since such things are clearly brought to light concerning the cities, such is the heavenly Jerusalem and consequently these cities, too, are heavenly. If, then, the Saviour dispenses control of these cities to his rational servants who behaved well in respect of the possessions with which they were entrusted, it should not be thought that a mortal governorship and sovereignty will be given in the earthly Jerusalem. Instead, those accepting power to lead the aforementioned cities will have led them in a manner closely resembling the archangels who lead the angels, as these holy cities are filled at once with inhabitants, that is, holy souls and spiritual powers.

They will bring this promise to pass who henceforth govern their own bodies, the irrational passions of the soul and the things related to them. Those who beat the body and enslave it [cf. 1 Cor 9.27], who mortify their members on the earth, will come into the office of ruling. Thus, after they have helped themselves, they are judged worthy to lead others into the discipline that they themselves have achieved, showing themselves to be teachers of these matters in deed and in word.[13] This is what is meant by saying that the rational possessions of the Master are divine instruction, in keeping with [the verse] 'the words of the Lord are chaste words, silver tested and purified by fire in clay' [Ps 11.7].[14] Gaining the assistance of those who are being instructed by them, they are similarly led to have faith in better things.[15] Thus they are declared rulers of the heavenly cities, having received leadership from God the Word himself, the Ruler of all.[16]

In the same way that the one who learns from us to govern himself through ethical instruction is directed toward the stewardship, the goal set before one who is entrusted with stewardship is to manage his responsibility well; upon discharging this task, he will receive his wages of leading a city. The life of Joseph offers a sign of this.[17] Learning from his father to govern himself, he was instructed in the divine laws so that, by prudence and the rest of the virtues, he withdrew higher than all pleasures and other passions; and he set his hand to managing the household under the rule of the one who owned him [Gen 39.1–4]. He was also placed in charge of the prison by the gaoler [Gen 39.21–23]. And when he had been shown to be the best person in charge, he accepted the superintendence of all Egypt and was appointed ruler after the king [Gen 41.39–44].

Consequently, men of piety first rule themselves through temperance and take care of their own houses, then they are ordained to lead the church (on which matter, Paul says, 'If one does not know how to superintend his own house, how shall he take care of God's church?'[1 Tim 3.5]). Therefore after each has taken care of himself and taken care of what is necessary for his children and his household and then the church, they will have as a trophy for these successes the power over the aforementioned cities. And the cities of Judea here below could be regarded as symbols of these cities. For as the earthly Jerusalem bears the image of the heavenly one, so too do the cities of this Judea below, I think. For as the earthly Jerusalem offers a reminder and a type of the cities of the Jerusalem above, so, too, the city is of the King [cf. Mt 5.35] – that is, the heavenly Jerusalem – and those who have suited themselves for it are approved by the king to reign over the other cities. For as the heavenly Jerusalem is the city of the Living God, the Lord is a great king. So they will become rulers of the other heavenly cities who have received from the Saviour the promise of having power over ten cities, or over five cities.[18]

19.28: 'When he had said this, he went on ahead, going up to Jerusalem.'

5. So he hastened to death, which he purposed to abolish, so that from its bonds he might release those who were formerly overpowered. And he gave himself up for all, having become the Lamb of God and bearing the sin of the world by his own slaughter, which

he voluntarily accepted. And this was his purpose: to give his blood for disbanding the wicked demons, so that he might lull them to sleep, making them drowsy. For his saving blood brought about their weakness, or rather death. Those who beforehand had chosen to contrive against him from the passion of envy, or rather from satanic activity, thought they had brought about his betrayal.

When the demons beheld souls removed day by day from every vice, and withdrawn from all deceit through the divine word of his teaching and his immaculate way of life which, being human, he had accepted when he set himself forth as a pattern for those who desire to live blamelessly, they thought to impede human salvation by subjecting the teacher and helper of mankind to death; but the fools were overthrown. For, by doing these things, they acted against themselves through them rather than contriving the villanies that they actually devised against Jesus. For he had voluntarily and with unforced zeal thought it right to head for death. And being able to submit to his own chosen end, he did not deem it safe for his death to happen either by his life perishing from some disease along with the flesh, or by putting away the body in some other way. For if in such manner he had accepted death, when he came back to life again in keeping with his undeceiving reports about his third-day resurrection, the wilful cowards would have seized upon this pretext for unbelief and, wishing to malign his resurrection, they would have said that he had never in fact died but had concealed himself and hidden himself from human eyes, and that only when he returned in their midst did he say that he was raised from the dead and had been brought back from the nether realm.

So that there would be no room for urging disbelief in his resurrection, he endured being handed over to the judge and judged by him in the sight of many. And indeed when the judge wished to dismiss him, in that he had not found in him one reason for death [cf. Lk 23.22], and when the Jews saw fit for a robber to be released in their midst instead of him, Jesus thought it right to keep silent when he was set before the tribunal. For if he had spoken out in his own defence, he would have been fleeing the sentence of death. Since the judge had no plea, he determined chastisement for him. For he had the aim, as I have already said, of immediately making with speed for the realm where souls freed from their bodies are kept, so there he might release from restraining misdeed, and fearful necessity, those of them who drew near his presence in that place.[19] And indeed that which he wished came to pass. Having been hanged on the gallows of the cross, he made his own celebrated death manifest and, working through it, established the faith of those whose minds were not excessively distracted.

23.44–47: 'And it was about the sixth hour, and there was darkness over all the earth until the ninth hour. And the sun was darkened, and the veil of the temple was torn down the middle. And when Jesus had cried with a loud voice, he said, "Father, into your hands I commend my spirit." And having spoken thus, he gave up the ghost. Now when the centurion saw what was done, he glorified God, saying, "Certainly this was a righteous man."'

6. So then having exercised his monstrous authority by the tree of the cross,[20] he confessed him to be truly the man of God. For the earth endured turmoil when it saw him hanging; even unbreakable rocks were broken when he was on the cross, and the veil of the temple was at once rent asunder, top to bottom [Lk 23.45]. Yes, even the tombs of the dead, standing suddenly open, sent forth those who had long lain dead but were now transformed by a life-giving power [cf. Mt 27.52]. Even the sun, that great bearer of light that was appointed by the Creator and Provider of all creation to begin the day [cf. Gen 1.16], did not give light to people though it was midday [Lk 23.45]. For darkness fell from the sixth hour even until the ninth hour [Lk 23.44].

But it did not fall as in the manner of an eclipse, as those who wish to discredit the Gospel try to say. From the hatred that is within them, they are of a contrary opinion to those things professed by the Gospels. Concerning the eclipse of the sun that customarily takes place, certain principles have been established.[21] For this does not happen at any other time than when the moon is traversing the same path as the sun. For they say that when the moon passes under the sun and directly behind it, it blocks the sun's beams by not permitting them to enter the realm around the earth. But they wilfully neglect that it was not the time of such a 'conjunction' when Jesus submitted to the cross: it is acknowledged by everyone that he suffered during the Jewish Passover – at which time the moon never passes beneath the sun, since the moon, being full, faces it and a fortnight would have already passed since the conjunction.[22] From these facts it is evident that the eclipse did not take place because of certain annual cycles, but by the power of the one who was working marvels from the cross, with the sun quickly desisting from completing its proper task as it saw the Master of all suffering outrages at the hands of worthless persons. And indeed the works of nature took place in order that it might be evident who it was who had accepted death, since he is the helmsman of all creation and the one who set it in order.

Each of the things that happened quickly was a sign and symbol of future things being successfully accomplished. The earthquake signified conversion from the ancestral customs of the whole earth and people withdrawing from the error of polytheism. The oracles of the whole earth were neglected, and the prophesying demons who ruled them of old, bewitching people with deceitful words, fell silent, as if they had never existed. The oracular springs dried up, as the demons in them were banished by fear of the power of the one who suffered. And the laws for each of the oracles languish henceforth, whilst the Gospel law alone directs and rules the human race. Now the cleaving of the rocks, being itself also a sign, hints at the bewilderment of foolish and sclerotic souls; and the rending of the veil reveals the withdrawal to come from the rites of the Jewish temple and all the miraculous epiphanies that occurred therefrom of old but which now reach out to all nations. And the prophecy had reached completion which said, 'For out of Zion shall go forth the law, and from Jerusalem the word of the Lord, and he shall judge among many nations' [Micah 4.3].

7. Now the opening of the graves prompted an idea of the freedom of the souls bound fast in Hades, and the resurrection of the dead, of which Jesus himself in his sufferings became the first born and the pledge [Col 1.18]. And the darkening of the sun revealed the withdrawal of the true light of the Sun of Righteousness [Mal 4.3] from the Jews, though it was midday. For this age was instituted, which in many places is allegorically called 'the day' by Scriptures, once all these prophecies had been fulfilled: 'the noon-day sun set and the light grew dark upon the earth during the day' [Amos 8.9 LXX]; and again, 'the sun went down for' them, 'though it was still midday' [Jer 15.9 LXX].

CHAPTERS

INTRODUCTION

The two most familiar works by Evagrius (at least, for the English-speaking world – thanks not least to J.E. Bamberger's fluid translations) are his *Praktikos* and his *On prayer*. These two works are written in an arrestingly terse style: they are respectively composed of one hundred and fifty-three *kephalaia* ('chapters'). A *kephalion*, or 'chapter', is a pithy saying – rather like a maxim – that is used very frequently in the Greek Christian tradition of ascetical literature. There are two great advantages to the genre that appeal to ascetic teachers. First, a chapter is readily memorised and thus can easily be absorbed into the monastic conscience. In this sense, it is the literary successor of the apophthegm (or 'saying'), which was the spoken word that was sought from a desert saint. Second, a chapter is structurally independent and so it is possible for the author of a collection of chapters to arrange them at will. This is not to say that the arrangement is necessarily arbitrary. On the contrary, there is very good evidence from Evagrius' pen that he deliberately ordered the chapters for maximum effect. Some sense of this is given in the 'prefatory note to copyists', found in his *Praktikos*:[1]

> I call upon the brethren who happen upon this book and wish to copy it *not* to join one chapter to another, *nor* to put on the same line the end of a chapter that has just been written and the beginning of what is about to be written. Instead, please begin each chapter with its appropriate beginning rightly and in keeping with the enumeration that we have introduced. For in this way the order of the chapters will be preserved and what is being said will be clear. We begin the first chapter with the question, 'What is

Christianity?' – which we answer by defining it as the teaching of our Saviour Jesus Christ, which is made up of ascetic struggle, natural contemplation and theology.

If the order is disrupted, the teaching will not necessarily emerge (or at least, not as clearly). To understand the teaching thus requires close consideration of the placement of the chapters in sequence, no less than serious attention to each chapter itself. The teaching is understood by appreciating the interconnection of elements within the overall arrangement.[2]

Evagrius' chapters, it is clear, are theoretically informed to their very foundations. He did not originate this technique – in fact, he himself seems to have been a careful student of the earlier collection of sentences by the pagan philosopher, Sextus[3] – but he popularised it to such an extent that it is tremendously well attested in the Byzantine tradition.[4] Because this style of writing is not likely to be familiar to modern readers (except, perhaps, for those who have already spent time studying the *Philokalia* and other related literature), it has seemed advisable to reserve it for the fourth and final section of this book, even though the contents of what Evagrius presents in this format cover the range of his teachings – from the relatively basic *Praktikos* to the highly advanced *Gnostic chapters*. The texts selected for translation here are similarly wide ranging, from the basic teachings of *To the virgin* to the abstract principles of *On prayer*. It is hoped that, after spending some time in reading the previous material, the reader will be prepared to recognise the allusions and references that are shot through these brilliant pieces.

A word of warning is in order, though: not all of the texts selected here go back to Evagrius' hand in their present form. This is manifestly true of *Definitions*, which were culled by a hostile source probably no earlier than the seventh century. It is difficult to know what to make of *Excerpts* and *Aphorisms*, which could have been prepared by Evagrius himself, but could as easily have been prepared by his followers. (We are still awaiting the publication of a similar collection made by Evagrius' disciples.)[5] So the reader might prefer not to expend too much effort in trying to make sense of the arrangement of chapters within those works. But even if the collections do not derive directly from Evagrius, they are still interesting and important insofar as they bear witness to the transmission, preservation and re-combination of his works by readers of subsequent generations.

TO THE VIRGIN
(*CPG* 2436)

INTRODUCTION

This relatively concise writing of Evagrius has been linked since the fifth century at least to his longer, better known and better studied work *To the monks*. Notwithstanding this virtual neglect, *To the virgin* enjoyed a wide circulation in the ancient world. Gennadius describes it as a 'short book for a virgin consecrated to God, appropriate to her profession and sex';[1] Socrates calls it one of 'two *stichera* [. . .], for a virgin';[2] and Jerome tells Ctesiphon that Evagrius 'wrote to the virgins'.[3] The Greek text was rediscovered in the early twentieth century and published by Hugo Greßmann in 1913. But in the years immediately before the Greek text was recovered, ancient translations in Latin, Syriac and Armenian were published. Add to this Rufinus' Latin translation (available in Holste's edition since the seventeenth century), Muyldermans' identification of four other Syriac MSS and the two incomplete Armenian versions – and one begins to appreciate the popularity of the work.[4]

We do not know for whom Evagrius wrote this piece in the first instance, though it is clear that eventually there was a copy of it at Melania's monastery on the Mount of Olives. From a discussion that can be traced across several letters,[5] it seems that the deaconess Severa intended to travel to Egypt, to consult Evagrius. Evagrius strongly discouraged her from undertaking the journey and tried to pre-empt it by sending her something he had already written. Hausherr, Bunge and Elm have argued that the writing that Evagrius sent is *Virgin*, and their collective case is very strong.[6] Elm has speculated that Evagrius may have originally written it for Melania herself.[7] Although some have accepted this suggestion with no ado,[8] it raises a serious question that has not yet received due consideration: if Melania were the original recipient, why would Evagrius have needed to send another copy to her monastery? In this connection, it may be more fruitful (and slightly less perilous) to think of Amma Syncletica, who seems to have known Evagrius, or similar virgins who were established in Egypt. For Syncletica at least we have the testimony of her hagiographer that she lived near a major metropolis such as the instructions seem to envisage. The instruction to 'honour your mother' (*Virgin* 2) does not accord well with Syncletica's presumptive role as leader of her community (which is an equally serious point against the hypothesis that Melania was the original recipient!), but it is possible that Evagrius was preparing a manual for the community's leader to distribute to the sisters.

Elm's suggestion is part of her intriguing, though ultimately unpersuasive, case for viewing *Virgin* as a monastic rule. Elm is surely right to point out that Evagrius' recipient was part of a community. But her further argument, that the contents of *Virgin* were 'of sufficient precision to allow a community to regulate its dealings with the outside world and to organize its life within', is poorly supported.[9] Her case is based chiefly on applying the criteria for recognising monastic rules set forward by Adalbert de Vogüé to *Virgin*; but, as Sinkewicz has very sensibly noted, *Virgin* hardly resembles anything from that period that is recognisable as a monastic rule.[10] Although Evagrius' instruction is addressed to a virgin in a community, it is not at all clear that he aimed to *direct* a community of virgins.[11]

Another important aspect of Elm's analysis is her claim that Evagrius' counsels for the anonymous virgin are different to his ascetic teachings as found in other writings. Elm has suggested (and been followed in suggesting) that in *Virgin* Evagrius' teaching has been reworked so as to be more feminine. In fact, Elm suggests that a significant difference in meaning underlies the difference in words used, with the result that the goal held forward for the virgins is different to that held forward for the monks.[12] This suggestion has not been universally accepted. Driscoll, for instance, claims that Elm's contrasts are too sharp and affirms that the goal of monasticism for men and women is the same.[13] Now it is undeniably the case that *Virgin* has a higher proportion of scriptural allusions and lower representation of technical terms than other writings of his have. But, as Josephine Williams has shown, it is more satisfactory to construe this difference as Evagrius' reaction to different states of perceived spiritual maturity in his readers, rather than as some reflection of gender inequality.[14] In sum, *Virgin* fails to provide evidence for Evagrius establishing a lower grade of monasticism to be observed by the women who putatively needed male guidance. To the contrary, as Williams has convincingly argued, the Scriptural content of *Virgin*, if taken seriously, points consistently to an intended reader who has not advanced far along the path of spiritual growth – a reader who could be male or female.

Source: This translation is based upon Greßmann (1913), though I have consulted the other ancient translations as well. In only one case has this resulted in a major divergence. At *Virgin* 54, Greßmann's text is considerably shorter than the agreed witness of two Latin versions; Frankenberg's published Syriac version and Greßmann's unpublished Syriac version (as reflected in his apparatus). Greßmann asserted that the lines in question were interpolated; but Muyldermans and Bunge have argued that they dropped out of the Greek.[15] Muyldermans' and Bunge's position has more intuitive appeal: it makes more sense to imagine that at some stage a Greek copyist would have excised the doctrinal statement by Evagrius than to suppose that someone interpolated it into the text early enough for both the Latin and the Syriac translations to reflect it. (The conjecture that a scribe omitted it is certainly in keeping with the general trend of the Greek reception of Evagrius' works, whereby his ascetic writings were embraced but his doctrinal writings treated with deep suspicion.) Bunge has advanced a detailed case for the affinities of the longer recension with other passages by Evagrius.[16] Thus, the material in question is supported by internal comparison with other writings of Evagrius. As the ancient translations offer widespread evidence for the longer recension of *Virgin* 54, and as Greßmann offers no argument for his claim on behalf of the shorter recension, I have included the material in my translation. It is, however, printed in brackets and marked with an endnote.

Translations: Bettiolo (1996): 132–43; Sinkewicz (2003): 131–35.

TRANSLATION

1) Love the Lord and He will love you;
   serve Him and He will enlighten your heart.
2) Honour your mother as Christ's mother,
   and do not provoke the grey hairs of her who bore you.
3) Love your sisters as your mother's daughters,
   and do not abandon the way of peace.

4) Let the rising sun find in your hands a book,
and after the second hour, your work.[17]
5) 'Pray without ceasing' [1 Thess 5.17],
and remember Christ who begot you.
6) Shun chance meetings with men,
lest they become an idol in your soul
and be a stumbling-block for you at the time of prayer.
7) You have Christ to love:
separate all men from yourself
and you will not live a reprehensible life.
8) Put irascibility and wrath far from yourself,
so that grudge-bearing likewise will not dwell in you.
9) Do not say, 'I shall eat today, but not tomorrow' –
for you do not do so wisely.
For it will cause damage to your body
and pain to your stomach.
10) Eating meat is not right, nor is drinking wine good;
but these things must be provided for the weak.[18]
11) An insolent virgin will not be saved,
nor will an indulgent one behold her bridegroom.
12) Do not say, 'My handmaiden has annoyed me and I will
punish her' –
for there is no slavery amongst God's daughters.
13) Do not give ear to idle talk,
and flee the prattle of old busybodies.
14) Do not attend the celebrations of drunkards,
nor go to the weddings of outsiders.[19]
Every virgin who does such things is sullied in the
Lord's eyes.
15) Open your mouth for the Word of God,
and still your tongue from chattering.
16) 'Humble yourself before the Lord,
and' His right hand 'will lift you up' [Jas 4.10].
17) Do not turn your back on the poor in the time of tribulation,
and oil will not be lacking for your lantern
[cf. Mt 25.1–12].
18) Do everything for the Lord,
and seek no glory from humans,
for humans' glory is 'as a flower of the field' [Is 40.6];
but the Lord's glory endures through the ages.
19) The Lord will love the meek virgin,
but the irascible one will be hated.

20) The obedient virgin will find mercy,
    but she who mightily resists is witless.
21) The Lord will destroy the petulant virgin,
    but deliver the grateful one from death.[20]
22) Laughter is shameful and shamelessness is reprehensible,
    and utter witlessness is woven from them.
23) She who has adorned herself with clothing
    is also far from prudence.
24) Do not abide with secular women,
    lest they divert your heart
    and turn your righteous desires into illegitimate ones.
25) Call upon the Lord with tears at night,
    and let no one see you praying and you will find grace.
26) Desire for roaming and yearning for strangers' homes
    upset the soul's stability and corrupt her purpose.
27) The faithful virgin will not fear,
    but the faithless one flees her own shadow.
28) Envy melts the soul,
    and rivalry devours her.
29) She who despises a weak sister
    is also far from Christ.
30) Do not say, 'This is mine, that is yours' –
    for in Christ Jesus, everything is common.
31) You should not concern yourself with another's life,
    and you should not gloat when your sister stumbles.
32) Help virgins who are in need,
    and do not brag about your hereditary status.
33) Do not utter a word from your mouth in the Lord's
    church,
    and do not let your eyes wander;[21]
    for the Lord knows your heart,
    and regards all your thoughts.
34) Drive every evil desire from yourself,
    and your enemies will not sadden you.
35) Chant psalms from your heart,
    and do not so much as move your tongue in your
    mouth.
36) The witless virgin will love money,
    but the wise one will even give away her last
    crumb.
37) Just as the raging of fire is hard to still,
    so, too, the wounded soul of a virgin is hard to heal.

38) Do not give your soul to wicked thoughts,
      lest they stain your heart
      and keep pure prayer far from you.
39) Sadness is burdensome and dejection, unbearable,
      but tears before God are stronger than both.
40) Hunger and thirst quench bad desires,
      and a good vigil purifies the mind.
41) Love discomfits wrath and anger,
      and gifts assuage grudges.
42) She who slanders her sister
      will be cast out of the bridal chamber,
    and will cry out in front of its doors,
      and there will be no one to hear her.
43) The merciless virgin's lamps will be extinguished,
      and she will not see her bridegroom approaching
      [cf. Mt 25.1–12].
44) Glass is shattered when it falls on a stone,
      and a virgin touched by a man will not be unharmed.
45) Better a meek wife
      than a wrathful and irritable virgin.
46) She who listens laughingly to a man's words
      is like a woman putting a noose around her
        own neck.
47) Like a pearl in a golden crown
      is a virgin protecting herself from shame.
48) The demons' songs and flutes relax the soul,
      and destroy her vigour,[22]
    which you must guard at all costs,
      lest you become shameful.
49) Do not delight in those who tell jokes flippantly,
      or take pleasure in those who tell jokes maliciously,
    for the Lord has abandoned them.
50) You shall not reproach your sister when she eats,
      and be elated about your continence.
    For you do not know what the Lord wants,
      or who will be made to stand before him.
51) She who laments her bloodshot eyes
      and the wasting of her flesh
      will not delight in the soul's impassibility.
52) Continence is burdensome and chastity, hard to endure,
      but nothing is sweeter than the heavenly
        bridegroom.

53) The souls of the virgins will be enlightened,
    but the souls of the impure will see darkness.
54) I have seen men corrupting virgins by their teachings[23]
    and annulling their virginity.
[As for you, my child, listen to the teachings of the
  Lord's Church,[24]
    and let no outsider win you over.
God established heaven and earth,
    and has forethought for them all and rejoices in them.
No angel is incapable of evil,
    and no demon is wicked by nature;
      for God made both by his own free will.
Just as a human consists in a corruptible body and a
  rational soul,
    even thus was Our Lord born (save for sin).
In eating, he truly ate,
    and when he was crucified he was truly crucified,
      nor was it an apparition to deceive the sense of men.
There will certainly be a resurrection of the dead,
    and this world will pass away,
    and we will receive spiritual bodies.]
For the righteous will inherit light,
    but the impious will dwell in shadows.
55) Virginal eyes will see the Lord.
    The virgin's ears will hear his words.
The virgin's mouth will kiss its bridegroom.
    The virgin's nose is carried off by the fragrance of his
      ointment.
Virginal hands will feel the Lord
    and chastity of the flesh will be easily borne.
The virginal soul will be crowned,
    and with her bridegroom will live forever.
A spiritual garment will be given to her,
    and she will rejoice with the angels in heaven.
She will enkindle an unquenchable lamp
    and oil will not be lacking for her vessels.
She will receive eternal riches
    and inherit the kingdom of God.
56) Let my words be read to you, my child,
    let your heart heed my sayings.
Remember Christ who protects you,
    and do not forget the venerable Trinity.[25]

EXCERPTS

INTRODUCTION

In a collection entitled 'A compilation in excerpts from various fathers on prayer' (Paris B.N. 2748 ff. 153–83ᵛ), Joseph Muyldermans identified over seventy extracts from Evagrius. Among other things, this collection features several passages taken from the *Sentences of Sextus*, about which, more anon. These *Excerpts* have been valuable for two reasons: first, they facilitated the critical edition of some of Evagrius' works (e.g., *Praktikos*, *To the monks* and *Gnostic chapters* are all cited in the collection); second, they bring to light previously unknown sayings. This means that, to a certain extent, the contents of *Excerpts* will be repetitious, but there are still reasons to include it in this dossier. One virtue of *Excerpts* is that it contains variant readings of certain passages, which gives the reader some sense of how fluid the ancient texts were. Another important point is that Evagrius himself recycled his material. Finally, the collection was produced by a later excerpter and as such it attests to the liberties that Evagrius' later editors took in re-arranging Evagrius' carefully constructed chapters.

In this regard, *Excerpts* can be compared to *Definitions*. The two can also be compared in that they preserve a wider range of Evagrian thinking that one finds elsewhere, so they give a flavour of some of his works that are too lengthy (or too complex) to be translated here – such as his *Gnostic chapters*. All the same, *Excerpts* is unlike the *Definitions* in that the former is not obviously datable, whereas the latter can be placed after the Second Origenist Crisis on grounds that it describes Evagrius as 'accursed', a dubious distinction for which we have no evidence of any real currency before the sixth-century controversies. There is no reason to assume such a late dating for *Excerpts*. Such pieces as *Excerpts* may help to fill in the history of how

Evagrius' works were transmitted from the time of his death until the Second Origenist Crisis.

With regard to the passages from the *Sentences of Sextus*, the impact of this material on Evagrius' thought cannot be overestimated. Henry Chadwick has rightly claimed that 'Evagrius had absorbed Sextus' morality';[1] it is very likely that Evagrius personally redacted a version of the collection. Versions of the *Sentences* attributed to Evagrius survive in both Greek and Armenian.[2] Further circumstantial corroboration comes from the fact that Rufinus, Evagrius' friend and Latin translator, was also responsible for translating the *Sentences*. Henry Chadwick has even raised the possibility that Evagrius may be the ultimate source for some aphorisms added by Rufinus for his Latin version.[3] It is worth noting that, despite the imprecations of Jerome in this instance, the boundaries between Christian and non-Christian literature were hardly impermeable.[4] The 'Teachings of Silvanus', which was transmitted under the name of Anthony the Great, provides a parallel instance.[5] In the case at hand, though, it seems reasonable to suppose that Evagrius was directly involved in transmitting the *Sentences*.

Source: Muyldermans (1932): 79–94.

Translations: This work as such has not previously been translated, though many of the works from which it has been excerpted have been translated into Latin or French.

TRANSLATION

1. Against the anchorites, the demons fight on their own; against those who work for virtue in monasteries or other communities, they arm the more negligent of the brethren. And this second form of warfare is by far lighter. For it is impossible to find a person bitterer than a demon.[6]

2. Reading, prayer and vigil stabilise the wandering intellect; psalmody, patience and mercy calm wrath that has been stirred up; hunger, thirst, toil and withdrawal extinguish desire that is enflamed. These things should be enacted at the appropriate time and to the appropriate measure. For untimely and immoderate practices are harmful.[7]

3. Spiritual knowledge purifies the mind; love heals anger; moderation stabilises the flowing desire.[8]

4. 'Let not the sun go down', he said, 'on your wrath' [Eph 4.26], lest by night the demons come and agitate the soul with terrifying fantasies – for such things happen from the anger, and so they make it more fearful for their warfare.[9]

5. When the irritable part of our soul, on some pretext, has become ferocious, then the demons suggest withdrawal to us, so that, not having resolved the causes of the trouble, we remain in that state. But when the concupiscible faculty is enflamed, then conversely they propose cordiality, so that we have dealings with bodies while lusting for bodies.[10]

6. When, during fantasies during sleep, we are tickled as we happen to meet familiar faces, then we are sick in our concupiscible faculty – and one must pay attention to this. But when we fantasise about crags and beasts and wars and panicked flights, then one must take thought for one's irascible part.[11]

7. Imageless fluxes during sleep are in keeping with nature; but when there are images, it is the token of an unwell soul. Likewise, unfamiliar faces are a sign of an old passion; but familiar faces are a sign of fresh passion.[12]

8. Battles bring us nightly fantasies, so that during the day they may more readily confound the anger or the desire – for once these things have been advanced, they are easily fastened on.

9. Some say that the demons set in motion the passion of fornication by fastening on to the bodily members by dreams; and this movement relates defiled fantasies to the mind. But some say that they set in motion the desire by appearing to the mind in shameful forms and lightly touching the members.

10. The tokens of imperturbability we recognise by day through separation from impassioned thoughts; but by night, through the idleness of shameful dreams.[13]

11. The soul that is imperturbable is not the one that does not suffer in the presence of things, but rather the one that is calm even at their memories.[14]

12. The sign of imperturbability is that the conceptions that mount up to the heart are always bare, both when the body is wakeful and by dreams.

13. It is necessary not to abandon the cell at the time of trials, weaving a fine-sounding excuse; but rather to stay there and courageously endure it and chiefly fight against the demon of despondency who is more overbearing than all the rest and makes the soul particularly well-proven. Fleeing such conflicts is for the ignoble and the weak.[15]

14. The demons presiding over the soul's passions persist against those fighting them until death, but those of the body retreat under pressure.[16]

15. The impure demons enlist the help of the more impure. Although they are by disposition at odds with each other, the one thing they will co-operate for is the soul's destruction.[17]

16. When the first demon grows weak in battle, another more powerful follows him; for which reason, whenever a passion that has been at rest for some time suddenly boils up again without our providing a pretext through indifference, then we shall know that a more difficult demon has taken up the fight.[18]

17. As the soul progresses, greater demons in succession fight against her, and they confirm this who conquer the former, but suffer ten thousand terrors from those who are next.[19]

18. When demons are impotent in battle, they fall back a bit; and if then they see weakening, they will charge in all at once and tear you to pieces.[20]

19. God alone sees the movements of the heart. The demons, who see nothing, seize on symbols of the passions that are in the soul, whether some word that has been uttered, or some movement or other of the body, or change of food, or some such – and through them infer what sort of thoughts we have within.[21]

20. One must watch the demons' thoughts closely: some sow them secretly; and their periods of intensity and relaxation and their interrelations and duration; and which demon follows which. And aid must be sought from Christ to stand arrayed against them. For they are particularly harsh to those who are wisely participating in ascetic struggle.[22]

21. Of them, there are keener ones who outstrip the movement of our mind – the demon of impurity and of blasphemy. Now the first is more violent, and the second does not stay long.[23]

22. It is not always possible to fulfil the customary rule, but it is necessary to discern the times and accomplish the undertaken commands as best one can. For the demons know the times: they will hinder things that can be done, and suggest doing things that cannot be done. For example, they would not have the sick giving thanks for their sufferings and bearing with those who minister to them; and they maliciously exhort those who are exhausted to remain abstinent and to pray the psalms.[24]

23. Unless it first rightly orders all the passion within, the mind cannot depart to heavenly contemplation: for problems in private matters are wont to turn it back.[25]

24. Both virtues and vices make the mind blind – but the former, so that it does not see vices; and that latter, so that it will not behold virtues.[26]

25. Demonic songs set our concupiscence and desire in motion in a shameful way; but spiritual ones set our concupiscence and desire in motion in a spiritual way.[27]

26. Hearing the trumpet calls soldiers to battle; so, too, does psalmody the angels, and impious songs the demons.

27. What follows upon thoughts sent from God is a peaceful condition; but those from the demons, a disturbed one.[28]

28. It is altogether shameful for a monk to be involved in legal action: as one wrongly done by, because he does not endure it; as a wrong-doer, because he has done wrong.[29]

29. Perception is the power by which we apprehend material things; the faculty of perception is that by which it naturally works; the perceptive is that which receives the perception; the perceptible is that which is subject to perceptions.[30]

30. God is said to be present where he is in action – and the more present where he is fully active. As one who acts fully in the mental powers, he is fully in them.[31]

31. True stillness is when one sits in one's cell, having not one memory of a worldly thing: perfect action is 'praying unceasingly' [cf. 1 Thess 5.17] to God alone.

32. Even though the fathers of Sketis directly redressed evil thoughts, they had more simplicity and fear of God. But such behaviour is not at all safe for us, for the Evil One is not at a loss for a word. As for the rest, talking idly all day long, we are cheated of conversation with God, conversing with the enemy.[32]

33. The one who bears grudges against his fellows, bears no grudges against the demons; for one who hates his fellow man is altogether a lover of demons.[33]

34. A strong wind drives away a cloud; and grudge-bearing drives the mind from knowledge.[34]

35. Fiery coals spit forth sparks; and the grudge-bearing soul, evil thoughts.[35]

36. The scorpion's sting has the sharpest pain, and the grudge-bearer's soul the harshest poison.[36]

37. The one who treasures up grudges in the soul, treasures up fire in chaff.[37]

38. The harsh things that are destructive to the soul's memory are stored-up grudges.

39. The one who bears grudges whilst praying, sows his seed on the stones [cf. Mt 13.5].

40. Praying for enemies, you will drive off grudge-bearing.

41. To love all equally is difficult; but to meet everyone without perturbation is possible.

42. Man cannot put away impassioned memories whilst taking care for his anger and desire: for one cannot conquer them who does not despise food and wealth and glory.[38]

43. When the mind obtains the beginning of imperturbability for many anchorites, and thereupon brings upon itself the horse of vainglory [cf. Ps 31.9], it will drive them through the cities; but through providential disposition of events, the spirit of fornication confronts the mind and encloses it in one of its pig-sties. This teaches them not to rise from bed before being perfectly healthy, nor to imitate the disarray of those who are sick. For those people, still carrying about the last traces of sickness, betake themselves to baths and diets prematurely and, taking a sharp turn, relapse into their malady.[39]

44. The demons agitate a man, now as rational, now as irrational; when the assault occurs with respect to the irrational part of the soul – I mean the anger and desire – then they set him in motion after the manner of irrationality; for the movement concerning them is the lot of even animals who are irrational.[40]

45. There are some of the jealous demons, who make an attempt on those who are reading for the sake of benefit from it; some others who constantly attend them confuse their mind at one point and at another, taking their points of departure from some words, bring unusual concepts into them. It is then that they prompt inopportune yawns and bring on deep fatigue, fastening on to the eyelids and brow and the whole head, chilling them along with the rest of one's own body. By their frost, the cool bodies of the demons discomfit those reading, as if they have learned to do so from experience. Now they do this so that, once the heat that was stored up in the skull has been cooled, the eyelids may be relaxed, the pupils covered over. So whereas a natural sleep warms the body and makes it radiant, a demonic sleep conversely cools and spoils it. So then, when we yawn, we seal the mouth in keeping with the ancient custom, to avert them who would stroke those things in the body. It is therefore necessary to pray immediately and endure till the end until we drive them away.[41]

46. Turbid water will not be pure as long as it does not remain unshaken; nor is the monk's soul stilled without perseverance.[42]

47. Meetings with many people make a good habit turbid.

48. A purified spring flows with clear waters, but a purified mind springs up lucid conceptions.

49. A king does not dwell in a befouled house, nor does Christ in a soul sullied with sins.

50. Like a plot of land, a soul is reclaimed through attentiveness.[43]

51. One who has been struck cannot fail to be wounded, and the one who accepts evil thoughts cannot fail to be struck.[44]

52. The source of salvation for you is to condemn yourself.[45]

53. Bread strengthens the body, but the word of God strengthens the soul.[46]

54. Thoughts agitate the prayer of the one who is indifferent.[47]

55. What is nourishment for the body in good condition is a temptation for the noble soul.[48]

56. The north wind ripens fruits, and temptation increases the soul's patience.[49]

57. It is not possible to be a Christian apart from temptation, just as it is not possible to be crowned without a competition.[50]

58. The angels, suggesting to us spiritual pleasure, call upon us to set anger in motion against the demons; but the demons, who intimate shameful pleasure, urge us to turn it against other people.[51]

59. Treat other people as you would be treated by them.[52]

60. When you govern your stomach, you also govern the parts below your stomach.[53]

61. One who is busy about many things becomes busy about wicked things.[54]

62. Of a shameful pleasure, the enjoyment quickly passes, but the shame remains.[55]

63. You will have your mind when you know that you do not have it.[56]

64. The body's limbs are burdens to those who do not use them.[57]

65. A word from the ancient wise men: the prudent profit from the imprudent, or rather the imprudent from the prudent – for the latter take care of the formers' sins, but the former do not remember the successes of the latter.

66. When the four are elevated, the five are also elevated; but when the five are elevated, the four are not also elevated. For when the four elements of the body are elevated by the soul's parting, the five senses are also elevated; but when the five senses are elevated

by the philosophic death of the body, its four elements are not elevated.[58]

67. The one progressing in knowledge has what goes with him; the one progressing in ignorance does not have what goes with him. Now ignorance is two, but knowledge is one. What precisely does this word mean? That ignorance is two-fold – one kind is from lack of learning, as with children; the other is from humility, as with virtuous men. For the one progressing in either one or the other would not credit himself for it – the child does it unwillingly, the humble man willingly. So then, ignorance is two: one from nature, another from resolve.[59] But there is one knowledge that is conceited, and the one progressing in it credits himself for it because of conceit.

68. The source of salvation is the fear of God [cf. Prov 9.10] – this begets disdain for all the delights of the world, which in turn produces humility. The signs of humility are the death of one's own will, heartfelt confession and taking to heart both actions and words; not trusting in one's conscience, but laying everything before one's father in the spirit and depending upon his words and unashamedly obeying all his commands; not daring to do anything at all spitefully, but rather enduring all spite from everyone; not measuring oneself; not setting one's hand to any new thing contrary to the rule of the fathers; being satisfied with thriftiness, even confessing oneself unworthy of it; making oneself last of all, in word and deed; in all confidence, prevailing over the tongue, neither being premature with words nor using harsh tones; not laughing readily. Accomplished in these and similar things, humility leads to the height of divine love, no longer having fear of correction but instead a most ardent desire for the bridegroom.

69. The distinguishing features of perfect love are loving one's enemies – for He says, 'Love your enemies'; benefiting those who hate you – for He says, 'Do well to those who hate you'; praying for the unrighteous – for He says, 'Pray for those who despitefully use you' [Mt 5.44]; not only not giving measure for measure, but doing good instead – for he says, 'Conquer evil with good' [cf. Rom 12.21]; rejoicing in a neighbour's successes, commiserating in his failures and abiding with him in both – for he says, 'Rejoice with those who rejoice and weep with those who weep' [Rom 12.15]; teaching the unlearned and leading them by the hand into salvation; giving mercy in cheerfulness of heart to those in need [cf. Rom 12.7]; making the discordance of sinners one's own and thus grieving and lamenting over them and fervently propitiating God as if for one's own sins;

and laying down one's soul for one's friends {cf. Jn 15.13}. These distinguishing features of perfect love make a man into an imitator of Christ; and with refined dinner companions and the like is a wandering and false shadow of love.

APHORISMS
(*CPG* 2445)

INTRODUCTION

The following twenty-six sentences by Evagrius are pithy and evocative. Like two other short collections of his sentences – *Capitula xxxiii* (*Definitiones passionum animae rationalis*) and *Capita paraenetica*[1] – this collection is not clearly structured. In this sense, it is unlike the otherwise similar collection *Spiritales sententiae per alphabeticum dispositae*. Evagrius' penchant for structure is evident, for instance, from the 'Prefatory note to the copyists' attached to the *Praktikos*, and in the light of how unsystematic the present collection is, one may wonder whether Evagrius himself is responsible for it. Without wishing to cast any doubt at all on the authenticity of this brief work, it can in fairness be noted that Evagrius' followers were perfectly capable of compiling gnomic works of this sort; perhaps this assortment of Evagrian *obiter dicta* is due to a similar impulse to gather the master's sayings.

Source: PG 40: 1269.

Translation: Sinkewicz (2003): 231–32.

TRANSLATION

1. A source of love: the presumption of good repute.
2. It is right and good to be wealthy in meekness and love.
3. A winnower of virtue: the proud thought.
4. The way is made smooth by almsgiving.

181

5. An unjust judge: the stained conscience.
6. It is fearful to serve the passions of the flesh.
7. If you wish to be free from grief, be keen to please God.
8. The one who rightly cares for himself is cared for by God.
9. A temperate heart: the receptacle of contemplations.
10. When you wish to understand who you are, compare [yourself] not to who you were, but to what you were made from the beginning.
11. A waterless lake: the glory-loving soul.
12. A proud soul, the pirates' chest; it hates the sound of knowledge.
13. The true man's evil error: not knowing Scripture.
14. Know from your tears, if you fear God.
15. An unbroken weapon: the soul's humility.
16. The tree of paradise: a virtue-loving man.
17. Jesus Christ is the tree of life. Make use of him as is necessary, and you will not perish forever.
18. Do good to the truly poor, and you eat Christ.
19. The body's true strength: to eat the body of Christ.
20. If you love Christ, do not forget to observe his commandments.
21. Thus is the benefactor after God revealed.
22. The friend according to God flows milk and honey with true words.
23. The soul that is indifferent will have no friend.
24. A cruel master: the pleasure-loving thought.
25. To silence the truth is to bury gold.
26. One who fears God does all in accordance with God.

DEFINITIONS

INTRODUCTION

The following definitions are found in the *Doctrina patrum* §34, which is entitled 'Definitions and illustrations anthologised from various writings'. The excerpts from Evagrius found in this work do not figure in the *CPG* and, perhaps as a result of this, they have not to my knowledge received any attention. That they are genuine can be inferred from three factors. First, *Definitions* 4–6 are taken from *KG* 1.36 and *Definition* 11 is a quotation of *Praktikos* 15. So a quarter of the definitions are positively identifiable as coming from Evagrius, which inspires some confidence at least in the accuracy of the collection as a whole. Second, the excerpts begin with a key used to identify the authorities from whom the definitions are taken. Those of Evagrius are marked *EY*, and he is significantly glossed as *tou epikatarátou Euagriou* – 'the accursed Evagrius'. How strange that the compiler would see fit to attribute the definitions in this way! Such a backhanded compliment would hardly be paid to any author other than Evagrius Ponticus, so we may confidently identify the Evagrius in question. It would also be difficult to imagine the compiler casually or erroneously ascribing definitions to an author from whom he had thus distanced himself. Third, the key terms found in these definitions are consistent with Evagrius' vocabulary, as are the definitions themselves. In all, there is no reason to doubt the accuracy of the compiler's identification and there are several prima facie reasons for trusting in it.

The presence of Evagrian excerpts in this anthology is interesting because it offers an unusual glimpse into the processes whereby a suspect author (such as Evagrius would have been to the Greek compiler of this seventh- to eighth-century document) was handled. It is also interesting because it indicates that, even at that relatively late date, right-thinking authors such as the compiler of the *Doctrina patrum* would have had access to sources by Evagrius in Greek that are now lost to us.

Source: Diekamp *et al.* (1981): 250, 254, 257, 258, 261, 263.

Translations: Previously untranslated.

TRANSLATION

1. Virtue is the excellent disposition of the rational soul, in keeping with which it becomes disinclined toward vice.[1]
2. The uncreated is not one of the beings that was thought of as beginning in its essence.[2]
3. Imperturbability is the state of the rational soul that is composed of meekness and moderation.[3]
4. Perception is the power by which we are accustomed to comprehend material things.[4]
5. The faculty of perception, however, is that in which the aforementioned perception is seated.[5]
6. The perceptive animal is one that acquires perceptions.[6]
7. The begotten is what has been begotten by another (such as by a father); the originated is what has come into being by another.[7]
8. A vow is the promise of good things being brought to God by people in keeping with a promise.[8]
9. A vow is the voluntary promise of the good.[9]
10. A petition is the invocation brought to God by one who is greater for the salvation of others.[10]
11. The nature of anger is to fight against the demons and struggle against their pleasures.[11]
12. Only-begotten is the one of whom no other has been brought forth and with whom no other is begotten.[12]

ON PRAYER

(*CPG* 2452)

INTRODUCTION

On prayer must rank, with *Praktikos*, as one of Evagrius' best-known writings. It has been often translated in many languages and in it we find his single best-known dictum: 'If you are a theologian, you will pray truly; if you pray truly, you will be a theologian' (*Prayer* 61). But this does not in any way mean that *Prayer* is an introductory writing. It is clear from Evagrius' reference at *Thoughts* 22 to *Prayer* that he intended it as a relatively advanced treatment of prayer. Indeed, it is better to think of *Prayer* as intended for an extremely accomplished readership. As prayer is a theological undertaking, the chapters on prayer are also theological and to that extent Evagrius would presuppose the readers of *Prayer* to bring to their reading of the text a mind that has been disciplined, purified and to some extent illuminated.

The tradition of modern commentary on *Prayer* is not as rich as that on *Praktikos*. The great exception is Hausherr's *Les Leçons d'un Contemplatif*, which I have profited from consulting. That book was the fruit of long study of *Prayer*; indeed, it was Hausherr himself who, in 1939, established that *Prayer* properly belongs to Evagrius (in keeping with the Oriental manuscript tradition) rather than to Nilus (in keeping with the Greek manuscript tradition).[1] But despite Hausherr's success in that regard, there is still no sign that a proper critical edition of the text is forthcoming. This problem is in part attributable to the incredible popularity of the text. A comprehensive analysis of the textual tradition would have to embrace not only the Greek versions, but also incorporate the indirect evidence from the Syriac and Arabic (which, for completeness, could be checked against the witness of the Ethiopic, Georgian, Armenian and Palaeoslavonic versions).

Sources: At present, there are two published versions – in Migne's *Patrologia Graeca* 79.1165–200, and in the *Philokalia* pp. 155–65 – and an unpublished *editio minor* that was prepared by Simon Tugwell, OP, several years before he brought out his translation and that he has very kindly allowed me to use. Tugwell's edition is based on the two printed editions, two MSS from the Bodleian Library, four from the Bibliothèque Nationale, and two from the Vatican. In addition to consulting Tugwell's edition, I have consulted the Syriac and Arabic texts prepared by Hausherr. For practical purposes, it can be assumed that, of the published versions, the present translation adheres most closely to that of the *Philokalia* (unless stated otherwise).

Translations: Hausherr (1960); Bamberger (1970): 45–80; Palmer *et al.* (1979–): 1: 55–71; Tugwell (1981); Sinkewicz (2003): 183–209.

TRANSLATION

Introduction

When I was burning with a fever from the passions, you refreshed me, as usual, by the touch of your divinely favoured letters and soothed my mind hard-pressed by shameful things, thus blessedly imitating the great guide and teacher.[2] And no wonder! Your part has always been distinguished, since you have been blessed like Jacob.[3] Having served well for the sake of Rachel and having received Leah, you are eager for your heart's desire since perhaps you have already 'fulfilled Leah's week' [Gen 29.27].

For my part, I would not deny that, having toiled all night, I have caught nothing. Yet, putting down my nets at your word, I took a plethora of fish – not big ones, I think, but a hundred and fifty-three of them all the same [cf. Jn 21.3–11]. I have sent them to you in a creel of love in the same number of chapters, to fulfil your command.

I am amazed by you and am very jealous of your excellent purpose in desiring the chapters on prayer, for you do not desire to have them simply at hand in ink on paper, but also settled in your mind through love and freedom from grudge-bearing. But since, according to the wise Jesus, 'everything is twofold, one facing another' [Ecclus 42.24], take them in the spirit and in the letter – but understand that the mind always comes before the letter; if it were not so, there would be no letter.[4] Accordingly, the mode of prayer is also twofold: one is ascetical, the other is contemplative. Likewise, the number's surface is quantity and its meaning is quality. By dividing the book on prayer into one hundred and fifty-three chapters, we have despatched to you gospel provender so that you may find delight in the symbolic number, along with the triangular figure and the hexagonal figure (where the former exemplifies the pious knowledge of the Trinity, and the latter the parameters of the universe's orderly arrangement).[5]

Now the number 100 is itself square, whereas 53 is triangular and spherical since 28 is triangular and 25 is spherical (since five fives make 25).[6] So you have a square figure, not only from the quaternion of seasons, but also from the wise knowledge of this age that resembles the number 25, due to the spherical character of time: week after week, month after month, time rolls on from year to year, season after season as we see from the movement of the sun and the moon, of spring and summer, and the rest. The triangular number might signify for you the knowledge of the Holy Trinity. But if you closely consider the number 153 as a triangle from many numbers, then think of ascetic practice, natural contemplation and theological contemplation, or faith, hope and love [1 Cor 13.13], gold, silver, precious stones [1 Cor 3.12].

So much, then, for the number. You will not look down on the humbleness of the chapters, as you are one 'who knows how to be full and how to go without' [Phil 4.12] and indeed one who has not forgotten him who, so far from rejecting the widow's two mites, received them before the wealth of many other people [cf. Mk 21.41–44; Lk 21.1–4]. So then as one who knows how to preserve for his genuine brethren the fruit of goodwill and love, pray for the one who is sick that he may be healed and finally take up his bed and walk [cf. Jn 5.8–9] by the grace of Christ.[7]

1. Should someone wish to prepare sweet-smelling incense, he will mix equal parts of clear frankincense, cinnamon, onycha and oil of myrrh according to the Law [cf. Ex 30.34–35]. Now these are the quartet of virtues and if they are fully and equally present, the mind will not be betrayed.

2. A soul purified by the fullness of the commandments prepares a steadfast organisation for the mind, making it receptive of the desired state.

3. Prayer is the mind's conversation with God – so what sort of state does the mind need to be able to reach out unalterably toward its Lord and commune with him without intermediaries?

4. If Moses was turned back when he tried to approach the burning bush on earth, until he took the sandals off his feet [Ex 3.5], how can you – who wish to see the one who is beyond all perception and conception and to be in communion with him – not put off from yourself every impassioned representation?

5. First pray to receive tears, so that through compunction you may be able to soften the savagery that exists in your soul and, once you have convicted yourself by announcing your sins to the Lord, perhaps you may obtain an acquittal from him.

6. Use tears to establish and accomplish every request, for your Lord rejoices greatly upon receiving a tearful prayer.[8]

7. Even should you pour out fountains of tears in prayer, never think highly of yourself as though you were superior to the masses – for your prayer has got assistance so abundant that you eagerly announce your sins and propitiate the Lord by your tears. So do not transform the remedy of passions into another passion, otherwise you will all the more enrage him who gave this grace.

8. Many who weep for their sins, but forget the purpose of the tears, have gone mad and strayed from the path.

9. Stand fast, pray vigorously and deflect the success of concerns and chains of thought – for they agitate and trouble you so that they may divert your attention.

10. When the demons see you yearning to pray truly, then they propose representations of certain things that are supposedly necessary and shortly thereafter they raise up and implant the memory of them, setting the mind in motion to search for them. When the mind does not find them, it is deeply grieved and discouraged. Then when it stands at prayer they remind it of the things sought and remembered, so that the mind, having become vain with the knowledge of them, will lose its fruitful prayer.

11. Fight to set your mind deaf and dumb at the hour of prayer, and you will be able to pray.

12. Whenever temptation or disputation should come upon you, or provoke you to set in motion your irascibility or mutter some ignoble word for the sake of exacting revenge, remember prayer and the judgement that comes with it, and the disorderly movement in you will quickly settle down.

13. Everything that you do to exact revenge against a brother who has wronged you will become a stumbling block for you at the time of prayer.

14. Prayer is the offshoot of meekness and freedom from wrath.

15. Prayer is the promontory of joy and thanksgiving.

16. Prayer is the remedy for grief and faintheartedness.

17. 'Go, sell your possessions and give to the poor, take up your cross' [Mk 10.21] and deny yourself utterly so that you may be able to pray uninterruptedly.

18. If you wish to pray commendably, deny yourself every hour and, suffering every last terrible thing for prayer, you will be a philosopher.[9]

19. At the hour of prayer, you will find the fruit of whatever hardship you endure philosophically.

20. When you desire to pray as you should, do not grieve a soul; otherwise, you 'run in vain' [cf. Phil 2.16].

21. 'Leave your gift', he says, 'before the altar and go, first be reconciled with your brother' [Mt 5.24] and then come and pray without disturbance. For grudge-bearing obscures the governing faculty of the one praying and darkens his prayers.

22. Those who accumulate their grief and grudges and suppose they are praying are like those draw water and pour it in a jar that has been worn through.[10]

23. If you are the enduring kind, you will always pray with joy.

24. Now when you pray as you ought, situations will happen to you such that you deem it entirely justified to make use of irascibility. But no anger at all against one's neighbour is justified. If you enquire further, you will find that it is possible to resolve the situation fairly without irascibility. So use every device to keep from rousing your irascibility.

25. See that, when you try to cure someone else, you do not make yourself incurable and cut deeply into your prayer.

26. When you are sparing with irascibility, you will find yourself spared and prove yourself wise and be among those who pray.

27. When you arm yourself against irascibility, then you will not maintain concupiscence, for it gives material to irascibility and so troubles the mental eye, ruining the state of prayer.[11]

28. Do not pray with merely external gestures, but with great fear turn your mind to the awareness of spiritual prayer.

29. Sometimes when you stand to pray you will immediately pray well; other times, even when you have toiled much you will not attain your goal, so that you will seek it all the more and guard your accomplishment inviolate once you do receive it.

30. When an angel approaches, immediately all those vexing us disappear and the mind will be found to pray in a state of healthy relaxation.[12] But sometimes when the usual war is waged against us,

the mind lashes out and is not permitted to rest, because it has been preconditioned by manifold passions. All the same, if it continues seeking, it will find, and it will be opened to the one who knocks vigorously [cf. Mt 7.7].

31. Do not pray that your will be done – for it is not always in accord with God's desire. Instead, pray as you have been taught, saying, 'Your will be done' in me [cf. Mt 6.10]. And ask him thus in every situation so that his will be done – for he wills what is good and expedient for your soul, whereas that is not always what you seek.[13]

32. Often in praying I requested that what seemed good to me would be done and persisted in my request, irrationally contending with God's will and not yielding to him so that he would providentially arrange what he knew to be more expedient. And in the event when I finally got it, I was deeply disappointed that I had requested instead that my own desire be done, for the thing did not turn out to be for me such as I had reckoned.[14]

33. What is good other than God [cf. Mk 10.18]? So then let us yield to him in all matters pertaining to us and it will be well for us. For the Good One is surely the purveyor of good gifts [cf. Mt 7.11].

34. Make your request from God, but not like someone who receives it quickly because of his might.[15] For God wishes to do well to you even more as you obstinately persist in praying to him. What is higher than conversing with God and being engaged in being with him?

35. Undistracted prayer is the highest function of the mind.[16]

36. Prayer is the mind's ascent to God.[17]

37. If you yearn to pray, abandon everything so that you can inherit everything.

38. Pray firstly to be purified of passions, secondly to be delivered from ignorance and forgetfulness and, thirdly, from all temptation and abandonment.

39. Only seek in your prayer righteousness and the kingdom – that is, virtue and knowledge – and all the rest will be added to you [cf. Mt 6.33].

40. It is just not to pray only for one's own purification, but also for the sake of all one's kinsmen, so that you imitate the angelic way.[18]

41. See if you truly stand before God in your prayers, or if you are overcome by human praise and are keen to chase it, using the exhibition of prayer for cover.[19]

42. Whether you pray with the brethren or by yourself, fight to pray not from habit but from perception.

43. Perception of prayer is mental focus with piety, contrition and pain of soul in announcing one's errors, with voiceless groaning.

44. If your mind looks around at the precise time of prayer, it has not yet realised that it is a monk praying; instead, it is still a secular 'adorning the external tent' [cf. 2 Cor 5.1–4].[20]

45. When you pray, guard your memory strongly so that it does not present you with its own passions, but instead moves you toward knowledge of the service – for by nature the mind is too easily pillaged by the memory at the time of prayer.

46. When you pray, the memory makes for you either appearance of old things, or new concerns, or else the face of one who has wronged you.[21]

47. The demon is very envious of one who prays and uses every device to damage his purpose. So the demon does not stop setting in motion representations of things through the memory and through the flesh forces open every passion, so that he might be able to impede the person's excellent course and departure to God.

48. When, even though he has done many things, the utterly wicked demon is unable to impede the prayer of the righteous, he pulls back a little and later exacts revenge against the one who had been praying. Either, having inflamed his wrath, he obliterates the excellent state that had been struck up in him by the prayer; or, having incited him to some irrational pleasure, he makes a mockery of his mind.

49. Having prayed as is right, anticipate what is not right and stand courageously guarding your gains. To this task you were ordered from the beginning: 'work and stand guard' [Gen 2.15]. So once you have worked, do not leave unprotected what you have worked hard for; otherwise, you profit nothing from praying.

50. All the warfare struck up between us and the impure demons is about nothing other than spiritual prayer – for it is particularly hostile and most grievous to them, but salvific and most pleasant to us.

51. Why do the demons want to activate in us gluttony, impurity, avarice, wrath, grudge-bearing and the other passions, unless it is that the mind, flaccid from them, be unable to pray as it ought? The passions of the irrational part, when they rule, do not allow the mind to move rationally and seek the word of God.

52. We pursue the virtues for the sake of the reasons of created beings, and we pursue them for the sake of the Word who exists and

makes other things exist – and he is accustomed to reveal himself in the state of prayer.

53. The state of prayer is an imperturbable habit, snatching the philosophic and spiritual mind to the heights by keenest love.

54. It is necessary for one who hastens to pray truly not only to rule his irascibility and concupiscence, but also to become separated from impassioned representation.

55. The one who loves God always converses with him as a father, deflecting every impassioned representation.

56. The one who has become imperturbable does not *ipso facto* pray truly; for he can be among bare representations and be engaged with tales of them and remain far from God.

57. Even when the mind does not abide among the bare representations of things, it has not *ipso facto* attained the place of prayer; for it can still be in contemplation of things and talk idly about their reasons. Even if they are bare words, insofar as they are contemplations of things, they imprint on and shape the mind and place it far from God.[22]

58. Even if the mind comes to be above the contemplation of bodily nature, it has not yet contemplated the perfect place of God; for it can be among the knowledge of representations and can be diversified by that knowledge.

59. If you want to pray, you need God who gives prayer to the one who prays [cf. 1 Kgs 2.9]. Therefore call upon him, saying, 'Hallowed be your name, your kingdom come' [Mt 6.9–10] – which means your Holy Spirit and Only-Begotten Son. He has taught you thus, saying that the Father is worshipped 'in Spirit and in Truth' [Jn 4.23–24].

60. One who prays in spirit and truth no longer honours the Creator for what he has created, but sings his praises for his own sake.[23]

61. If you are a theologian, you will pray truly, and if you pray truly, you will be a theologian.

62. When your mind in great yearning for God as it were withdraws by degrees from the flesh and, being filled with piety and joy, deflects all representations from perception, memory or temperament, then reckon that you have come near to the boundaries of prayer.

63. The Holy Spirit, sympathising with our weakness [cf. Rom 8.26], regularly visits us even when we are impure. And if he should find the mind praying to him alone from love of truth, he lights upon it and obliterates the whole battle-array of thoughts or representations that encircle it, advancing it in the love of spiritual prayer.

64. Whereas all the rest implant in the mind thoughts or representations or contemplations through changing the body, God does the opposite.[24] Descending upon the same mind, he inserts in it the knowledge of such things as he wills, and through the mind he lulls the body's bad temperament.

65. No one who loves true prayer and is wrathful or bears grudges is anything other than deranged, for he is like one who wishes to have keen vision and wounds his own eyes.

66. If you yearn to pray, do nothing opposed to prayer so that God, having drawn near, will travel alongside you.

67. Never give a shape to the divine as such when you pray, nor allow your mind to be imprinted by any form, but go immaterial to the Immaterial and you will understand.[25]

68. Look out for the snares of the enemies. It may happen when you are praying in purity and without disturbance that some strange and foreign shape suddenly appears to you to lead you into the notion of rashly putting the divine in a place, so that you will be persuaded that the quantity which has suddenly revealed itself to you is the divine. But the divine admits of neither quantity nor shape.[26]

69. When the envious demon is unable to set the mind in motion by memory during prayer, then he forces the temperament of the body into making some strange apparition in the mind and shaping the mind. And the mind will bend easily since it has the habit of being linked with representations, and the mind that was rushing toward immaterial and formless knowledge is cheated, accepting smoke instead of light.

70. Stand guard, protecting your mind from representations at the time of prayer, and make your stand on your own state of rest so that he who sympathises with the ignorant may also regularly visit you and then you may get the most glorious gift of prayer.

71. You will not be able to pray purely while being tangled up with material things and shaken by unremitting cares.[27] For prayer is the setting aside of representations.

72. It is not possible for one in chains to run, nor is it possible for a mind enslaved to the passions to see the place of spiritual prayer.

73. When at length the mind is praying purely and imperturbably, then the demons no longer overtake it from the left, but from the right. They suggest to it the glory of God and some shape familiar from perception, so that it would seem to have attained the perfection of its goal with respect to prayer.[28] An ascetic and knowledgeable man declared that this happens because of the passion of

vainglory and the demon who, having attached himself to the area around the brain, plucks the veins.[29]

74. I think that the demon, by touching the place just mentioned, manipulates the light around the mind at will, and the passion of vainglory thus sets in motion a thought that shapes the mind into frivolously limiting the divine and existent knowledge.[30] Such a mind is not disturbed by fleshly and impure passions, but standing purely (as he thinks) it supposes that no opposing activity is still at work in itself. So it supposes the apparition that has come to it is divine – though in fact, as we said before, it is from a demon using terrible cunning, and through the brain changing the light that is joined to it, and shaping it.

75. God's angel, when he is present, stops with a single word all the opposing activity for us and sets in motion the light of the mind to work unwaveringly.

76. When it says in Revelation [8.3] that the angel takes incense so that he may add it to the saints' prayers, I think this refers to the grace worked by the angel. For he implants the knowledge of true prayer so that thereafter the mind stands outside every turmoil of despondency and contemptuousness.

77. The phials of incense that the twenty-four elders offer are said to be the saints' prayers [Rev 5.8]. Now 'phial' is to be understood as *philia* for God, that is, perfect and spiritual love, in which prayer is made 'in spirit and in truth' [Jn 4.23–24].[31]

78. When you suppose tears on account of sin are no longer necessary in your prayer, see how far removed from God you are – you who ought to always be in him! – and you will weep more fervently.

79. Indeed, when you have understood your own measure,[32] you will delight in compunction and call yourself a wretch, in the manner of Isaiah. For how, being impure and having impure lips and being in the midst of such a people (that is, of adversaries), how have you dared stand before the Lord Sabaoth [Is 6.5]?

80. If you pray truly, you will find great assurance and the angels will accompany you as they did Daniel [cf. Dan 2.19] and illumine for you the reasons of things coming to be.

81. Know that the holy angels exhort us to prayer and stand by us, at once rejoicing and praying for us. So if we are negligent and accept opposing thoughts, we provoke them deeply. Although they fight so much for us, we are not only unwilling to supplicate God for ourselves, but we even despise our own liturgy[33] and abandon their Lord and God, joining ourselves to unclean demons.

82. Pray suitably and without disturbance and chant psalms with understanding and rhythmically, and you will be like a young eagle soaring in the heights.[34]

83. Psalmody calms the passions and silences the body's bad temperament; prayer prepares the mind to put its own activity into action.

84. Prayer is activity that befits the dignity of the mind, that is, its best and uncontaminated activity and use.

85. Psalmody is the part of diversified wisdom [cf. Eph 3.10]; prayer is the prelude to immaterial and undiversified knowledge.

86. Knowledge is exceedingly fair, for it is prayer's collaborator, rousing the mind's mental power to the contemplation of divine knowledge.

87. If you have not yet received the gift of prayer or of psalmody, keep watch and you will receive it.

88. 'He told them a parable that they should always pray and not be faint-hearted.' So do not be faint-hearted or discouraged for as long as you do not receive it – for you will receive it. He goes on in the parable, ' "Even though I do not fear God or respect man, still because the woman is making trouble, I will judge her case." So, too, God will also do vengeance soon for those who cry out to him day and night' [Lk 18.1–8]. So then, courage! Persist in the labour of holy prayer.

89. Do not want for your affairs to transpire as seems best to you, but as pleases God, and you will be undisturbed and thankful in your prayer.[35]

90. Even if you seem to be with God, beware the demon of impurity, for he is quite the deceiver and is very envious and wants to be quicker than the movement of your mind so as to remove it from God when it is standing by him in reverence and fear.

91. If you are intent on praying, make yourself ready for the demons' onslaughts and boldly endure their lashes – for they will come upon you suddenly like ferocious animals and harm your whole body.[36]

92. Prepare yourself like an experienced warrior not to be driven in confusion, even if you should suddenly see an apparition; not to be troubled, even if you should see a scimitar drawn against you or a torch running down your face; not let your spirits flag, even if you should see some unpleasant, gruesome shape. But stand fast, making a good confession [cf. 1 Tim 6.12], and you will look upon your enemies easily.[37]

93. The one who undergoes grievous pains will also receive joys in excess; the one who stands strong in unpleasant matters will not lack a share of pleasant ones.

94. See that the wicked demons do not deceive you through any vision, but focusing your mind and turning to prayer, invoke God so that he may enlighten you as to whether the representation is from him and, if not, drive the wandering thought quickly from you. Be confident that the dogs will not stand against you if you expertly use the stick of petitioning God. Being lashed invisibly and inaudibly by God's power, they will be driven away directly.[38]

95. It is right for you not to be unaware of this trap: the demons sometimes break up into groups and if you seem to be calling for help some of them draw near in the guise of angels and drive off the others – in order that you will be thoroughly deceived by them into thinking that they are really angels.

96. Be intent on much humility and courage and no insolence from the demons will touch your soul and 'the scourge will not draw near your tent, for God will give his angels charge over you to protect you' [cf. Ps 90.10–11], and they will chase away the whole enterprise opposed to you.

97. The one intent on pure prayer will hear noises, crashes, voices and tortured sounds from the demons, but he will not fall or forsake his thought, saying to God, 'I will not fear, for you are with me' [cf. Ps 22.4], and so forth.

98. In the time of such temptations, make use of brief, intense prayer.

99. Even if the demons threaten you by appearing suddenly from thin air, astounding you and snatching your mind, or injuring you like wild animals, do not be distraught or have any care from all their boasts. They scare you to test whether you are paying attention to them or despise them utterly.

100. If in prayer you make your stand with God Almighty, the Creator and Supervisor of all, why are you so irrational in standing by him that, disregarding his unsurpassable awe, you are alarmed by mosquitoes and dung-beetles? Or have you not heard it said, 'You shall fear the Lord your God' [Dt 6.13], and again, 'whom all shudder and tremble at, before the face of his power' [Dan 6.27 *Theodotion*], etc.?

101. Just as bread is nourishment for the body and virtue is for the soul, so, too, spiritual prayer constitutes nourishment for the mind.

102. Pray in the holy place of prayer, not like the Pharisee, but like the Publican, so that you, too, may be justified of God [Lk 18.10–14].

103. Fight not to pray against anyone in your prayer, lest by making your prayer disgusting you destroy what you have built.

104. Let the man who owed ten thousands talents convince you that if you do not forgive your debtor, you will not receive forgiveness yourself – 'for he handed him over', he said, 'to the torturers' [cf. Mt 18.24–35].

105. Dismiss the needs of the body during the service of your prayer, lest being stung by a flea, louse, mosquito or fly you are deprived of the great profit of your prayer.

106. It has come to our attention that the Evil One so attacked one of the saints who was praying that, as he was raising his hands, the Evil One changed into the shape of a lion. Raising his front paws upright, he sank his claws into both of the fighter's thighs from either side and did not let go until he lowered his hands – but he never lowered them even a little before he had completed his usual prayers.

107. We knew another to have been like that and he practised stillness in a pit – I mean the monk John the Little, or rather, the Mighty, who remained unmovable from his communion with God, though a demon in the form of a dragon coiled around him and chewed his flesh and belched in his face.[39]

108. You have surely read the lives of the Tabennesiot monks, where it is said that, as Abba Theodore was saying a word to the brethren, two vipers came toward his feet. Being untroubled by this, he made for the vipers a kind of vaulted chamber and took them in until he had finished saying his word; then he revealed them to the brethren, explaining what had happened.[40]

109. Again, we have read about another spiritual brother that when he was praying a viper drew near and fastened on to his foot. But he did not lower his hands before he had completed his usual prayer and, loving God more than himself, he was not harmed.[41]

110. Keep your eyes fixed downward when you pray and, denying your flesh and soul, live according to the mind.[42]

111. There was another of the saints living in stillness in the desert, vigorous in prayer, whom the demons, when they attacked, played with like a ball for two weeks: they tossed him in the air and caught him in a rush-basket,[43] but they were not in the least able to lead his mind down from its fiery prayer for even a moment.

112. Again, there was another friend of God who made provision for his prayers as he walked through the desert, whom two angels, descending, accompanied – but he paid not the slightest attention to them, lest he should be deprived of something better. For he recalled that apostolic utterance, that 'neither angels, nor principalities, nor powers will be able to separate us from the love of God' [Rom 8.38–39].

113. Through true prayer, the monk becomes 'equal to the angels' [Lk 20.36], yearning to 'see the face of the Father who is in heaven' [Mt 18.10].[44]

114. Do not seek at all to receive a form, shape or colour at the time of prayer.

115. Do not yearn to see angels or powers or Christ perceptibly, lest you become utterly insane, accepting a wolf in the place of the shepherd and paying reverence to your enemies the demons.

116. The source of a wandering mind is vainglory, by which the mind is moved to try circumscribing the divine by a shape or figures.

117. I shall say my part that I have said to the novices:[45] blessed is the mind that at the time of prayer has attained total freedom from figures.

118. Blessed is the mind that at the time of prayer becomes free from matter and from possessions.

119. Blessed is the mind that, whilst praying without distraction, always conceives a greater desire.[46]

120. Blessed is the mind that at the time of prayer attains total freedom from perception.

121. Blessed is the monk who thinks himself 'the off-scouring of all' [1 Cor 4.13].

122. Blessed is the monk who thinks of everyone as God after God.

123. Blessed is the monk who beholds with all joy and pleasure everyone's salvation and the visitation as though it were his own.

124. The one who is separated from all and united with all is a monk.

125. The one who reckons himself one with everyone, because he seems to see himself unceasingly in each one, is a monk.

126. The one who prays is he who dedicates to God every first-fruit of his mind.

127. As you yearn to be a monk and pray, put away every lie and oath; otherwise, you are vainly wearing a habit that is not your own.

128. If you wish to pray in the spirit, draw up nothing[47] and you will not have an obstructing cloud in the time for prayer.

129. Trust God for bodily needs and it will be clear that you also trust him for spiritual ones.

130. If you attain to the promises, you shall rule – so keeping an eye on them, you will bear the present suffering with joy.

131. Do not decline suffering and tribulation, which are the stuff of unburdened prayer.

132. Let the body's virtues be for you a pledge for the soul's, and the soul's for the spirit's, and the spirit's in turn for the knowledge that is immaterial and truly real.

133. If you pray against the thoughts and they easily disperse, look for the reason it has happened, lest, having been misled, you suffer an ambush and surrender yourself.

134. It happens sometimes that the demons suggest thoughts to you whilst encouraging you to pray against them and refute them;[48] then they voluntarily withdraw, so that you will be cheated into thinking that you have begun to conquer thoughts and frighten demons on your own.

135. If you pray against a vexatious passion or demon, remember him who said, 'I will pursue my enemies and overtake them and not return before they fall; I will crush them and they will be unable to stand, they will fall beneath my feet' and so on [Ps 17.38–39]. In praying, you should say these things at the appropriate times, arming yourself with humility against your adversaries.

136. Do not reckon that you have acquired a virtue until you shed blood for it. According to the divine apostle, it is necessary to contend strenuously and blamelessly against sin to the point of death [cf. Heb 12.4].

137. If you help someone, you will be harmed by someone else – so that you will say or do something bad to your neighbour as though you had been wronged, and you will scatter in wickedness what you had gathered in goodness.[49] And that is the aim of the wicked demons. So it is necessary to be discreet and attentive.

138. Always expect attacks brought on by the demons, considering how to avoid being enslaved by them.

139. By night the wicked demons claim the spiritual teacher to distress him by themselves, but by day they assault him with circumstances and accusations and dangers through other people.[50]

140. Do not decline the fullers: even if they strike and trample, stretch and fret you, after all this is how your clothing becomes radiant.[51]

141. To the extent that you have not abandoned the passions and instead your mind is opposed to virtue and truth, you will not find fragrant incense in your bosom.

142. The one who yearns to pray is the one who has stood apart from everything here and holds a citizenship in heaven [Phil 3.20] all the time, not simply with a mere word, but with angelic struggle and divine knowledge.

143. If it is only when things go ill that you recall that the Judge is awe-inspiring and cannot be bribed, then you have never learnt to 'serve the Lord with fear and rejoice in him with trembling' [Ps 2.11]. Know, then, that even in times of spiritual relaxation and good cheer it is necessary to serve him with piety and modesty.

144. One who does not forsake the grievous memory of his own sins, and their just retribution in eternal fire, before he has obtained perfect repentance, is a wise man indeed.[52]

145. One who dares to strive for knowledge of divine things or embark upon immaterial prayer whilst still ensnared in sins and wrath, must embrace the apostolic evaluation, since it is not without danger for him to pray with a naked and uncovered head. As he says, 'Such a soul needs to have control over its head for the sake of the angels present' [cf. 1 Cor 11.10], clothing it in befitting modesty and humility.

146. Just as directly and intently contemplating the sun at its keenest radiance at high noon does not benefit one with watery eyes, likewise the imitating of fearful and supernatural prayer in spirit and truth is not beneficial in the least to an impassioned and impure mind.[53] On the contrary, it provokes the divine to indignation against it.

147. If he who wants nothing and cannot be bribed does not receive the one who came to the altar with his gift, until he was reconciled with his neighbour, who was angry with him [cf. Mt 5.24], look at what precaution and judgement is necessary if we are to give God acceptable incense on the intelligible altar![54]

148. Rejoice in neither reputation nor words, or else the sinners will 'set to work' on your face no less than your back [cf. Ps 128.3], and you will be a laughing-stock for them at the time for prayer, as you are dragged away and caught in unnatural thoughts by them.

149. Attentiveness seeking prayer will find prayer: if prayer follows anything, it is attentiveness – which must therefore always be zealously sought.

150. Just as vision is the best of all the senses, so, too, prayer is the highest of all the virtues.

151. It is not simply quantity that is praiseworthy in prayer, but rather quality; this is demonstrated by those going up to the Temple {Lk 28.10–14}, and again, by 'When you pray, do not babble' {Mt 6.7}, and by other such {verses}.

152. In proportion as you are paying attention to the body and your mind is busy with the Tabernacle's delights, you have not yet beheld the place of prayer and in fact its blessed way remains far from you.

153. When you surpass every other joy in offering your prayers, then you have truly found prayer.

NOTES

PART I

1 WHY EVAGRIUS MATTERS

1 See, *inter alia*, Louth (1998): 1–11 and (2002).

2 EVAGRIUS' LIFE AND AFTER-LIFE

1 The classic treatment of Evagrius' influence on Cassian remains Marsili (1936).

2 On the various concerned parties in the aftermath of the Council of Nicea and the Arian controversy, see now Richard Vaggione, *Eunomius of Cyzicus and the Nicene Revolution* (Oxford: OUP, 2000); for concise information, the entries in Cross and Livingstone (1997) are useful.

3 Thus, Palladius, *HL* 38.2.

4 The modern site is Iverönü, Turkey – see Leclercq (1907–53) and the detailed description of Guillaumont (2004): 25–26. We arrive at the date of Evagrius' birth by inference and subtraction: Palladius, his first biographer and sometime pupil, tells us that Evagrius died aged 54 (*HL* 38.1) but he does not mention Evagrius in connection with the great exodus from Egypt of 399–400 – see nn. 50 and 68, below. It is generally assumed that Evagrius had already died, and therefore that he was born around the year 345. On Basil's retreat to Annisa, see esp. his *Letter* 14. Macrina's proximity to Ibora is inferred not least from the fact that it was likely that the bishop of Ibora performed her funeral: *Life of Macrina* 34 (SC 178: 250–51 n. 1).

5 Palladius, *HL* 38.2, Latin; ed. Wellhausen (2003): 621.

6 I incline to the view that Gregory *is* talking about Evagrius Ponticus, but this perspective is not uncontroversial. (See the thorough discussion of Guillaumont (2004): 34–35 n. 5.) In the end, the question comes down to what to make of Gregory addressing the elder Evagrius as 'Your Excellency' (*timiotêti*). I accept Courtonne's dating of the letter to 359, and it is quite easy to imagine the prodigious – but as yet unordained – Gregory addressing a clergyman in that way.

7 On the father's social standing, see Butler (1898–1904): 2: 116 app. crit.; on the olive grove and the question of the children dividing their patrimony, *Letter* 57.4; see further Guillaumont (2004): 26, 68.

8 Lackner (1966), Guillaumont (2004): 31–32.

9 Basil, *Letter* 201; see further Rousseau (1994): 61–62.

10 Gregory Nazianzen, *Letter* 3; but note that some scholars have rejected the possibility that this letter refers to Evagrius Ponticus – see n. 6, above.

11 Thus, Guillaumont (2004): 34–35 n. 5.

12 Kaster (1999) offers a pithy overview of the curriculum and the social relevance of a classical liberal education.

13 See Rousseau (1994): 1–26.

14 Palladius, *HL* 38.2.

15 *Gnostikos* 45.

16 Babai the Great (ob. *c.*629) is the earliest known person to make this claim, but it has been widely accepted; see his biographical sketch of Evagrius in the introduction to *Commentary on the Gnostic chapters* (Frankenberg (1912): 20). For a list of scholars who have subsequently endorsed the idea, see Guillaumont (2004): 26–27.

17 *Pace* Guillaumont (2004): 29 and 38 n. 1, who wants to see Evagrius as a deacon – and a deacon *only* – during his time with Gregory Nazianzen in Constantinople. Guillaumont's strongest argument is that, in his will (a precise legal document), Gregory fails to describe Evagrius as a monk. One could contrast this to his mention of 'Marcellus, deacon and monk' and 'Gregory, deacon and monk'. There is, however, another solution: it was not Evagrius Ponticus who inherited the thirty pieces of gold and the rest in 381; rather, it was another deacon from Nazianzus, also named Evagrius (thus McGuckin (2001): 366). This is not at all implausible. There were, after all, numerous men named Evagrius at this time: between the entries in the *Dictionnaire d'Histoire et de Géographie Ecclésiastiques* 16: 101–09 and in Jones *et al.*, *Prosopography of the later Roman Empire* (Cambridge: CUP, 1971): 1: 284–86, about a dozen Evagrii have been identified between 260 and 395.

18 Thus, *On the faith* 1.3.

19 *On the faith* 1.2–3.

20 In support of this, I suggest not only Gregory's *Letter* 3 (with its attendant difficulty: see n. 6, above), but also Evagrius' expansive way of talking about Gregory's impact upon him – e.g., 'Gregory the Righteous who planted me' (*Praktikos*, epilogue); cf. *Letters* 21, 26 – which prompts the thought that the roots of their relationship may well go very deep indeed. This would be a very strange way of talking indeed if from the age of 34 Evagrius had spent merely two years with Gregory.

21 That they need not be is clear from the case of Evagrius' younger contemporary, John Cassian, whose excursion from the monastery in Bethlehem went worryingly over curfew (see *Conference* 17). Evagrius may well have written *On the faith* in part as an example of what he was learning, in the hopes that his confreres would be suitably impressed and thus tolerate his protracted absence from the monastery for a little longer.

22 Perhaps the 'unexpected event' was Gregory's ascension to the archiepiscopal see.

23 McGuckin (2001): 229–369.

24 Thus, McGuckin (2001): 278 n. 271.

25 On Nectarius, see Socrates, *Church history* 5.8, and Sozomen, *Church history* 7.8.

26 Palladius, *HL* 38.2; cf. Sozomen, *Church history* 6.30; see further Richard Vaggione, *Eunomius of Cyzicus and the Nicene revolution* (Oxford: OUP, 2000).

27 On Evagrius' good looks and taste in clothing, see Sozomen, *Church history* 6.30.

28 Palladius, *HL* 38.3; Guillaumont (2004): 41–42 n. 5 provisionally identifies the cuckolded husband as Sophronius, the city's prefect and a Cappadocian known to Gregory Nazianzen – which may account for how Evagrius met with his wife.

29 I understand Palladius' comment at *HL* 38.8 ('making a complete change in his clothing and discourse, vainglory stupefied him') to mean that it was at this point – and not earlier – that Evagrius reverted to a completely secular way of life. This sorry affair gives piquancy to Evagrius' words about 'adultery in the heart' at *Thoughts* 25.

30 Palladius, *HL* 46 and 54; see further Butler (1898–1904): 2: 222–23 nn. 85–86; on Evagrius' relationship with Melania, see Hunt (1982): 186–89.

31 Palladius, *HL* 38.9.

32 Palladius (*HL* 38.9) says that Evagrius 'received a change of clothing' (*metêmphiasthê*) from Melania; but Evagrius says that he was 'given the sacred habit' and 'admitted to the number of monks' in a letter probably addressed to Rufinus (*Letter* 22.1; see Bunge (1986): 184). It was likely Melania's idea.

To be clear, my view of what happened is that Evagrius abandoned the monastic life decisively in Jerusalem (see n. 29, above) after a period of gradual estrangement from its practices in Constantinople; I therefore regard the event of Easter 383 as Evagrius' *return* to the monastic life, rather than his inauguration into it, even if he did make monastic vows at that time (see *Letter* 57.1).

33 Evelyn White (1932): 85; Guillaumont (2004): 44–46, with the suggestion *inter alia* that Evagrius may well have studied with Didymus the Blind shortly after arriving in Alexandria, at Rufinus' recommendation.

34 Thus, famously, *Apophthegmata* Evagrius 7; this is not meant to disparage the intellectual accomplishments of the Egyptian fathers, however, and any attempt to reduce the desert fathers to a pitched battle between unwashed, ignorant Copts and Greek scholastic poseurs is utterly to be rejected. The best assessment of the theological and intellectual milieu of Christian Egypt during Evagrius' age is Sheridan (2002).

35 Rufinus, *HM* 21.1.2.

36 Palladius, *HL* 7.5; discipline would include corporal punishment – hence, one of the three whips hanging from the palm trees near the Church (*HL* 7.3).

37 See Evelyn White (1932): 170–71, with reference to Palladius, *Dialogues on the life of John Chrysostom* §7 (SC 341: 141.11) and Jerome, *Letter* 22.33.

38 Palladius' *HL* 7 is the chief source for all that follows; see further Regnault (1999).

39 Palladius, *HL* 7.5.

40 Evagrius the scribe: Palladius, *HL* 38.10 (and see further Casiday, 2005); flax weaving: *HL* 7.5.

41 Evelyn White (1932): 173 infers that Nitria had a steward from the fact that Palladius mentions a steward at Kellia and Cassian mentions one in Sketis.

42 Thus, Evelyn White (1932): 173.

43 Apollonius was one such monk: Palladius, *HL* 13.

44 Evelyn White (1932): 69.

45 Palladius, *HL* 38.10; on the pattern of retiring to Kellia from Nitria, see Rufinus, *HM* 22.2.2 – the best single source for information on life at Kellia.

46 Rufinus, *HM* 27.7.2: 'ut multo tempore instructus fuerit a beato Macario'; see further Bunge (1983).

47 *Apophthegmata* Isaac the Priest 8.

48 *Apophthegmata* Isaac the Priest 7.

49 E.g., Palladius is described as being part of the 'fellowship of Evagrius' (*HL* 35.5).

50 On the uncertainty of the year of Evagrius' death, see now Guillaumont (2004): 63 n. 6.

51 Cf. *Coptic life* §17 (Amélineau (1887): 114–15). N.B. The internal numbering for this material is taken from Vivian (2004).

52 *Coptic life* §§17–18 (Amélineau (1887): 114–15); Evagrius' visitors are also mentioned in his *Letters* 10 and 22 (Frankenberg (1912): 572, 580) and implied in the discussion of Severa's abortive plans to travel to Egypt in *Letters* 7–8 and 19–20, translated below.

53 See *Coptic life* §18 (Amélineau (1887): 115); the money was a gift from benefactors.

54 On the question of Anatolios' identity, see Bunge (1986): 33–36.

55 See Palladius, *HL* 26.1, cited below.

56 See Butler (1898–1904): 1: 131–37 for the Greek text of this anecdote and a comparison of it to the Coptic version (*Coptic life* §29 [Amélineau (1887): 121–24]); for summary information on the three controversies, see the respective entries in Cross and Livingstone (1997).

57 *HM* 20.15.

58 Coaxing the monk: Syriac version of *HL* 72.3 (ed. R. Draguet, *Les formes syriaques de la matière de l'Histoire Lausiaque, II*, CSCO 398–99 [Louvain: CSCO, 1978]: 366–67); consulting John the Seer: Evagrius, *Antirrheticus* 6.16 (Frankenberg (1912): 524) – and on the time it took to travel from

Kellia to Lycopolis, Palladius, *HL* 35.4; dodging Theophilus: *Coptic life* §§19, 27 (Amélineau (1887): 115, 118), Socrates, *Ecclesiastical history* 4.23 and Evagrius, *Letter* 13 (on which, see Guillaumont (1962): 62 n. 65 and Bunge (1986): 187).

59 Cf. *Causes* 5.

60 Palladius, *HL* 38.1.

61 Evagrius, *Great letter* 33.

62 See Palladius, *HL* 38.12 and, for a somewhat more detailed version, *Coptic life* §13 (Amélineau (1887): 112). The Revd Dr Luke Dysinger, who is a physician as well as a patrologist, has suggested to me that the extreme dehydration of Evagrius' diet probably contributed to urinary tract stones.

63 *Coptic life* §§14, 24 (Amélineau (1887): 113, 116).

64 *Coptic life* §21 (Amélineau (1887): 115–16); cf. Palladius, *HL* 38.10.

65 Palladius, *HL* 38.11; *Coptic life* §§22–23 (Amélineau (1887): 116).

66 The only surviving record of Evagrius being attacked to his face is related by Palladius (*HL* 26.1): the monk Heros told him that 'those persuaded by your teaching are deceived – for it is unnecessary to attend to any master other than Christ'. It must be noted that Heros is not attacking some particular aspect of Evagrius' teaching, but rather the very fact that Evagrius is a teacher who has disciples. In other words, this anecdote does not enable us to conclude that Heros represents a larger group of monks who objected to the content of Evagrius' teaching.

67 See Evelyn White (1932): 125–44 and Clark (1992) – an important and influential study. But for a timely note of caution on (among other things) the presumption that Evagrius was himself central to this controversy, see the review by Sheridan (1996).

68 The most detailed account of this unedifying episode written by a contemporary (albeit some time later) is found in Palladius' *Dialogues on the life of John Chrysostom* esp. §§7–8 (SC 341: 130–54).

69 Theophilus, *Letter to Constantinople* §1, ed. Richard (1975): 61.

70 Theophilus, *Letter to Constantinople* §7, ed. Richard (1975): 63.

71 Theophilus, *Letter to Constantinople* §11, ed. Richard (1975): 64–65.

72 See, e.g., Guillaumont (1961) and (1962).

73 This line of thinking may have been inspired by writings such as Origen's *First Principles* 5.3.9–12.

74 On this, and what follows, the most important study is Sheridan (2002).

75 *Apophthegmata* Arsenius 6.

76 E.g., Rubenson (1995): 141–44 and Hombergen (2001): 206–52.

77 Jerome, *Letter* 133.

78 See further Casiday (2001): 367–72.

79 For an overview of the sometimes-shifting alliances of the period, see esp. Clark (1992).

80 E.g., Evelyn White (1932): 86.

81 Bunge (1986): 25–26 comments upon the absence of Evagrius' name from the earlier phases of the controversy. Guillaumont (1962): 122 fn. 177 calls into question the 'evidence' of *Letter* 133, finding in it merely an opportunistic attack by Jerome who was casting aspersions on all of Rufinus' friends.

82 One example of the anthologies, *Excerpts*, is translated below.

83 See Guillaumont (1985) and, for specific details, *CPG* items 2430–82.

84 Barsanuphius and John, *Letters* 600–03 (SC 451: 804–14); NB: Evagrius' name almost always recurs with Origen's and Didymus' in the disputes of the Second Origenist Controversy.

85 Anonymous *ap.* Barsanuphius and John, *Letter* 602 (SC 451: 812).

86 One example is Abba Sopatrus' sensible advice to a novice about not embroiling oneself in debates about 'the image': see *Apophthegmata* Sopatrus.

87 See further Hombergen (forthcoming).

88 Cyril, *Life of Kyriakos* 12–13 (Schwartz (1939): 229.32–230.26).

89 On the reception of these claims by some modern Evagrian scholars – and the dissenting view of other Evagrian scholars – see Casiday (2004). It is possible that Kyriakos' views were a catalogue of the possible errors to which speculation might lead, rather than specific accusations about what his opponents were actually claiming (thus, Louth (2003): 1170–71; but for our purposes what is striking is how closely Kyriakos' denunciation fits with the ideas about Origenism that were normative for a very long time indeed and that have been systematically challenged over the last three generations or more. See, e.g., A.-J. Festugière, 'De la doctrine "origéniste" du corps glorieux sphéroïde,' *Revue des sciences philosophiques et theologiques* (1959): 81–86; the general introduction to Henri Crouzel and Manlio Simonetti's edition of *Origène. Traité des principes*, SC 252 (Paris: Cerf, 1978); and B. Daley, 'What did "Origenism" Mean in the Sixth Century?', in Gilles Dorival and Alain le Boulleuc (eds), *Origeniana Sexta* (Leuven: Peeters, 1995): 627–38.

90 It is not strictly accurate, with reference to Kyriakos' description, to speak categorically of 'all rational creatures'; he merely says that they claim 'we' (presumably, us humans) will be 'equals to Christ at the Resurrection'. But it is very clear from subsequent developments that those who issued the condemnations of Origenism envisaged (and anathematised) the extending of this eschatological equality to the demons and even Satan himself. Such being the case, I hope that the lack of precision vis-à-vis Abba Kyriakos will be forgiven.

91 See especially Hombergen (2001).

92 Philoxenus, *To Abraham and Orestes.*

93 Such is the argument of Frothingham (1886), who follows Gregory Barhebraeus and other Syrian authorities. A more detailed case is advanced by Marsh (1927): 227–32.

94 It should be noted that this combination of characteristics is commonly ascribed to Evagrius' 'Origenist' theology as well. For more on 'Hierotheos', see especially Marsh (1927): 210–46 and Guillaumont (1962): 311–23.

95 Evagrius Scholasticus, *Church history* 4.38–39.

96 See Louth (2003).

97 See Tanner (1990): 1: 125, 135, 161.

98 Guillaumont (1961) and (1962). To be clear, however, we are talking here about *allusions, echoes and phrases* rather than extended quotations; it is not

often (or at least not often enough) realised that Guillaumont's discovery means at most that Evagrius' pithy style was, for better or worse, amenable to sloganeering.

99 Thus, Casiday (2004b).

100 The standard treatment of Maximus' relationship to Evagrius remains Viller (1930).

101 This excerpt from the anonymous 'Iambs on the words of the holy fathers' is quoted as the epigraph for this book. It is to be noted that the 'three books' mentioned are in all likelihood to be understood as *Praktikos*, *Gnostikos* and *Gnostic chapters*. The poem can thus be taken to indicate that, at the time it was written, Evagrius' trilogy was still available in Greek.

102 John Climacus, *Ladder* §14 (PG 88: 865); on *Doctrina patrum*, see the introduction to *Definitions*, translated below.

3 EVAGRIUS' WRITINGS AND HIS THINKING

1 Barhebraeus, *Ethicon* 1.2.7 (CSCO 534 (*Scriptores syri* 218): 35; CSCO 535 (*Scriptores syri* 219): 31).

2 Thus, Muyldermans (1952): v–vi: 'In the Syriac manuscript tradition, Evagrius' name assuredly covers a vast literature – of which, part is ascribed in Greek to Neilos. But the breath of doctrine that animates the unedited material and the technical vocabulary that characterises it leave no doubt concerning their Evagrian origin, as it is asserted in the manuscript tradition. And even if the critic does not ascribe one page or another to our author, the very publication of these new sources will have permitted their authenticity to be examined.'

3 See C. Chahine, 'Le témoinage de Thomas de Marga sur les écrits d'Abraham Nethpraia dans le *Livre du Paradis* de "Nanisho"', *Augustinianum* 40 (2000): 439–60.

4 See Rondeau (1960).

5 See n. 2, above.

6 For further discussion, see the introductions to the translations of the respective texts, below.

7 For my part, I find H.G. Gadamer's essays on hermeneutics particularly helpful; e.g., the essays edited and translated by David Linge in Gadamer, *Philosophical Hermeneutics* (Berkeley, CA: University of California Press, 1976).

8 This overview is not intended to be comprehensive. For a wider view of the developments, see Casiday (2004) and Géhin (2004).

9 Balthasar (1965): 183–84.

10 Hausherr (1960): 88–90.

11 See esp. Darling Young (2001) and Driscoll (1991), building on the work of Pierre Hadot.

12 Darling Young (2001): 62–63.

13 Hadot (1995): 137–38.

14 Thomas Aquinas, *Summa Theologiae* I^a q. 1, a. 1, resp. ad primum (paraphrasing Gregory the Great, *Moralia in Job* 5.36.66).

15 For an extended consideration of this aspect of Thomas' theology, see Pieper (1957): 92 *et passim.*

16 Louth (1981): 109–10 n. 21.

17 See Guillaumont (1958) for both versions of the *Gnostic Chapters* – wherein S_1 is Frankenberg's text and S_2 is the putatively unexpurgated version; Guillaumont (1961) for a detailed analysis of the anathemas; Guillaumont (1962) for an account of the reception of Evagrius.

18 See Casiday (2004).

19 See esp. Guillaumont (1961).

20 See Daley (1995) and Louth (2003).

21 This has been established by the work of Hombergen (2001); for discussion of the implications for Evagrian studies, see also Casiday (2004): 269–71. Note that Guillaumont (1962): 129 takes Cyril's works as 'un guide sûr' ('a reliable guide') to the conflict.

22 I use the term 'Gnostic' advisedly; see M.A. Williams, *Rethinking 'Gnosticism'* (Princeton, NJ: Princeton University Press, 1996).

23 Cf. *On the faith* 7.23 to *KG* 4.36 and *Great letter* 13; and *On the faith* 2.7–3.9 to *KG* 1.1–9.

24 E.g., cf. *Great letter* 26 to Origen, *Principles* 2.8.3.

25 Parmentier (1985): 21.

26 E.g., Guillaumont (1962): 37 n. 67: 'Evagre a cependant exposé une fois clairement les grandes lignes de sa pensée, dans sa grande *Lettre à Mélanie*: ce texte peut servir de clé pour les *Képhalaia gnostica* . . .'; see also Guillaumont (2004): 144, 392–93.

27 In view of the research of Driscoll (1995) and (2000) and of Sheridan (2002), it is not implausible in the least to take Evagrius seriously when he claims that his ascetic and gnostic teachings are drawn from what he heard from the abbas. This is a departure from conventional wisdom – on which, see the various studies mentioned at Casiday (2004): 266 fn. 37.

28 The further implication of Evagrius' esotericism is that the secret teachings are available only to fully initiated Christians – and here he is in good company. See Amand de Mendieta (1965): 45–56 and Perler (1950): 671–76.

29 If I understand it correctly, O'Laughlin (1997) argues for an interpretation of Evagrius that is in some ways similar to the one from which I wish to distance myself.

30 Casiday (forthcoming).

31 See Basil, *On the Holy Spirit* 27.66–67 (SC 17: 232–38) and Origen, *Homilies on Numbers* 5.1 (GCS 30: 24–26).

32 How to conceive of the relationship between the groups is a disputed question. Amand de Mendieta (1965): 47–50, following Hanson (1954): 73–90, uses the term elite to describe the intellectuals and accordingly sees the 'secret teachings' as their preserve. By contrast, Florovsky (1972): 87 sees the elite as being the Church as a whole and denies that the 'secret teachings' are reserved for intellectuals. Although he does not speak to the point, Florovsky's view is consistent with the idea that the intellectuals are

distinguished from the plebeians by the fact that they *teach* them. I incline toward Florovsky's view, not least because the idea of an intellectual elite over and against the great unwashed is fraught with unexamined presuppositions and it is invoked far too readily in modern scholarship.

33 Origen, *Homilies on Numbers* 5.1 (GCS 30: 24–25).

PART II

LETTERS

INTRODUCTION

1 These are *Letters* 17, 18 and 30.
2 See especially Clark (1992).
3 These are *Letters* 21 (to Eustathios), 48 (to Theophoros), 58 (to Hymettios) and 59 (to Kekropios). Theophoros, Hymettios and Kekropios are otherwise unknown, but Bunge (1986): 178–79 notes that Evagrius writes to Eustathios on the death of their 'common father' and connects this to Gregory Nazianzen's reference to one of his slaves, a monk named Eustathios.
4 These letters are as follows. To Melania: *Letters* 1, 8, 31, 32, 35, 37, 64; to Rufinus: 5, 7, 10, 19, 22, 32, 36, 40, 44, 49; to Anatolius: 25; to Severa: 20; to John of Jerusalem: 2, 9, 24, 50, 51; to Theophilus: 13; to Gregory Nazianzen: 12, 23, 46.

ON THE FAITH

1 See Bousset (1923): 335–41; another monograph demonstrating Evagrius' authorship of the letter appeared simultaneously – R. Melcher's *Der achte Brief des hl. Basilius, ein Werk des Euagrius Ponticus* (Münster-i-W.: Aschendorff) – but I have not been able to consult it.
2 The essay by Gendle (1985) is important, but much work remains to be done in this connection.
3 McGuckin (2001): 276–78 esp. at n. 271 thinks that Evagrius' influence may be detected in Gregory's five great *Theological Orations*.
4 E.g., Bettiolo (2000) and the papers therein.
5 'Leading' translates *paidagôgôn*, which has significant overtones of educational and cultural formation. For Laban and Esau, see Gen 28.5, 29.13–14.
6 To be more specific, he means Gregory Nazianzen; see also *Praktikos*, epilogue.
7 Cf. Gregory Nazianzen, *Oration* 30.5 (PG 36.108–09).
8 Cf. *KG* 2.3, 3.1; Bunge (1989).
9 'Considerations' translates *epinoias*; on the *epinoiai* of Christ in Origen, see McGuckin (1986).
10 For 'Jesus the Christ', I follow the variant reading noted by Gribomont.

11 This description of Christ's life recalls the pattern (and the phrases) found in the Byzantine Eucharistic anaphora immediately before the Invocation (see Brightman (1896): 385–86). It is hardly implausible that a deacon who had spent time in Constantinople – such as Evagrius (see *HL* 38.2) – would spontaneously resort to liturgical phrases to describe Our Lord's life.

12 Cf. Evagrius' description, at sch. 10 in Ps 104.15 and sch. 2 in Ps 118.3, of Christ as 'the Lord who has made his home [*epidêmêsanta*] with God the Word'.

13 Cf. sch. 13 on Eccl 2.25.

14 Evagrius contrasts the speechless and unreasoning baby to God the *Logos* dwelling in the baby.

15 Cf. *Prayer* 57, *KG* 3.88, *Praktikos* prol.

16 On 'the object of desire', cf. Aristotle, *Anima* 3.10 (433a18–b11).

17 'Rudimentary', or 'thick', doctrine (*pachytera didaskalia*), recalls the typical use of the word *pachytera* by Gregory Nazianzen and others to describe the 'thickening' of the *Logos* that occurred at the Incarnation.

18 Cf. *Gnostikos* 42.

19 Cf. *Praktikos* 2, 3; *KG* 4.81.

20 Cf. *Skemmata* 1; *KG* 6.33. For the *Skemmata* (*CPG* 2433) see Muyldermans (1913): 38–44.

21 Cf. *KG* 3.9, 3.11, 5.22, 5.25.

22 Cf. *KG* 4.36.

23 On 'considerations' (*epinoia*), see n. 9 above; for the Scriptural references, see Jn 14.6, 10.9, 10.11; Is 9.6, 53.7; and Heb 3.1, respectively.

24 Cf. Gregory Nazianzen, *Oration* 30.5 (PG 36.108–09): Gregory rejects the argument from 1 Cor 15.28 (presumably advanced by the Eunomians) that Christ's being insubordinate makes him 'unlike' (*anomoios*) the Father. Evagrius follows Gregory in countering that being insubordinate is one of our infirmities that Christ bore for our sake.

25 Cf. *KG* 1.4.

26 See *On the faith* 2.

27 See *On the faith* 2.

28 At *On the faith* 2, Evagrius defines angels as 'essence plus holiness'.

29 Cf. Basil, *Holy Spirit* 19.49.

30 Evagrius derives *theos* from either *theasthai* or *tetheikenai*. This folk etymology has a distinguished pedigree; see, e.g., Plato, *Cratylus* 397C–D; Gregory Nazianzen, *Oration* 30.18 (PG 36.128); Clement of Alexandria, *Protrepticus* 2.26; ps.-Iamblichos, *Theologoumena arithmeticae* 1.5.

31 Cf. *Praktikos* 3.

32 This proverb is ultimately attributed to Cleoboulos (in Diels (1951–52): 1:63.2), but a proximal reference is found in Gregory Nazianzen, *Oration* 43.60 (PG 36.573).

LETTERS 7, 8, 19 AND 20

1 Bunge (1986): 179.

2 Hausherr (1934): 44; Bunge (1986): 220–21, 232–33; Elm (1990): 399–400 and (1991): 97–120.

3 Bunge (1986): 203 n. 60, referring to MS Mingana 68, fol. 68b–70a.

4 See the *Coptic life* § 18.

5 Palladius, *HL* 26.1.

6 Cf. *KG* 1.27.

7 Cf. *Prayer* 145; *Thoughts* 37.

8 Cf. *Praktikos* 12: the demon of despondency inspires similar thoughts.

9 The river Gihon is one of the four that flowed from Paradise (cf. Gen 2.13), and the Children of Israel were forbidden from drinking of its waters (Jer 2.18); Evagrius also refers to it at *KG* 1.83. Bunge (1986): 336 n. 5 notes that Evagrius also identifies Egypt as the symbol of sin (*KG* 5.88, 6.49) and therefore concludes that ' "drinking of the waters of Gihon" means polluting oneself with the sins of the world'.

10 Cf. sch. 1 on Luke 10.25–37; this claim ultimately rests on Jesus' teaching as reported at Mt 5.27–48.

11 Evagrius' trenchant views notwithstanding, such pilgrimages by women were not unheard of. Melania herself travelled through Egypt before settling in the Holy Land (see *HL* 10.2); we also know of the pilgrimage of Silvia of Aquitaine (Hunt (1972)), not to mention the famous travels of Egeria.

12 Evagrius means that the messengers ('those in haste') were unable to wait for him to compose 'something profitable for her life'; although he does not specifically identify the 'prudent virgin', Bunge is surely right to identify her as the 'prudent deaconess Severa' mentioned in *Letter* 7.2.

13 Bunge (1986): 344 nn. 3–4 has noted that the principles listed here are also found in *To the virgin*: 'Pray unceasingly': cf. *To the virgin* 5; self-control: cf. *To the virgin* 9, 10, 40; meekness: cf. *To the virgin* 12, 19, 41, 45.

14 Cf. *Thoughts* 1.

15 On the bridegroom, cf. *To the virgin* 11, 43, 52, 55.

16 Bunge (1986): 345 n. 5 has suggested that 'full knowledge of the truth' mentioned here should be understood as the orthodox teaching related at *To the virgin* 54.

17 The 'writing' is in all likelihood *To the virgin*.

THE GREAT LETTER

1 Hausherr (1946): 290.

2 *Dictionnaire de Spiritualité* 10: 959.

3 Parmentier (1985): 5–6.

4 Vitestam (1964): 4–5 n. 4.

5 Bunge (1986): 194.

6 Bunge (1986): 197–200.

7 Sight is the best of all senses, after all; thus, *Prayer* 150.

8 Cf. *KG* 3.57.

9 This example is based on the fact that, in Syriac (as indeed in Greek), the same word means both 'breath' and 'spirit'/'Spirit.'

10 But cf. *Faith* 7.23.

11 Guillaumont (1962): 121 n. 174 has suggested that Syriac: *thar'e* ('passes' or 'doors' – here translated loosely as 'pathways') could be a copyist's error for Syriac: *tha'yatha* ('ideas').

12 Evagrius has previously spoken of the mind that is 'renewed *into* the image' of God, so that his claim here need not imply that some people were created incapable of God's image. Rather, they are 'not according to his image' precisely because they are 'far away' from God; cf. *Great letter* 46.

13 Here as before, 'Spirit' and 'breath' translate the same Syriac (and Greek) term so that the parallel of 'Word/word' and 'Spirit/breath' is stronger in the ancient versions than it can be in English.

14 Cf. *Thoughts* 37.

15 The charge of pantheism made against Evagrius is based on this segment of the *Great letter* – yet care must be taken in reading it. It is entirely possible, and consistent with the text, to conceive of the union Evagrius describes as making no more ontological claims than the 'Great High Priestly Prayer' (quoted here) does. With reference to the 'concord of wills', it is perfectly legitimate to interpret this passage as Evagrius speaking of a moral union between Creator and creation.

16 On God's names as derived from his providential actions, see also sch. 1 in Luke 10.25–37, Origen's *Principles* 4.4.1 and Gregory Nazianzen's *Oration* 31.21 (PG 36.132–33).

17 To this discussion of the unity of creation with God, cf. Evagrius' relatively terse remarks at sch. 25 in Eccl 4.4.

18 See Origen, *Principles* 2.8.3; Evagrius, *KG* 2.37, 3.70.

19 It is initially surprising that Evagrius mentions the sea at two points in this letter – here and at 65–66 (he is writing from the Egyptian desert, after all); but the recurrent image suggests that growing up near the Black Sea must have made a deep impression upon him.

20 If God's unity is indeed endless and inseparable, there would be no question for Evagrius of the cycles of falls and reconciliations that Jerome accuses Origen of having taught (see Jerome, *Letter* 124.5, 14). Please note that no claim is here intended about the accuracy of those allegations.

21 The text is lacunose between the words for 'earth' and for 'it happened to be'; on the claims made here, see also *KG* 5.72, *Monks* 128.

22 Cf. Origen, *Principles* 1.4.4.

23 The text is lacunose between the words 'but' and 'to them'; on the derivative endlessness of rational creatures, see also Gregory Nazianzen, *Oration* 29.13 (PG 36.92).

24 Cf. *Causes* 10: 'Eat once per day, and do not desire a second meal, otherwise you will become extravagant and trouble your purpose.'

25 The distinction made here is important throughout the letter: Evagrius distinguishes between what is *according to nature* (natural), what is *contrary to nature* (unnatural) and what *goes beyond nature* (supernatural). In what follows, I frequently translate his periphrastic expressions with a single word.

26 Cf. Origen, *Principles* 2.1.4, 3.1.2, 4.4.6–7.

27 Throughout this chapter, Evagrius is referring to the body and looking back to the categories he enumerated in §35.

28 This discussion elaborates on a distinction Evagrius drew at §34, above. See also *Praktikos* 56, 60; and Cassian, *Conferences* 12.7.

29 From study of the manuscript, Bunge (1986): 339 n. 80 concludes that the words in brackets are a later 'dogmatic' correction.

30 Literally, 'the proofs of her virginity who bore him remained'; in other words, Evagrius affirms Our Lady's virginity *in partu*.

31 'Hidden leaven' recalls the Lord's parable at Mt 13.33 and Lk 13.21. In the Gospels, the leaven is the Kingdom of God, but here it is Christ.

32 The modern interpretations of this teaching neatly exemplify the two major trends of scholarship. It can be taken as a statement of the teaching condemned by the eighth anathema of 553, along the lines laid down by Guillaumont (1962): 151–56. On the other hand, Bunge observes that Evagrius here 'formulates in a rich way the patristic teaching of the *deification of man* through the *humanisation of God*' (1986: 400 n. 92 – with references to Athanasius, Gregory Nazianzen and Origen) and notes that the slight echoes of this passage in the condemnation do not inspire confidence.

33 Claiming that he is bound by 'the mighty chains of loving those things that ceaselessly please me' is perhaps Evagrius' rather poetic way of describing the effects of habitual pleasures.

TREATISES

THE CAUSES FOR MONASTIC OBSERVANCES, AND HOW THEY COMPARE TO STILLNESS

1 On this topic generally, see also Gould (1989).

2 Paul of Tamma, *On the Cell*; see esp. Vivian (1997).

3 On that expectation, and for a response to it, see Casiday (2004b).

4 'Delightful' comes from reading *terpnê* rather than *sternê*.

5 Evagrius exhorts the novice to be *aülos* ('free from matter'), *apathês* ('free from perturbations') and *pasês epithumias ektos* ('set apart from every desire'). There is no indication that Evagrius is describing progressive development in monastic virtue; indeed, since these characteristics are his gloss on what it means to 'abandon the care of this world', it seems more likely that they should be understood as different facets of the state at which the novice should aim.

6 For a more advanced discussion of the ambiguous urge to hospitality, see *Thoughts* 7.

7 The word translated here is *paida* – which, like the English 'boy' or the French 'garçon', can refer to a servant as well as to a male youth. If the word is understood in the latter sense, the 'scandal' to which Evagrius refers is presumably pederasty. The passage can be understood in that way if we recall that gluttony is related to sexual excess; see, e.g., *Thoughts* 1. So the

abrupt transition in this passage from 'some scandal about you' to caring about sumptuous food is not as incongruous as it might seem at first glance. Evagrius teaches that, if a monk mollified his fasting practices to suit a servant boy, he would run a greater risk of falling into sexual temptation.

8 Evagrius warns his readers against living with men who are *emperistatoi* – 'encumbered', or preoccupied in worldly matters. Lampe (*s.v.*), citing this work only, glosses the word as 'involved in business', and Sinkewicz (2003): 7 similarly translates the term as 'involved in business affairs'. But the term as used elsewhere in these paragraphs does not easily reduce to the category of 'business affairs', so it seems prudent to translate it otherwise. Cf. Bettiolo (1996): 170: 'uomini ilici e *affaccendati*'.

9 Bettiolo (1996): 178–79 notes that the need for respite is well attested in Evagrius and also in Gregory the Theologian. He quotes Evagrius, sch. in Ps 45.11 ('Rest and see that I am God'): 'There is need for rest in order to know God'; and Gregory Nazianzen, *Theological orations* 27.3: 'It is necessary to rest really and know God and "when we have taken a moment, judge" [Ps 74.3] the precision of theology.'

10 For 'noises', I follow the reading in the *Philokalia*; this preference is in some measure corroborated by Evagrius' words at *Thoughts* 23, where he describes the fearful – and loud – attacks of the demons.

11 The ps-Athanasian fragment of *Causes* ends here.

12 The demon of despondency (*akêdia*) features prominently in Evagrius' teachings. See esp. Bunge (1995).

13 It is worth remembering in this connection that Evagrius had a steward who appears to have acted as his agent in financial transactions: thus, e.g., *Coptic life* §18, 28 (Amélineau (1887): 115, 120–21).

14 Cf. *Prayer* 144.

15 Here and in the following sentence, the word that Evagrius uses is *phronêma*, which is 'purpose' in the sense of a determined thought, or care.

16 Evagrius himself ate only once a day: see the *Great letter* 33.

17 Suspending one's normal fasting regimen for the sake of hospitality is an established convention among the desert saints: see *Apoph* Joseph of Panephysis 1, Moses 5, Matoes 6; Cassian, *Institutes* 5.24.

18 The further rationale for these practices is revealed at *Thoughts* 3.

19 Cf. *Prayer* 10.

20 Cf. *Prayer* 28.

ON THOUGHTS

1 See Zeno in von Arnim (1903–24): 1: 39; for Evagrius, see especially *Thoughts* 41.

2 For Jerome, Augustine and Cassian and a further discussion, see Casiday (2001).

3 Evagrius reiterates that these three preoccupations are the fundamental temptations at *Letters* 6.3, 19.2 and 39.2–3. This teaching is taken up in the Byzantine tradition: see Maximus the Confessor, *Centuries on love* 3.56 (PG 90: 1033) and Gregory of Sinai, *Acrostic chapters* 91 (PG 150: 1268).

4 Evagrius uses the same Greek word to describe the appearance of created things as he does to describe the appearance of God: *tôn gegonotôn . . . tas phantasias* on the one hand, and *Theou tên phantasian* on the other; from this it is clear that Evagrius does not understand the word *phantasia* to be inherently negative.

5 Cf. *Letter* 58: God 'appears to the heart after the suppression of all representations of things'. This sentiment is echoed by Hesychius the Sinaite and the Xanthopouloi brothers; see SC 438: 157 n. 11. For Evagrius' teaching on the illumination of the mind at prayer, see Guillaumont (1984).

6 Here, Evagrius returns to a theme that he has already announced at *Causes* 11.

7 Cf. *Praktikos* 31.

8 On the reconciliation of opposites in Christ, see also *KG* 2.17; cf. Maximus the Confessor, *Difficulty* 41. (PG 91: 1304–16), Eng. trans. and notes Louth (1996): 155–62.

9 *Organon*, a term frequently met in Evagrius' *KG* (2.48, 80; 3.20, 45, 51; 4.60, 62; 6.72), is used by Plato to mean 'the organ of sense or perception' in many passages; see, e.g., *Republic* 508B, 518C; *Theatetus* 185C; *Phaedo* 250B. In this context, the Platonic meaning gives a better sense than the less specific 'organ' or 'organism'.

10 Cf. *Praktikos* 56: 'We recognise the proofs of imperturbability in one's thoughts during the day, and one's dreams during the night.'

11 These 'false images' (Greek: *eidôla*) are not innocuous, as is clear from *Thoughts* 16.28, 25.55 and 36.17. In every case, Evagrius uses this term to describe images that distract the Christian from God. As such, they bear comparison to his warning at *Thoughts* 37.24 against 'making a god' of the face of one's enemy while praying.

12 Cf. *Prayer* 24.

13 On the dog, see also *Thoughts* 13 and *Prayer* 94; it is clear that the metaphor is ambivalent from Evagrius' positive descriptions of the mind as a dog that hunts down wicked thoughts: *Skemmata* 9–10. See also sch. 324 on Prov 26.11.

14 The 'pagan sage' is Menander, whose *Dyskolos* (vv. 451–53) was quoted to this end by Clement (*Stromata* 7.31.1). Bile – and, by extension, the gall-bladder – is classically linked to anger (see Plutarch, *Advice to Bride and Groom* 27 [= *Moralia* 141]); elsewhere, Evagrius takes the loin as symbolic of lust: see *Praktikos* prol. 5. On Evagrius' knowledge of secular literature, see Lackner (1966).

15 Contrast to this Evagrius' explanation of the scapular: *Praktikos* prol. 4.

16 Evagrius gives precisely this example at *Letter* 18.4, where he also draws on *Thoughts* 31; it will also be noted that his exposition of the perils of hospitality here is far more nuanced than what is found at *Causes* 3.

17 The final clause of this sentence (*mê di' anthropous tauta prattein hêmas katanankazontos*) presents a difficulty. If we are to be hospitable at all, there must be a sense in which we do so 'for the sake of other people' (*di' anthropous*). But if we keep in mind the previous sentence, the final clause appears to mean that the 'better thought' prevents us from acting hospitably for

the sake *of being made known to* other people. Furthermore, in his note to Luke 10.25–37, Evagrius indicates that hospitality is enjoined upon us; we do it because we are obliged to do it by precepts from the New Testament such as Rom 13.8: 'Owe no one anything, except love.'

18 Evagrius may also have learnt this difference after reading Origen's *Principles* 3.2.4.

19 Géhin interprets this angelic thought in keeping with Origenian speculation about the pre-existence of souls (SC 438: 179 n. 4), and Sinkewicz follows him point for point in his note ad loc. (268 n. 16). This is not inherently unreasonable, but it should be noted Evagrius' words do not necessarily imply an Origenian metaphysics: for example, there is nothing in the passage that corresponds to pre-existent souls, falling into bodies or indeed restoration to an original state.

20 This demon – *Planos* – is also mentioned by Cassian, *Conference* 7.32 and in the *Life of Anthony* 94.2. He is an obvious opponent to monastic stability of place.

21 At *Causes* 8 and *Excerpts* 46, Evagrius likens the mind to wine and water (respectively) that is made turbid through lack of stability.

22 Cf. Evagrius' description of the physical effects of attack by the demon who besets a monk as he reads: *Excerpts* 45.

23 Cf. Driscoll (1997).

24 Cf. *Skemmata* 41.

25 This passage probably refers to the demon of grief displacing other demons; cf. *Skemmata* 61, where Evagrius comments that the thought of grief 'destroys all thoughts'.

26 Cf. Evagrius, sch. 27 in Job 30.24; there, as here, Evagrius is warning against suicide. See also Géhin's remarks about Evagrius' views on suicide (SC 438: 194–95 n. 2).

27 I adopt Géhin's emendation, reading *chysis* ('secretion') in place of *physis* ('nature'); see SC 438: 195 n. 3.

28 Evagrius gives these four examples in the same order in *Letter* 56.7–9.

29 On vainglory's 'abundance of material', see also *Skemmata* 44; on the 'material' of wicked thoughts, see *Thoughts* 36.

30 Evagrius describes how the other thoughts' defeat contributes to the cause of vainglory at *Praktikos* 31.

31 Cf. *Excerpts* 43.

32 Cf. *Definitions* 1; *KG* 6.21.

33 As Géhin notes, this progression from progress in virtue, through renewal in knowledge, to elevation in prayer is, in fact, a summary of Evagrius' teaching on the three stages of the Christian life: ascetic struggle, natural contemplation and theological knowledge (SC 438: 204–05 nn. 7–9). We should remark on two significant features of this gloss on theological knowledge. First, prayer is placed at this stage, which reinforces the idea that *Prayer* is a sublime work of Evagrian theology (rather than an introductory treatise); second, Evagrius focuses theological knowledge on the light of Our Saviour, that is, Christ, and he thus gives pride on place to Christ within his overall scheme.

34 In several passages, Evagrius expresses an unwillingness to state himself clearly; see, e.g., *Praktikos* prol. 9; *Antirrhetikos* 2.65; *Great letter* § 17. Reticence of this kind has, in some instances, fuelled speculation about what precisely Evagrius was trying to hide; see the discussion in the general introduction, under the heading 'Esoteric teachings'.

35 On the demon of impurity making physical contact with the monk, see *Excerpts* 9.

36 Cf. *Great letter* § 41.

37 Evagrius is returning to the example of David – in this case, how he slew Goliath with a stone before decapitating him with his own sword; see 1 Sam 17.50–51.

38 Evagrius takes as his example a monk who is thinking about whether he will be consecrated a bishop. The point is that it is one thing for the monk to dismiss the thought because it is simply ridiculous to suppose he will become the bishop of Constantinople, but another for him to dismiss the (comparatively more plausible) thought of simply becoming a bishop. Géhin gives other references for Evagrius using the case of episcopal ordination (SC 438: 225 n. 6). It may be significant to note that, according to the *Coptic life of Evagrius* 19 (Amélineau (1887): 115), Theophilus of Alexandria tried to make Evagrius the bishop of Thmuis but, when he learnt of the plan, Evagrius fled to Palestine.

39 Evagrius is again talking about a monk who fantasises of being made a clergyman (and of all the powers which that would entail).

40 Hausherr (1960): 5 has suggested that the chapters mentioned here are probably *Prayer* 43, 55–57, 67–68, 70, 112 and 115. Evagrius rarely makes explicit cross-references such as this one, which is also significant because it establishes a relative chronology: *Prayer* is at least no earlier than *Thoughts*. This reference is also interesting because Evagrius typically reserves such discussions for treatment in more advanced works. By that standard, *Prayer* is a more advanced treatise than *Thoughts* (and consequently far more advanced than *Causes*).

41 A rather more basic description of these noises and visions is found at *Causes* 6 (at n. 10). See also *Praktikos* 13, where Evagrius describes how the thought of vainglory causes insecurity, with similar results.

42 This vivid image is an interesting echo of Evagrius' city life, and perhaps indicates that he expected his early readers to be living in or near cities. Such an example would not be very apposite in the deserts of Egypt.

43 According to the textual transmission, what appears in Ch. 17 is not at all what Evagrius describes here. A much closer fit is found in what is now Ch. 2. This has been taken as evidence that the chapters have been rearranged (see SC 438: 154–55 n. 1 and 237 n. 3). Another possibility is that Evagrius was mistaken in his internal reference.

44 Evagrius expresses the same teaching elsewhere through the proverb that one nail drives out another: *Praktikos* 58 (SC 171: 636–38; see especially Guillaumont's notes on the proverb as found in Aristotle and Cicero).

45 Modern commentators have not remarked on this strange assertion, even though it is clear that, for Evagrius, the 'face' is a theologically important symbol (cf. sch. 1 in Ps 33.1: '"face" means the condition [*katastêma*] of the soul ... Often when Scripture mentions a man's face, it means his *logos*.'). For one attempt to explain it, see Casiday (forthcoming).

46 'Schema' (Gk: *schema*) is a form, shape or representation; Evagrius appears to use it here interchangeably with terms such as representation and shape, but even though it seems to be a synonym I have thought it best to follow his lead in using a different word.

47 This is a difficult passage and it is therefore surprising that no commentator as yet has made anything of it. The crux of the passage seems to be that the 'incomplete' schema (which Evagrius will shortly call an 'incomplete icon') lacks its face. Now in one of his notes on the Psalter, Evagrius calls Christ 'the face of the Father' (see his sch. 4 in Ps 79.8 (PG 12: 1544)) and it is consistent with Evagrius' conception of Christ's mediating role that he should also regard Christ as the face that perfects the otherwise incomplete icon described here. For further development of this analysis, see Casiday (forthcoming).

48 This last sentence is quoted at *Skemmata* 13.

49 On the 'materials' of thoughts, see *Thoughts* 36.

50 This account of the three renunciations also appears in *KG* 1.78–80, which may indicate that Evagrius excerpted some of the chapters of *KG* from his other works.

51 This reference to the shepherd's cloak and little flock signifies the clergy.

52 The image of monks cast down from ladders had enduring value; in the literary tradition, it is implicit in *The Ladder of Divine Ascent* CPG 88: 632–1164) by John Climacus and, in the iconographic tradition, it is found in the famous icon of the same name from St Catherine's (which is widely available in books and on the internet).

53 On the 'feathers of imperturbability', cf. Cassian, *Conference* 9.4.

54 This chapter is found in *Letter* 17.2–3. The odd phrasing of the Septuagint for Ps 139.6 (*echomena tribou skandala*) has attracted Evagrius' attention, and so it is translated oddly here. It should be noted that Evagrius is correct in his conjecture of the Septuagint's reading; for other evidence that he may have had a serious interest in Hebrew, see sch. 27 in Job 30.24 and the notes ad loc.

55 This much of *Thoughts* §31 is also found in *Letter* 18.1–2.

56 This rather convoluted observation on being and non-being is also found in *KG* 1.39.

57 The remainder of *Thoughts* §31 is attested in several other writings: *KG* 1.40; *Letters* 43.3, 59.3; sch. 62 in Prov 5.14. Géhin interpolates the material translated here in square brackets, which does not in fact appear in the manuscript tradition, on the basis of the parallel passages in *KG* and *in Prov* (see SC 438: 263 n. 9).

58 Evagrius also uses the image of someone deliberately harming his eyes at *Prayer* 65 and *Gnostikos* 5.

59 For another account of how the demons attack those who are reading, see *Excerpts* 45 and the notes ad loc.

60 The cupping-glass (*sikuê* – so named because its shape resembled a cucumber or gourd) was used in ancient medical procedures and the sound it produces was described by Plato at *Timaeus* 79e–80a. Evagrius also mentions it at *Antirrhetikos* 4.36, where he talks of the attacks of the demons leaving a mark like that left by a cupping-glass!

61 Géhin has noted that Macarius of Alexandria is said to have seen demons putting their fingers in the mouths of sleepy monks (SC 438: 269 n. 9; cf. *HM* 29). On Evagrius' relationship with Macarius, see especially Bunge (1983) and Vivian (2004: 37–38). The practice of making the sign of the Cross over one's mouth when one yawns, lest a demon might enter one's mouth, can still be found amongst eastern European Christians, as this translator has learnt (in Evagrian fashion) from having observed it many times.

62 Cf. *Excerpts* 16.

63 Regnault (1999): 61–81 has shown that bread, oil and water are the dietary staples of Sketis and Kellia.

64 Contrast to this the materials that make for good prayer: poverty and tribulations (*Prayer* 131).

65 That is, one who has been wounded by a sin can expect to be reminded of it (by the demon of grief) during prayers.

66 Evagrius also claims that God is able to insert knowledge directly into the mind, whereas everyone else can merely 'implant thoughts or representations or contemplations' through the body: *Prayer* 64. That the demons must watch the body for signs of the soul, cf. *Great letter* §§ 15–21 ('the soul is unknown apart from the body').

67 Géhin conjectures that the priest in question is probably Macarius of Alexandria, whom he further identifies as the 'Macarius' mentioned in *Thoughts* 33 (SC 438: 281 n. 3).

68 Evagrius reiterates the danger for one praying of imagining the face of an enemy at *Prayer* 46. For some discussion of Evagrius' use of *theopoiôsis* here in the context of his teaching on deification, see Casiday (2003).

69 Géhin notes the following interesting passage from Hesychius the Sinaite's *Centuries* 2.49 (PG 93: 1528), which may be in reference to Evagrius: 'the celebrated gnostic fathers, in some of their writings, have called the demons "men" on account of their faculty of reason' (see SC 438: 285 n. 10).

70 A slightly modified version of this chapter is cited in the Syriac *ps-Suppl. to KG* 24 (see SC 438: 286 n. 1).

71 This chapter is also cited, with some modification (see SC 438: 287 n. ad loc.), at *Skemmata* 25; on the 'sapphire' colour, see further Harmless and Fitzgerald (2001) and Harmless (2004): 370–71.

72 Géhin has interpolated the word *noêmata* here on the strength of the parallel text of *Skemmata* 23, where this chapter is cited with some modification (see SC 438: 289 n. 1).

73 The last phrase of *Thoughts* 40 (*ektupountos ton topon ton tou Theou*) has attracted scholarly attention. Géhin, who translates it as 'modèle le lieu de

Dieu', expresses his surprise on the basis that *Thoughts* 41 explicitly states that God does not make an imprint on one's mind (SC 438: 290–91 n. 6); he is followed in this by Sinkewicz (2003): 180, whose translation ('leave an impress of the place of God') throws the perceived problem into higher relief (273 n. 62). On the other hand, Bunge (2000): 12 and 12 n. 56 has criticised the translation found in SC and argued that the phrase is better understood as meaning 'exprime le lieu de Dieu', in the sense that this light makes the place of God visible to the mind. Because Bunge's analysis resolves the apparent conundrum without doing violence to the text, this translation follows him. It should also be noted that the problem arises if 'the place of God' at *Thoughts* 40 is thought to be an exact equivalent of 'God' at *Thoughts* 41 – a presumption which may be sound with respect to LXX where 'the place of' is a reverential pleonasm, but which is not self-evidently warranted here.

74 Elizabeth Clark (1992): 65 has adduced these examples in support of her claim that Evagrius was opposed to liturgical worship on ground that it is 'defective' and 'produces images in the mind'; I have argued elsewhere that her interpretation relies on ascribing to Evagrius a theory of representation that is not borne out by the evidence: see Casiday (2004b).

75 This contrast between created things that are bodily (the 'corporeals') and created things that are not (the 'incorporeals') is found elsewhere in Evagrius' writings – e.g., at *Letter* 7.1, sch. 52 in Eccl 6.10–12. The difference between the respective meanings (or reasons: *logoi*) of these different created beings is the stuff of advanced theological contemplation; cf. *KG* 1.27.

76 The claim that God, as a non-physical entity, does not create mental impressions underlies Evagrius' denunciation of giving a 'shape' to the deity as one prays: *Prayer* 67.

77 This chapter gives the background that is presupposed at *Prayer* 57.

78 = *Skemmata* 24.

79 Evagrius elsewhere associates the right side with God and the left with demons; see *Prayer* 72, *KG* 2.12 and 4.21.

80 None of the appendices is widely attested in the manuscript tradition; 1 and 2 essentially reiterate *Thoughts* 1; as for 3, although it resembles *Praktikos* 5, Géhin, who pithily observed that 'son authenticité évagrienne est douteuse', is surely right in doubting whether Evagrius wrote it.

A WORD ABOUT PRAYER

1 Wright (1871): 2:448 (MS 567 item 38) and 757 (MS 779 item 3*u*).

2 Cf. *Causes* 11.

3 The plural form of the Syriac *dwbra* typically refers to monastic discipline in particular.

4 Cf. *Prayer* 126.

5 Making the sign of the cross is evidently profitable upon returning to one's cell – especially if one finds the door locked! See Palladius, *HL* 38.12.

6 This passage contrasts the sequence of temptations described at *Thoughts* 1: gluttony, avarice and vainglory are the 'front line'. The difference may be attributable in part to a shift in focus. In *Thoughts*, Evagrius describes temptations generally; in this treatise (as in *Prayer* 51), his attention is restricted to temptations during prayer.

NOTES ON SCRIPTURE

INTRODUCTION

1 See *Gnostikos* 18–21.
2 For an example of this technique being used to great effect (albeit chiefly on a different corpus), see esp. Sheridan (2002). In a chapter on Evagrian prayer from my doctoral thesis, I argue for an interpretation of various passages from Evagrius' *Gnostic chapters* that resolves their seeming contradictions by distinguishing references to the Pauline corpus from references to Revelation: see A.M.C. Casiday, 'Tradition and Theology in John Cassian', PhD thesis (University of Durham: Department of Theology, 2002): 103–08.
3 E.g., sch. 42 on Eccl 5.17–19.
4 Sch. 38 on Eccl 5.7–11 and the reference to Origen in the note ad loc.
5 Sch. 27 on Job 30.24 and sch. 6 on Lk 23.44–47; on the breadth of Evagrius' interests in the text of Scripture, see Casiday (2005).

NOTES ON JOB

1 See *CPG* 2458(2). The most important secondary material on these scholia are as follows: Balthasar (1939): 204–05; Hagedorn (1994–2004): 1: 109–10; Devreesse (1928); Mercati (1914).
2 Hagedorn (1994, 1997, 2000, 2004).
3 Iunius (1637).
4 The thirty scholia in question (with references to the Hagedorns' volumes) are as follows: 2.34 (I.202); 3.73, 75 (I.304–05); 6.60 (I.457; ascribed by one MS to Evagrius, but attributed by the editors to Polychronios); 7.124 (II.40; ascribed by one MS to Evagrius, by another to Olympiodoros); 7.178 (II.58; one MS ascribes it to Evagrius); 8.17 (II.75; multiple ascriptions, attributed by the editors to Didymus); 9.87 (II.120); 11.91 (II.248); 19.28–30, 85 (III.48, 68); 20.9, 92, 148 (III.81, 108, 127); 22.20 (III.163); 24.27 (III.205; cf. Evagrius' scholion on Ps 35.13); 25.9 (III.213); 26.56, 111, 137 (III.277, 296, 306); 27.6 (III.315); 28.22–23, 34, 54, 60, 66, 72, 93 (III.327, 331, 338, 340, 342, 344, 352); 29.10 (III.377; cf. Evagrius' remarks in *Ep fid* on the Holy Spirit).
5 Devreesse (1954): 108–11. The general acceptance of Devreesse's argument can be inferred from the notice at *CPG* 1503(10).
6 = Hagedorn 1.41 (I.185); for an argument in favour of ascribing this scholion to Evagrius, see Casiday (2005).

7 = Hagedorn 2.24 (I.190).

8 = Hagedorn 2.45 (I.206).

9 This variant is attested in two MSS in the Bodleian: Laud. gr. 20 and Auct. e. 2.19.

10 = Hagedorn 2.128 (I.233); = sch. 41 in Eccl 5.14–15.

11 = Hagedorn 2.129 (I.233); NB: this scholion is not attributed to Evagrius by the Hagedorns, but MS B ascribes it to Evagrius. The use of Origenian terms found in it (e.g., *synpegnumi*, *protê demiourgia*, *aülos*) and the eschatological vision that it presupposes both support this ascription.

12 = Hagedorn 2.132 (I.235); cf. *Skemmata* 15.

13 = Hagedorn 2.151 (I.241).

14 = Hagedorn 2.156 (I.243); for the reference to Phil 3.20, cf. *Prayer* 142.

15 Cf. *Life of Anthony* 29.3. This variant is recorded at Iunius (1637): 68–69.

16 = Hagedorn 6.59 (I.457).

17 = Hagedorn 7.128 (II.41).

18 = Iunius (1637): 225.

19 = Hagedorn 7.134 (II.43).

20 = Hagedorn 7.172 (II.56); NB: this scholion is not attributed to Evagrius by the Hagedorns, but it is ascribed to Evagrius by the four MS of the γ-redaction (Venetus Marcianus gr. 538, Vat. gr. 338, Mediolanensis Ambrosianus M 65 sup., and Patmensis gr. 171) as well as Bodleianus Auct. e. 2.19.

21 = Hagedorn 7.173 (II.56).

22 = Hagedorn 8.20 (II.76); cf. *KG* 6.59.

23 = Hagedorn 9.31 (II.104).

24 = Hagedorn 9.32 (II.104–05); NB: the Hagedorns provisionally attribute this scholion to Olympiodoros on the basis of its similarity to a known writing by him, but the only MS ascription of it is to Evagrius (MSS H and C) and seven others imply that he wrote it by ascribing the next scholion to 'the same one' when the nearest antecedent name is Evagrius'. Furthermore, the use of *nous* and *gnôsis* in this scholion is consistent with Evagrius' general practice.

25 = Hagedorn 9.33 (II.105).

26 = Hagedorn 9.88 (II.120).

27 = Hagedorn 9.130 (II.133).

28 = Hagedorn 11.48 (II.234–35).

29 = Hagedorn 11.54 (II.237); Evagrius heartily recommended restraint in drinking water (even to the point of dehydration) – see, e.g., *Historia Monachorum in Aegypto* 20.16.

30 = Hagedorn 12.10 (III.21); NB: the Hagedorns do not attribute this scholion to anyone, but I follow Pragensis Státní knihovna XXV B 3, the only witness that identifies it, in ascribing it to Evagrius.

31 = Hagedorn 19.82 (III.67).

32 = Hagedorn 19.102 (III.73); NB: the Hagedorns do not attribute this scholion to anyone, but I follow MS G in ascribing it to Evagrius. The identification of Christ as the Lord of creation is consistent with Evagrius' teaching.

33 = Hagedorn 20.46 (III.92).

34 = Hagedorn 20.52 (III.94).

35 The Tetraselides, also known as the Tetrapla, was Origen's synoptic compilation of the Greek Old Testament translations of Aquila, Symmachus, Theodotion and the Septuagint; see Origen, *Selecta in Genesim* 17.4 (PG 12.141); Eusebius, *Church history* 6.16.4 (PG 20.557); the Hagedorns' note, III.110; and O. Procksch, 'Tetraplarische Studien', *Zeitschrift für die Alttestamentliche Wissenschaft* 12 (1935): 240–69, esp. 257–60.

36 = Hagedorn 20.99 (III.110); they conjecture that the original reading of the scholion might have been *diacheirosasthai* ('to put hands on oneself thoroughly', or – to be blunt – 'to commit suicide'), which would have preserved the parallel with the verse from Job. This scholion is one of three (the others are 1 and 35) that indicate an exegetical technique far more sophisticated in practical terms than one might expect. Here, Evagrius indicates that he has compared multiple versions of the Greek text for his commentary; at sch. 35, he comments on the Hebrew meaning of the name *Leviathan* and at sch. 1 on the various Hebrew names for God. Evagrius may have cribbed his information from Symmachus, as he certainly did for sch. 50 on Eccl 6.9.

37 = Hagedorn 20.123 (III.118).

38 = Hagedorn 20.151 (III.127).

39 = Hagedorn 23.21 (III.186).

40 = Hagedorn 23.33 (III.191); NB: the Hagedorns do not attribute this scholion to anyone, but I follow Pragensis Státní knihovna XXV B 3, the only witness that identifies it, in ascribing it to Evagrius.

41 = Hagedorn 23.34 (III.192); NB: the Hagedorns do not attribute this scholion to anyone, but I follow Pragensis Státní knihovna XXV B 3, the only witness that identifies it, in ascribing it to Evagrius.

42 = Hagedorn 28.14 (III.325); abandonment (*enkataleipsis*) by God is a recurrent theme in Evagrius' writings: see Driscoll (1997).

43 = Hagedorn 28.37 (III.332).

44 = Hagedorn 28.68 (III.342–43).

45 = Hagedorn 28.117 (III.362).

46 = Hagedorn 28.131 (III.367).

47 = Hagedorn 29.8 (III.377).

48 = Hagedorn 31.7 (III.390); the Hagedorns note that this scholion is probably to be attributed to Evagrius on the strength of the parallel phrasing found at sch. 28 on Job 38.5 (= Hagedorn 20.123 (III.118)).

49 = Hagedorn 33.40 (III.415).

NOTES ON ECCLESIASTES

1 Talmud *Shabbath* 30*b*: Epstein (1935–52): Mo'ed 1: 135–37.

2 Beth Shammai: Misnah *'Eduyot* 5.3 (Epstein (1935–52): Tohoroth 2: 558); R. Nathan, *Aboth* 1 (vers. B): Saldarini (1975): 27 and 27–28 n. 20.

3 My translation is different to Géhin's, who takes the Greek *ho logos* (here, '*the Word* says') as referring to the biblical text: '*le texte* dit' (SC 397: 59).

His argument is palaeographical, based on the fact that *logos* is written with a minuscule and thus does not indicate the Word of God ('si c'était le cas, il faudrait naturellement mettre une majuscule au mot' – SC 397: 61 n. ad loc.). I rather incline to the view that Evagrius *was* referring to the Word of God. My argument is based on Evagrius' claim that the Preacher is Christ (sch. 1 on Eccl 1.1), which I take it was in his mind when he commented on Eccl 1.2, so that when he glosses the Scripture's *Ecclêsiastês* as *logos*, this should be understood as the Word (irrespective of the size of the lambda). But Evagrius' meaning is clear regardless of how one understands that particular word.

4 In distinguishing between God *doing* something and God *allowing* something, Evagrius follows the teaching that Paphnutius related to him when he, Albinus and Palladius visited him: see *HL* 47.5. For Evagrius' perspective on what it means to be abandoned by God, see Driscoll (1997).

5 The Greek text (as reported in the Tetrapla and the Alexandrian text) is ambiguous as to whether the wood shoots up the thicket or vice versa. It is interesting that, in clarifying this matter, Evagrius' remarks are consistent with the underlying Hebrew.

6 In Greek, the word *pneuma* means both 'breath' – even 'breeze' – and 'spirit'. Since in the passage from Ecclesiastes, the former sense is primary (as indeed Evagrius takes it to be when he comments on this expression at sch. 27 on Eccl 4.6 and sch. 51 on Eccl 6.9), but in the quotations from other biblical works the latter sense is primary, it seems good to translate the Greek into two English words.

7 Cf. *On the faith* 14.

8 Here, as elsewhere, the word translated 'business' is *perispasmon* – literally, 'distraction' or 'pre-occupation' – and it should be understood broadly as 'being busy' rather than narrowly as 'being involved in commerce'. The sense of being distracted insofar as one is busy ought to be kept in mind when Evagrius describes the *perispasmon ponêron* ('wicked business'): part of what makes it 'wicked' is precisely that it causes the person who is involved in it to be distracted from God; thus, sch. 40 in Eccl 5.14; cf. *Causes* 2, 4, 7. On the other hand, Evagrius acknowledges that some forms of business are godly: see sch. 42 and 45 in Eccl 5.17–19.

9 At *KG* 2.2, Evagrius cites Eph 3.10 by way of describing how Christ made the universe.

10 Evagrius' syllogism depends upon the Greek word *diôkô* (to pursue), which occurs in the verse as 'that which has followed' – *diôkomenon* – and in the scholion's quotation from the Beatitudes as 'those who are persecuted' – *dediôgmenoi*.

11 Cf. *On the faith* 6.

12 The final clause is obscure, but it seems to preclude any kind of reincarnation or metempsychosis whereby a person who has died in a sinful condition could return to earthly life in order to regain a good spiritual standing (or, 'come here again to do things conducive to possessing' spiritual rejoicing). See also Géhin's note, ad loc.

13 Cf. *Great Letter* 22–27, for an expanded treatment of the creation's union with God.

14 Géhin has noted that Evagrius does not make as much of the phrase *proairesis pneumatos* (here translated as 'the resolve of a breeze') as one might expect. He translates it as 'choix de l'espirit', but Evagrius' scholia do not necessitate thinking of the *pneuma* in question as spirit in the sense of the 'breath of life' – nor indeed do they necessitate thinking of *proairesis* according to the categories of Greek philosophy. On the contrary, the interpretations advanced by Evagrius (here and at sch. 51 on Eccl 6.9) are consistent with the underlying Hebrew phrase, רעות רוח, which is a paradox alluding to the impermanence of a blast of air. For this reason, I am not persuaded by Géhin's assertion (SC 397: 18) that 'it goes without saying that such an interpretation gives the biblical book a voluntarist dimension that it does not have, but that accords well with our author's Origenist conceptions, in which free will plays an important role'.

15 'Speak of God' translates *theologein*, which I suppose must be more or less what people mean when they talk about 'doing theology'. Evagrius also advises against rashly speaking of God at *Gnostikos* 27, sch. 310 on Prov 25.17, and *Exhortation to Monks* 2.39.

16 Cf. sch. 1 on Luke 10.25–37: 'Whatever one does of one's own resolve – virginity or ascetic withdrawal – is by way of a gift.'

17 Chance (*automatismos*) is an important concept in Epicurean cosmology and was probably attractive to Egyptian Christians: apart from Evagrius' rejection of the concept here, we also find it denounced by Clement of Alexandria (*Strom* 5.14.90.2) and by Didymus the Blind (sch. on Eccl 3.14c–d (fol. 88.17–21)).

18 Cf. Origen, *Principles* 2.9.5–7.

19 = sch. 4 on Job 1.21.

20 In the two scholia that follow, Evagrius conspicuously fails to comment about a person living for 'cycles of millennia' (*chiliôn etôn kathodous*) mentioned here. Such silences do not sit well with the idea that he was responsible for the teachings that were condemned in the sixth century as Origenism; for the condemnation of 'terms [*periodous*] of bodies and souls', see, e.g. canon 1 of the Council *in Trullo*.

21 The quotation from Symmachus is imprecise, though not entirely inaccurate. What he actually said was, 'Better to look ahead than to wander according to one's fancy' (Field (1875): 2: 391).

22 'To flow' translates *rheusai*, which the editor has emended to *rhepsai* ('to incline') despite the fact that *rheusai* is well attested (see SC 397: 153). While I agree that 'inclining' is more to be expected than 'flowing' in this context, 'flowing' is not entirely meaningless and so I refrain from the emendation.

23 Géhin has rightly compared Evagrius' claim that the names given to bodiless nature reflect the status (*katastasis*) of the given being, to Origen's concern for retaining meritocracy and divine impartiality in his account of Creation (see *Principles* 1.8.1). It should be noted that Evagrius' analysis

of names is ambivalent: he might mean that knowledge transforms the human rational nature into an angelic or a demonic rational nature (as suggested by the condemnations of Origenism); but he need not mean more than that the rational nature of a human admits of several different names. The latter view has this to recommend it: Evagrius does not talk of a change in the 'quality' of the rational nature, merely of a change in its 'state', and there is no reason to suppose that he confused quality with status in such a way as to think that the human would become an angel (or archangel, or throne . . .) or a demon (or Satan . . .).

24 In the Allegory of the Cave (Plato, *Rep* 7.1 (516B)), Socrates relates that the one who has been freed is ultimately able to contemplate the sun 'as it is'. Perhaps Evagrius recalled this passage in writing his scholion.

25 Cf. *Thoughts* 25.

ON THE 'OUR FATHER'

1 For an overview of the Copto-Arabic Evagriana, see Samir (1992).

2 Muyldermans (1963).

3 Amélineau (1887).

4 E.g., Quecke (1989), Schenke (1984).

5 Bunge (1987): 44–61.

6 Hausherr (1960): 83–84.

7 I am grateful to Dr Tim Vivian for his suggestions in preparing this translation and for a helpful discussion of various particular points that arise in it.

8 'Our first nature': *pefkataphysis*.

9 'With boldness': *nouparrêsia*.

10 'Every rational soul': *têrf nlogikon*; 'mental powers': *nijom nnoeron* – from the context of this passage, we can tell that the former refers to every creature endowed with reason (namely, angels, demons and humans) and that the latter refers specifically to angels.

11 'Kind' (*helje*) is related to the word 'kindness' (*hloj*), used in the immediately preceding comment. In the Bohairic version of Prov 2.21, it translates *chrêstos*, which is a term often met in Evagrius' *Notes on the Psalms* and which perhaps underlies the Coptic translation here.

NOTES ON LUKE

1 Fabricius and Harles (1780–1809): 8: 687.

2 Corderius (1628)

3 Mai (1825–38).

4 See Corderius (1628): 'Index patrum' n. 19.

5 Balthasar (1939): 204–05.

6 I wish to thank Prof. Andrew Louth for his comments and suggestions regarding this translation.

7 Cf. *Letter* 8.3: 'Moses' command averts us from sinning by action, but Our Saviour's from sinning by thought.' Evagrius' assertion is ultimately based on Jesus' words related at Mt 5.27–48.

8 Or 'with foresight': the Greek word is *pronoia*.

9 Cf. *Great letter* 24.

10 Corderius (1628): 313 translates the scholion to this point; according to his system, it appears as 10.57.

11 Cf. sch. 36 in Eccl 5.3–4.

12 This is a dense and challenging passage. Evagrius' basic purpose is to insist on the fundamental identity of God's law and God's love. Evagrius says of such offerings as virginity and monastic retreat that they are, in effect, gifts that are above and beyond what is required. Since he has identified the requirements of the law as being the requirements of love, Evagrius specifies that the gifts of hospitality are not required by the law and therefore (paradoxically) they are 'not offered out of love'. The ambiguities of hospitality exercised Evagrius greatly; see further *Causes* 3 and *Thoughts* 7.

13 'Discipline' here translates *paideusis*, a word that also has overtones of 'culture', in the sense of a way of thinking and living that has been cultivated through discipline.

14 For Evagrius, the contemplation of God's creation (here, 'the Master's rational possessions') is a crucial part of the Christian life. This terse phrase and the citation from Ps 11.7 are linked by a suggestive similarity in the Greek that is not obvious in English: the 'rational possessions' are *logika* and the 'words of the Lord' are *logia kuriou*.

15 Three times in the immediately preceding lines, Evagrius uses the word *paideia* (and cognates) to describe what the rulers have accomplished and what they consequently lead others into. The word means instruction, but also the training and discipline by which one is instructed, and the culture that results from being thus instructed.

16 Corderius (1628): 483–84 translates the scholion to this point, as 19.26.

17 Similar use of the life of Joseph for ethico-political instruction was made by Philo in his *On Joseph*. See eds F.H. Colson and G.W. Whitaker, *Philo. Works* (London: Heinemann, 1929–43), vol. 6: 140–271.

18 Cf. *Letters* 23 and 37.3.

19 Canonical scripture reports Jesus preaching to the souls in 'prison' (see 1 Pet 3.19) – but Evagrius' words go well beyond that and bear comparison with the results of Jesus' preaching as described in a number of non-canonical sources (e.g., *Gospel of Nicodemus*, *Questions of Bartholomew*). The theme is traditionally called 'the Harrowing of Hell' and a convenient overview can be found in Elliot (1996): 97–108.

20 The *skolops* (here paraphrased as 'the tree of the cross') is in the first instance a stake or pole, and, by extension, a tree.

21 Cf. Julian, *Oration* 2.80d ed. W.C. Wright, *The Works of the Emperor Julian* (London: Heinemann, 1913–23), vol. 1: 214–15; Dio Cassius *Roman history* 60.26 ed. E. Cary, *Dio's Roman history* (London: Heinemann, 1914–25), vol. 7: 432–35.

22 Evagrius' knowledge of astronomy and his unexpected knowledge of how the date of Passover is calculated are quite detailed, and may suggest an

interest in Judaica that goes beyond what has previously been assumed of him (see further Casiday, 2005). For the 'conjunction', and a general description of the Jewish calendar, see now Stern (2001), esp. ch. 3.

CHAPTERS

INTRODUCTION

1 This note is found in only three manuscripts, but Guillaumont (SC 170: 384–85) plausibly argues that it goes back to Evagrius himself.

2 The pioneering work in this field is Driscoll's analysis of *To the monks*; see especially (1990) and, in greater detail, (1991).

3 See the introduction to *Excerpts*.

4 See von Ivanka (1954).

5 See Antoine Guillaumont's initial report: 'Fragments syriaques des *Disciples d'Évagre*', *Parole de l'Orient* 6/7 (1975–76): 115–23; the forthcoming edition is being prepared by P. Géhin for SC.

TO THE VIRGIN

1 Gennadius, *Famous Men* 11 (TU 14: 65).

2 Socrates Scholasticus, *Church history* 4.23 (PG 67: 516); I have translated the Greek into blank verse in deference to Socrates' claim that the work was written in verses.

3 Jerome, *Letter* 133.3 (CSEL 56: 246).

4 On Holste, see Wilmart (1911); Syriac texts: Muyldermans (1952): 30 n. 30; Armenian texts: Sargisean (1907): 355–59 and Muyldermans (1940).

5 These are *Letters* 7, 8, 19 and 20, translated herein.

6 Hausherr (1934): 44; Bunge (1986): 220–21, 232–33; Elm (1990): 399–400 and (1991).

7 Elm (1990): 399 and (1991): 116.

8 E.g., Clark (1992): 22 at n. 87; Sinkewicz (2003): 117; Driscoll (1996): 255.

9 Elm (1991): 116. Counter to that claim in particular, the reader may wish to consider the following questions while reading *Virgin*. How does the community financially support itself? Does it offer hospitality to outsiders? Who represents it publicly? Who is responsible for cooking and cleaning? How often do they assemble to pray, at what times and where? . . . and so on.

10 Sinkewicz (2003): 117–19. One might go further: Elm advances an open-ended definition of 'regula', then argues against hypothetical objections to applying that definition to *Virgin*. But this is tantamount to making an assertion then saying, 'Well, why not, after all?' – which hardly makes for a compelling argument.

11 This is assumed by Elm (1991): 102.

12 Elm (1991): 110–14.

13 Driscoll (1996): 255–56.

14 Mrs Williams is currently engaged in writing a doctoral thesis on *Virgin* in the University of Glasgow, Department of History and I am grateful to her for having shared some of her findings with me. Her insights have influenced my thinking about the work.

15 Muyldermans (1938): 208–14; Bunge (1986): 32.

16 See Bunge (1986): 32–35.

17 In the ancient Greek world, the day begins at dawn and the second hour is therefore two hours after dawn.

18 This chapter is missing from Wilmart (1911) – henceforth, 'W'.

19 W gives 'seculars'.

20 W adds: 'She who constantly takes care for her work will find a great reward; but she who ignores it will be ignored.'

21 Cf. *Prayer* 110.

22 The image Evagrius uses here is of a bow being unstrung and thus losing the tension that makes it useful.

23 W specifies 'their heretical teachings'.

24 I translate the material in angular brackets from the Latin (with an eye to the Syriac). The Greek only preserves the shorter recension, but the Latin and Syriac versions witness to the longer recension. As noted in the introduction, a strong case has been made for accepting the longer recension as authentic.

25 W has 'to adore the *homousion*, that is, consubstantial, Trinity'.

EXCERPTS

1 Chadwick (1959): 162

2 See Conybeare (1910): 131–37.

3 Chadwick (1959): 118, following Bardenhewer.

4 Jerome's shifting views are traced in Chadwick (1959): 117–37.

5 See Funk (1976), Hausherr (1933).

6 cf. *Praktikos* 5.

7 cf. *Praktikos* 15.

8 cf. *KG* 3.35.

9 cf. *De octo vitiis*, 'De ira' (PG 79: 1453).

10 cf. *Praktikos* 22; this version is terser and so its use of the verbs *agrainô* and *eraô* (where the critical edition has *ektarassô* (to be stirred up) and *epithumeô* (to desire)) is all the more striking.

11 cf. *Praktikos* 54 (PG 40: 1245); NB: *Praktikos* survives in two redactions; for the second redaction, the reader should consult the text reprinted by Migne.

12 cf. *Praktikos²* 55 (PG 40: 1248).

13 cf. *Praktikos²* 56 (PG 40: 1248).

14 cf. *Praktikos* 67.

15 cf. *Praktikos* 28; for further discussion of the monk's cell and its importance, see *Causes* 6.

16 cf. *Praktikos* 36.

17 cf. *Praktikos* 45.

18 cf. *Thoughts* 34.

19 cf. *Praktikos*[2] 59 (PG 40: 1248).

20 cf. *Praktikos*[2] 44 (PG 40: 1244–45).

21 This appears to be a composite of *Mal cog* (PG 79: 1232 §27) and *Praktikos*[2] 47 (PG 40: 1245).

22 cf. *Praktikos* 50.

23 cf. *Praktikos* 51.

24 cf. *Praktikos* 40 (= PG 40: 1244); there, the verb is *apokôliousin* (lit., 'they will not be disposed'), but here it is *ouk eôsin* (lit., 'they would not be').

25 cf. *Praktikos* 61.

26 cf. *Praktikos* 62.

27 cf. *Praktikos* 71.

28 cf. *Praktikos* 80.

29 cf. *Gnostikos* 8; for Evagrius' views on entering into legal action, see also *Letters* 33 and 60.3.

30 cf. *KG* 1.36; *Definitions* 4–6.

31 cf. *KG* 1.42.

32 For 'conversation with God', see *Prayer* 3.

33 *Evlogius* 21 (PG 79: 1121A).

34 *Monks* 13.

35 *Evlogius* 21 (PG 79: 1121B).

36 *Evlogius* 21 (PG 79: 1121B).

37 cf. *Monks* 10.

38 cf. *Thoughts* 3.

39 cf. *Thoughts* 15.

40 cf. *Thoughts* 18.

41 cf. *Praktikos*[1] 66 (PG 40: 1240); for another account of the demons acting against those who are reading, see *Thoughts* 33 and the supporting description of demons at *KG* 4.25.

42 cf. *Causes* 8, where the comparison is to a jar of wine.

43 Evagrius may have earned his own livelihood by working as a scribe, but he was clearly aware of the realities of agricultural work in the desert communities.

44 cf. *Inst mon* (PG 79: 1237B).

45 cf. *Cap paraen* 1 (PG 79: 1249).

46 cf. *Cap paraen* 17 (PG 79: 1252), where it is wine – not bread – that is said to strengthen the body.

47 cf. *Ad mon* 37, where thoughts are said to trouble the heart.

48 cf. *Spir mal* 13 (PG 79: 1157).

49 cf. *Spir mal* 13 (PG 79: 1157).

50 cf. *Inst mon* (PG 79: 1236).

51 cf. *Praktikos* 24.

52 cf. Sextus, *Sentences* 210a.

53 = Sextus, *Sentences* 240, Clitarchus' variant.

54 cf. Sextus, *Sentences* 262.

55 cf. Sextus, *Sentences* 272.

56 cf. Sextus, *Sentences* 333.

57 = Sextus, *Sentences* 335.
58 The first sentence is a quotation from *KG* 1.15; the following gloss may well be a later addition.
59 Evagrius' positive evaluation of ignorance (*agnoia*) has been well treated by Hausherr (1936) and (1959).

APHORISMS

1 *CPG* 2442, 2443.

DEFINITIONS

1 *DP* 250.10–11.
2 *DP* 250.12–13.
3 *DP* 250.14–15 (= Syriac *ps-Supplements to KG* 3 (Frankenberg (1912): 427)).
4 *DP* 250.20–21 (= *KG* 1.36); another version of this definition is found at *Excerpts* 29.
5 *DP* 250.22–23 (= *KG* 1.36).
6 *DP* 250.24–25 (= *KG* 1.36).
7 *DP* 254.11–12.
8 *DP* 257.21–22; cf. Cassian, *Conference* 9.12.1.
9 *DP* 257.23.
10 *DP* 258.10–11.
11 *DP* 261.22–23 (=*Praktikos* 15).
12 *DP* 263.10–11.

ON PRAYER

1 Hausherr (1939).
2 Hausherr (1934): 44 has suggested that Evagrius' use of the word *makariôs* ('blessedly') is a punning reference to the name of his teacher, Makarios the Egyptian.
3 The mention of Jacob's 'distinctive' or 'marked' part is probably another pun, in this case referring to Jacob's dealings with Laban, his father-in-law, for a share of the livestock; see Gen 30.27–43.
4 Cf. *Life of Anthony* 73.1–3.
5 The word translated here as 'the universe's orderly arrangement' (*diakosmêsis*) is familiar from Pythagorean usage; cf. Zaleucus the Pythagorean in Diodorus Siculus, *Historical library* 12.20.1–2 and more generally Aristotle, *Metaphysics* 1.5.1–5 (985b–986a).
6 The modern reader may take comfort in knowing that, judging from the numerous textual variants, this account of numbers was also confusing to the ancients (see Muyldermans (1952): 41–42). Some explanation is in order.

Modern commentators (Hausherr (1960), Tugwell (1981), Sinkewicz (2003) and especially Muyldermans (1952): 39–46) unanimously agree that guidance is best sought from the *Introduction to mathematics* by Nicomachus of Gerasa (fl. *c.* AD 100–150; trans. D'Ooge (1952)), to which the reader is referred for the theoretical underpinning of what follows. A triangular number is one obtained by counting consecutive numbers from one $(1 + 2 + 3 \ldots;$ *Introduction* 2.8); a square number, by counting alternate numbers from one $(1 + 3 + 5 \ldots;$ *Introduction* 2.9); a hexagonal number, by counting every fourth number from one, then adding the two resulting numbers $(1 + 6 + 15 \ldots;$ *Introduction* 2.11 – Muyldermans (1952): 45 formulates this helpfully as $2n^2 - n$, where n = the ordinal number of the hexagonal sought; thus, the ninth hexagonal number is $2(9)^2 - 9 = 153$); a spherical number is one which, when raised to any power, can always be found at the end of the product $(5^2 = 25; 25^3 = 15,625; 625^4 = 152,587,890,625 \ldots;$ *Introduction* 2.17.7).

Thus, 153 is hexagonal because $1 + 5 + \ldots 29 + 33 = 153$, and triangular because $1 + 2 + \ldots + 16 + 17 = 153$; 100 is square because $1 + 2 + \ldots + 17 + 19 = 100$; 28 is triangular because $1 + 2 + \ldots + 6 + 7 = 28$; 25 is spherical because $5^2 = 25$ (as Evagrius states), but also because $25^2 = 625$.

7 Evagrius is putting himself in the role of the sick person.

8 I have used two words for *katorthôsis*: 'setting aright' and 'accomplishing'. The former sense is important because Evagrius would be misunderstood if he were thought to advance here a kind of magical formula for getting one's desires.

9 Several translators have resorted to circumlocutions for the final word (*philosophei* – literally, 'you will philosophise') – e.g., Sinkewicz (2003): 194, 'practice love of wisdom'; Bamberger (1970): 58, 'playing the part of a wise man' – but this blunts the directness of an assertion that is parallel in form to *Prayer* 61. In much the same way that *Prayer* 61 prompts us to rethink what being a theologian means for Evagrius, *Prayer* 18 should prompt us to rethink what being a philosopher means for him.

10 The futility of carrying water in a jug full of holes is well attested in antiquity (see Liddell and Scott (1968): *s.v.*, *pithos* I.2), but Hausherr is right to point out that Evagrius' source as likely as not was Arsenius (*Apoph* Arsenius 33; see Hausherr (1960): 37).

11 On the 'material' of wicked thoughts, cf. *Thoughts* 36.

12 For an amusing account of a secular who rebuked some monks who were relaxing, and the sharp retort by their leader, see *Apoph* Anthony 13 (PG 65.77–80).

13 Evagrius dilates on this theme in *Letter* 42. Hausherr (1960): 50 has noted that this teaching may reflect Evagrius' knowledge of the *Life of St Pachomius* (cf. *Vita prima* n. 45), which is not implausible in the light of the reference to Tabennisi at *Prayer* 108.

14 Cf. *Prayer* 89.

15 This translation is based on the majority of the texts, the *Philokalia* being the only exception. Despite my preference for the *Philokalia*, I adopted the other reading on the principle of *lectio difficilior*: since the majority reading (*mê hôs en dunamei komizomenos* ...) is less clear than the reading in the *Philokalia* (*mê odunô mê komizomenos* ..., meaning, 'Do not be distressed if you

do not quickly receive from God the request that you make'), it is more likely that it is the original and the *Philokalia* text is quite probably an editorial correction. The meaning of the text as translated here is that one ought not to make a request of God as though the request would be granted owing to one's own power. One should instead make requests persistently and humbly.

16 This chapter does not appear in some versions (e.g., Migne's) and in other versions it is attached to §34 – which obviously affects the numbering of the chapters for those versions. We, however, follow the text (and also chapter numbers) of the *Philokalia*'s version.

17 Evagrius did not portray this ascent as a matter of rising into the sky, along the lines of Christ's ascension (Acts 1.9); instead, as Hausherr (1960): 53–54 suggests on the comparison with *KG* 4.49, 5.40, 5.60 and *Letters* 39 and 58, it should be visualised as climbing a mountain – either Mt Zion, or Mt Sinai.

18 Not all humans are one's kinsmen in this specialised sense (cf. *Letter* 53). This use of 'kinsmen' (*homophyloi*) is found in other authors, but the most striking anticipation of Evagrius' teaching is found in Gregory of Nyssa, *Life of Moses*, esp. at 2.15, 2.310.1–311.4. That a major function of the angels is to mediate salvation to other creatures is clear e.g., from *KG* 3.65, 5.7, 6.90.

19 According to Evagrius' *Letter* 25, prayer presents an exceptional opportunity to judge one's spiritual status.

20 Evagrius perhaps developed this from a lesson that he learnt from Macarius: 'A monk is called a monk for this reason: he converses with God night and day and imagines nothing but the things of God, possessing nothing on the earth' (see Hausherr (1960): 64; I regret that I have been unable to coordinate Hausherr's reference to the 1861 Constantinople edition of the *Evergetinos*, which is unavailable to me, to the 1993 Athens edition). He also compared the 'monk-mind' implicit in this chapter to Evagrius' distinction between the 'monk-man' and 'monk-mind' in the prologue to *Antirrhetikos* (on which, see also Bunge (1997)).

21 On the face, cf. *Thoughts* 37.

22 See also *Thoughts* 41.

23 As Hausherr (1960): 85 has observed, this chapter summarises the message that Evagrius relates in his *Great letter*.

24 Evagrius asserts that God knows the heart directly, whereas the demons only infer the heart's contents by close observation of bodily movements: *Thoughts* 37.

25 Evagrius' emphasis on refusing to form an image of God flows from his insistence that God has no body and therefore makes no mental impression himself: *Thoughts* 41. His memorable instruction, 'go immaterial to the Immaterial', is comparable to Plotinus' dictum about going 'alone to the Alone': *Enneads* 5.1.16, 6.9.11.

26 Because Evagrius warmly endorses recognising the 'place of God' in oneself while praying (e.g., *Thoughts* 39–40), his warning against putting the divine in a place is a call for probity in evaluating one's spiritual experience.

The obvious difference between what he encourages in *Thoughts* and discourages here is that he does not want the person praying to limit God. After all, God is everywhere, rather than anywhere (*KG* 1.43). For his assertation that God has neither quantity nor shape, see *KG* 1.1.

27 For the first sentence of §71, MS Paris BN gr. 873 reads: 'You will not be able to pray purely while being entangled with material things and disciplined by continuous cares, namely, distractions and circumstances.'

28 Cf. *Thoughts* 42: 'The demonic thoughts blind the soul's left eye, which is directed toward contemplation of created things; but those representations that imprint on and shape our governing faculty darken the right eye ....' Hausherr (1960): 104 comments that the 'glory' here described should be understood as an apparition or hallucination.

29 Note that the precise description of this exceptional man varies in the manuscripts: in three, he is *gnôstikos*; in one, he is *thaumastos kai gnôstikos*; and in another, *praktikotatos*. Evagrius uses both as terms of praise (cf. *Praktikos* 29, 98), so in default of any clear means of deciding which he intended here, I have opted to translate both. Hausherr (1960): 106 has reasonably proposed that the man in question may be John of Lykopolis, whom Evagrius often cites for information of this sort – e.g., *Antirrhetikos* 2.36, 5.6, 6.16 and 7.19.

30 According to *KG* 2.47, such knowledge is specifically knowledge of the Holy Trinity; see Viller (1930): 248 n. 140. The word translated as 'limiting' is *topasmon*, literally, 'placing' or 'locating'.

31 In Migne and several manuscripts, the second sentence constitutes a new chapter.

32 Cf. *KG* 3.20: 'the measure of your status'.

33 In Migne, this clause reads, 'we even despise *their* service'; the word translated 'service' here and 'liturgy' in the text is *leitourgia*, which can mean service in the sense of either public service or of worship service.

34 Cf. Evagrius, *Thirty-three sentences*, 33: ' "Young eagles" are the holy powers charged with casting down the impure ones.' Hausherr (1960): 115 has remarked that, in the light of that passage, Evagrius' claim about being 'like the young eagles' here is a foreshadowing of his claim that true prayer makes a person 'equal to the angels' (*Prayer* 113).

35 Cf. *Prayer* 32.

36 Cf. *Life of Anthony* 51.5–52.3.

37 Cf. *Life of Anthony* 53.

38 On thoughts as dogs, see *Thoughts* 5 and the note ad loc.

39 On John the Little, see Mikhail and Vivian (1997).

40 Abba Theodore made the 'vaulted chamber' by enclosing the vipers between his feet. Another version of the story is related in the *Letter of Amon* 19 and the question of how Evagrius' account relates to it, together with the modern scholarship on this point, is thoroughly discussed by Goehring (1986): 255–57.

41 In his notes ad loc., Hausherr (1960) follows L.-Th. Lefort, *Les Vies coptes de saint Pachôme et de ses premiers successeurs* (Louvain 1943) – a work I have

not been able to consult – in finding another parallel to the Pachomian literature; in this case, it is to SBo99, wherein we read that Paul continued his prayers after being bitten by a scorpion. (See further Goehring (1986): 255–57.) But as Bamberger (1970) has subsequently pointed out in his notes ad loc., a far closer parallel is to be found in Talmud *Berakoth* 33a (Epstein (1935–52): Zeraʿim 203): 'Even if a snake is wound round his foot he should not break off [sc., his prayers].' One can be pardoned for imagining Evagrius may have found something of a kindred spirit in R. Hanina b. Dosa, who was bitten by a *yarod* ('apparently a cross-breed of a snake and a lizard': Epstein (1935–52): Kodashim 204 n. 2) – which promptly died.

42 Cf. *Virgin* 33.

43 The monk was caught in a *psiathion*; the precise meaning is unclear, but in a nearly contemporary papyrus, the word is used to describe something that coals could be carried in: see Liddell and Scott (1968), s.v. *psiathion*.

44 Elsewhere, Evagrius identifies Christ as the 'face of the Father' (see *in Ps* 16.2α´, 23.6γ´, 29.8ζ´, 68.29ιζ´, 79.8δ´), from which we may deduce that the monk wishes to see Christ. As regards becoming 'equal to the angels' (*isangelos*), Evagrius' immediate precedents for taking the Lord's saying seriously are found in Clement, Origen and Gregory of Nyssa. See, e.g., Clement, *Paedegogus* 1.6.36.6; *Stromateis* 6.13.105.1.2, 7.10.57.5, 7.12.78.6, 7.14.84.2; Origen, *Against Celsus* 4.29, *Commentary on John* 2.22.140, 13.16.99.5; and Gregory of Nyssa, *Making of Man* 17, 18, *Creation of Man* 1. It is worth noting Gregory's gloss on 'the one equal to the angels' as 'the one equal *in honour* to the angels' at *Making of Man* 17. What is clear from Evagrius' teaching is that a monk can emulate the function of angels; what is not altogether clear is whether this means that a human can *become* an angel.

45 The manuscripts differ concerning this word. Most of the manuscripts previously studied read *neôterois* – 'to the rather young' or 'novices'; but BN Coislin 109 reads *en eterois* – or 'elsewhere'. See the discussion by Hausherr (1960): 151–52.

46 Cf. *Praktikos* 57.

47 The *Philokalia* specifies 'from the flesh'.

48 The practice of refuting the demons is what Evagrius aims to encourage with his *Antirrhetikos*.

49 Cf. *Monks* 35: 'Anger scatters knowledge, // but patience gathers it.'

50 Cf. *Praktikos* 5.

51 Evagrius also compares the demons to fullers at *Monks* 55 and 60.

52 Cf. *Praktikos* 33, *Causes* 9.

53 Cf. *Letter* 58.3.

54 Cf. *Skemmata* 6: 'The incense-altar is the pure mind that, at the time of prayer, offers nothing perceptible.'

SELECT
BIBLIOGRAPHY

EVAGRIUS' WRITINGS (TEXTS)

Corderius, B. 1628. *Catena sexaginta quinque graecorum patrum in S. Lucam, quae quatuor simul Evangelistarum introducit explicationem; luce ac latinitate donata, et ex alijs patribus tam Graecis quam Latinis suppleta et annotationibus illustrata, a Balthasare Corderio* (Antwerp: Plantiniana)

Diekamp, F. 1907. *Doctrina patrum de incarnatione verbi: ein griechisches Florilegium aus der Wende des 7. und 8. Jahrhunderts* (Münster-i-W.: Aschendorff)

Frankenberg, W. 1912. *Euagrius Ponticus* (Berlin: Weidmann)

Géhin, Paul. 1993. *Évagre le Pontique: Scholies à l'Ecclésiaste*, SC 397

——. 1994. 'Nouveaux fragments grecs des lettres d'Évagre', *Revue d'Histoire des Textes* 24: 117–47

—— et al. 1998. *Évagre le Pontique: Sur les Pensées*, SC 438

Greßman, Hugo. 1913. *Nonnenspiegel und Mönchsspiegel des Euagrios Pontikos*, TU 39.4 (Leipzig: Hinrichs)

Gribomont, Jean. 1983. (ps-)Basil, 'Epistula 8', in ed. M. Forlin-Patrucco, *Basilio di Cesarea, Le Lettere* (Torino: Società Editrice Internazionale) 1: 84–112

Guillaumont, Antoine. 1958. *Les six centuries des 'Kephalaia Gnostica'*, PO 28.1 (Paris: Firmin-Didot)

—— and Claire Guillaumont. 1989. *Évagre le Pontique: Le Gnostique*, SC 356

Guillaumont, Claire. 1987. 'Fragments grecs inédits d'Évagre le Pontique', in ed. J. Dummer, *Texte und Textkritik*, TU 133 (Berlin: Akademie-Verlag): 209–21

Hagedorn, Ursula and Dieter. 1994–2004. *Die älteren griechischen Katenen zum buch Hiob*, PTS 40, 48, 53, 59

Hausherr, I. 1933. *De doctrina spirituali Christianorum orientalium. Quaestiones et scripta I*, Orientalia Christiana 30.3 (Rome: PIOS)

——. 1939. 'Nouveaux fragments grecs d'Évagre le Pontique', *OCP* 5: 229–33

Iunius, Patricius. 1637. *Catena Graecorum patrum in beatum Iob* (London: Ex typographio regio)

de Lagarde, P. 1886. *Catenae in Euangelia Aegypticae* (Göttingen: Hoyer)

Mai, Angelo. 1825–38. *Scriptorum veterum nova collectio* (Rome: Burliaeum)

Muyldermans, J. 1931. 'Evagriana', *Mus* 44: 37–68; 369–83

——. 1932. *A travers la tradition manuscrite d'Évagre le Pontique*. *Essai sur les manuscrits grecs conserves à la Bibliothèque Nationale de Paris* (Bureaux du Muséon: Louvain)

——. 1952. *Evagriana Syriaca* (Louvain: Publications universitaires)

Quecke, Hans. 1989. 'Auszüge aus Evagrius' Mönchsspiegel in koptischer Übersetzung', *OCP* 58: 453–63

Rondeau, M.-J. 1960. 'Le commentaire sur les Psaumes d'Évagre le Pontique', *OCP* 26: 307–48.

Sargisean, B. 1907. *Vark`ew matenagrut`iwnk`: t`argmanealk`i hune i hay barbar i hingerord daru* (Venice: S. Ghazar)

Schenke, H.-M. 1984. 'Ein koptischer Evagrius', in ed. P. Nagel, *Graeco-Coptica: Griechen und Kopten im byzantinischen Agypten* (Martin-Luther-Universität: Halle): 219–34

Tugwell, S. 1981. *Evagrius Ponticus. De oratione* (Oxford: privately printed)

Vitestam, Gösta. 1964. *Seconde partie du traité qui passe sous le nom de 'La grande lettre d'Evagre le Pontique à Mélanie l'Ancienne', publiée et traduite d'après le manuscrit du British Museum Add. 17192* (Lund: Glerrup)

Wilmart, André. 1911. 'Les versions latines des sentences d'Évagre pour les vierges', *Revue Bénédictine* 28: 143–53

EVAGRIUS' WRITINGS
(MODERN TRANSLATIONS)

Bamberger, J.E. 1970. *The Praktikos. Chapters on Prayer* (Spencer, MA: Cistercian Publications)

Bettiolo, P. 1996. *Evagrio Pontico. Per conoscere lui* (Magnano: Qiqajon-Monastero di Bosè)

Bunge, G. 1986. *Evagrios Pontikos. Briefe aus der Wüste* (Trier: Paulinus-Verlag)

—— and S. di Meglio. 1995. *Lettere dal deserto* (Magnano: Qiqajon-Monastero di Bosè)

Deferrari, R.J. 1926. *Collected Letters of St Basil*, LCL (London: Heinemann): 1: 47–93 (ps.-Basil, *Letter* 8 (= Evagrius' *On the faith*))

Hausherr, I. 1960. *Les leçons d'un contemplatif* (Paris: Beauchesne)

Parmentier, M. 1985. 'Evagrius of Pontus' "Letter to Melania"', *Bijdragen, tijdscrift voor filosofie en theologie* 46: 2–38; reprinted in ed. E. Fergusson, *Forms of Devotion* (New York: Garland, 1999)

Sinkewicz, R. 2003. *Evagrius of Pontus. The Greek Ascetic Corpus* (Oxford: OUP)

Tugwell, S. 1981. *Evagrius Ponticus: Praktikos & On Prayer; Dionysius the Areopagite: Mystical Theology* (Oxford: Faculty of Theology)

OTHER PRIMARY SOURCES

Apophthegmata Patrum, alphabetical collection: PG 65: 71–440

Aristotle. *Soul*: ed. D. Ross. 1961. *De anima. Aristotle* (Oxford: Clarendon Press)

——. *Metaphysics*: ed. D. Ross. 1924. *Metaphysics. Aristotle* (Oxford: Clarendon Press)

Athanasius. *Life of Anthony*: ed. G.J.M. Bartelink. 1994. *Vie d'Antoine. Athanase d'Alexandre*, SC 400

Babylonian Talmud: ed. I. Epstein. 1935–52. *The Babylonian Talmud* (London: Soncino Press)

Basil. *Holy Spirit*: ed. B. Pruche. 1946. *Traité du Saint-Esprit*, SC 17

Book of Hierotheos: ed. F.S. Marsh. 1927. *The Book which is called the Book of the Holy Hierotheos with extracts from the Prolegomena and Commentary of Theodosios of Antioch and from the 'Book of Excerpts' and other works of Gregory Bar-Hebraeus* (London: Williams & Norgate)

Cassian. *Conferences*: ed. E. Pichery. 1955–59. *Conférences. Jean Cassien*, SC 42, 54, 64

Clement of Alexandria. *Paedegogus* and *Protrepticus*: ed. G. Stählin. 1936. *Clemens Alexandrinus, 1. band: Protrepticus und Paedagogus*, GCS

——. *Stromateis*: ed. G. Stählin. 1960–70. *Clemens Alexandrinus, 2. und 3. bände: Stromata*, GCS

Cyril of Scythopolis. *Lives of the Palestinian Monks*: ed. E. Schwartz. 1939. *Kyrillos von Skythopolis*, TU 49

Decrees of the Ecumenical Councils: ed. N. Tanner. 1990 (London: Sheed & Ward)

Didymus the Blind. *Scholia on Ecclesiastes*: ed. L. Koenen, G. Binder *et al.* 1969–83. *Kommentar zum Ecclesiastes (Tura-Papyrus)* (Bonn: Habelt)

Diodorus Siculus. *Historical Library*: ed. C.H. Oldfather *et al.* 1933–67. *Diodorus of Sicily*, LCL (London: Heinemann)

Doctrina patrum de incarnatione Verbi: ein griechisches Florilegium aus der Wende des 7. und 8. Jahrhunderts: ed. F. Diekamp, V. Phanourgakes and E. Chrysos. 1981. (Münster: Aschendorff).

Egeria. *Travels*: ed. V. du Bierzo. 1982. *Journal de voyage (Itinéraire). Egérie*, SC 296

Evagrius Scholasticus, *Church History*: eds J. Bidez and L. Parmentier. 1898. *The Ecclesiastical History of Evagrius, with the Scholia* (London: Methuen)

Gregory Nazianzen. *Orations*: eds J. Bernardi *et al.* 1978–. *Discours. Grégoire de Nazianze*, SC 247, 309, 405, 270, 284, 250, 318, 358, 384

Gregory Nyssen. *Creation of Man*: ed. H. Hörner. 1972. *Auctorum incertorum vulgo Basilii vel Gregorii Nysseni Sermones de creatione hominis; Sermo de paradiso*, Gregorii Nyssenis Opera, suppl. (Leiden: Brill)

——. *Life of Moses*: ed. J. Daniélou. 1955. *La vie de Moïse: ou, Traité de la perfection en matière de vertu. Grégoire de Nysse*, SC 1 bis

——. *Making of Man*: PG 44: 125–356

Historia Monachorum in Aegypto: ed. A.-J. Festugière. 1961. *Historia Monachorum in Aegypto: édition critique du texte grec* (Bruxelles: Société des Bollandistes)

(ps.-)Iamblichos. *Theology of Arithmetic*: ed. V. de Falco. 1922. *{Iamblichi} Theologoumena arithmeticae* (Leipzig: Teubner)

Jerome. *Letters*: ed. J. Labourt. 1949–63. *Lettres. Saint Jérôme* (Paris: Belles Lettres).

Menander. *Dyskolos*: ed. E.W. Handley. 1965. *The Dyskolos of Menander* (London: Methuen)

Nathan. *Aboth*: trans. A. Saldarini. 1975. *The Fathers According to Rabbi Nathan* (Leiden: Brill)

Nicomachus of Gesara. *Introduction to Arithmetic*: trans. M. D'Ooge. 1952. In *Great Books of the Western World*, vol. 11 (Chicago, IL: Encyclopedia Britannica): 811–48; reprinted from D'Ooge *et al*. 1926 (New York and London: Macmillan)

Nikodimos. *Philokalia*: trans. G.E.H. Palmer *et al*. 1979–. *The Philokalia: The Complete Text Compiled by St. Nikodimos of the Holy Mountain and St. Makarios of Corinth* (London: Faber & Faber)

Origen. *Hexapla*: ed. F. Field. 1875. *Origenis Hexaplarum quae supersunt* (Oxford: Clarendon)

——. *Principles*: eds H. Crouzel and M. Simonetti. 1974–89. *Traité des principes. Origène*, SC 252–53, 268–69, 312

Palladius. *Coptic Life of Evagrius*: ed. E. Amélineau. 1887. *De Historia Lausiaca* (Paris: Leroux): 92–104.

——. *Lausiac History*: ed. G.J.M. Bartelink. 1990. *Palladio. La Storia Lausiaca* (Milan: Mondadori)

——. *Lausiac History*, Latin: ed. A. Wellhausen. 2003. *Die lateinische Übersetzung der* Historia Lausiaca *des Palladius*, PTS 51

Philoxenus of Mabbug. *To Abraham and Orestes*: ed. A.L. Frothingham, Jr. 1886. *Stephen bar Sudaili the Syrian Mystic and the Book of Hierotheos* (Leiden: Brill): 28–48

Plotinus. *Enneads*: ed. A.H. Armstrong. 1966–88. Plotinus, LCL (London: Heinemann)

Plutarch. *Moralia*: ed. F.C. Babbitt *et al*. 1927–. *Moralia*, LCL (London: Heinemann)

Rufinus. *Historia Monachorum*, Latin: ed. E. Schulz-Flügel. 1990. *Historia monachorum, sive De vita sanctorum patrum*, PTS 34

Sextus. *Sentences*: ed. H. Chadwick. 1959. *Sentences of Sextus* (Cambridge: CUP)

Socrates. *Historia ecclesiastica*: PG 67: 33–841.

Sozomen. *Historia ecclesiastica*: PG 67: 843–1630.

Theophilus of Alexandria. *Letter written to Constantinople*: ed. M. Richard. 1975. 'Nouveaux fragments de Théophile d'Alexandrie', *Nachrichten der Akademie der Wissenschaften in Göttingen. I. Philologisch-historische Klasse*. Jahrgang 1975, Nr. 2: 57–65 (reprinted in his *Opera Minora*, II (Turnhout: Brepols, 1977), item 39)

SECONDARY LITERATURE

Amaduzzi, G.C., ed. 1773. *Anecdota litteraria ex MSS codicibus eruta* (Rome: Fulgonio)

Amand de Mendieta, E. 1965. *The 'Unwritten' and 'Secret' Apostolic Traditions in the Theological Thought of St Basil of Caesarea* (Edinburgh: Oliver & Boyd)

Arnim, H. von. 1903–24. *Fragmenta Stoicorum Veterum* (Leipzig: Teubner)

Balthasar, H.U. von. 1939. 'Die Hiera des Evagrius', *Zeitschrift für Katholische Theologie* 63: 86–106; 181–206

——. 1965. 'The Metaphysics and Mystical Theology of Evagrius', *Monastic Studies* 3: 183–95 (an anonymous translation from the German: 'Metaphysik und Mystik des Evagrius Ponticus', *Zeitschrift für Aszese und Mystik* 14 (1939): 31–47)

Bettiolo, P., ed. 2000. *L'EPISTULA FIDEI di Evagrio Pontico: Temi, Contenti, Sviluppi* (Rome: Augustinianum)

Bousset, W. 1923. *Apophthegmata* (Tübingen: Mohr)

Brightman, F.E. 1896. *Liturgies Eastern and Western* (Oxford: Clarendon)

Bunge, G. 1983. 'Evagre et les deux Macaire', *Irénikon* 56: 215–27, 323–60

——. 1986. 'Origenismus-Gnostizismus. Zum geistesgeschichtlichen Standort des Evagrios Pontikos', *Vigiliae Christianae* 40: 24–54

——. 1987. *Das Geistgebet* (Cologne: Luthe-Verlag)

——. 1989. 'Hénade ou Monade? Au sujet de deux notions centrales de la terminologie évagrienne', *Mus* 102: 69–91.

——. 1995. *Akedia. Die geistliche Lehre des Evagrios Pontikos vom Überdruß*, 4th edn (Würzburg: Verlag 'Der Christliche Osten')

——. 1997. 'Evagrios Pontikos: Der Prolog des "Antirrhetikos"', *SM* 39: 77–105

——. 2000. 'La montaigne intelligible: De la contemplation indirecte à la connaissance immédiate de Dieu dans le traité De oratione d'Évagre le Pontique', *SM* 42:7–26

Butler, C. 1898–1904. *The Lausiac History of Palladius: A Critical Discussion Together with Notes on Early Egyptian Monachism* (Cambridge: CUP)

Casiday, A. 2001. '*Apatheia* and Sexuality in the Thought of Augustine and Cassian', *St Vladimir's Theological Quarterly* 45: 359–94

——. 2003. 'Deification in Origen, Evagrius and Cassian', in ed. L. Perrone, *Origeniana Octava* (Leuven: Peeters): 995–1001

——. 2004. 'Gabriel Bunge and the Study of Evagrius Ponticus: Review Article', *St Vladimir's Theological Quarterly* 48: 249–97

——. 2004b. 'Christ, the Icon of the Father, in Evagrian Theology', in eds M. Bielawski and D. Hombergen, *Il Monachesimo tra Eredità e Aperture*, SA 140: 31–60

——. 2005. 'Evagrius Ponticus' Use of Different Versions of Scripture (with Special Reference to his Scholia on Job)', *Adamantius* 11: 143–57

——. Forthcoming. 'Contemplating the Faceless Icon: An Exercise in Evagrian Psychology.' To appear in ed. A. Casiday, *Re-thinking Evagrius Ponticus* (Crestwood, NY: SVS Press)

Clark, E. 1992. *The Origenist Controversy* (Princeton, NJ: Princeton University Press)

Conybeare, F.C. 1910. *The Ring of Pope Sixtus* (London: Williams & Norgate)

Cross, F.L. and E.A. Livingstone, eds. 1997. *The Oxford Dictionary of the Christian Church*, 3rd edn (Oxford: OUP)

Daley, Brian. 1995. 'What did "Origenism" mean in the Sixth Century?', in eds Gilles Dorival and Alain le Boulleuc, *Origeniana Sexta* (Leuven: Peeters): 627–38

Darling Young, R. 2001. 'Evagrius the Iconographer: Monastic Pedagogy in the Gnostikos', *Journal of Early Christian Studies* 9: 53–71

Devreesse, R. 1928. 'Chaînes exégétiques grecques', *Supplément au Dictionnaire de la Bible* 1: 1145

———. 1954. *Introduction à l'étude des manuscrits grecs* (Paris: Imprimerie Nationale)

Diels, H., ed. 1951–52. *Fragmente der Vorsokratiker*, 6th edn (Berlin: Weidmann)

Driscoll, J. 1990. 'A Key for Reading the *Ad Monachos* of Evagrius Ponticus', *Augustinianum* 30: 361–92.

———. 1991. *The 'Ad Monachos' of Evagrius Ponticus*, SA 104

———. 1995. 'Exegetical Procedures in the Desert Monk Poemen', in eds M. Löhrer and E. Salmann, *Mysterium Christi: Symbolgegenwart und theologische Bedeutung: Festschrift für Basil Studer*, SA 116: 155–78

———. 1996. 'Spousal Images in Evagrius Ponticus', *SM* 38: 243–56

———. 1997. 'Evagrius and Paphnutius on Causes for Abandonment by God', *SM* 39: 259–86

———. 2000. 'The Fathers of Poemen and the Evagrian Connection', *SM* 42: 27–51

Elliot, J.K. 1996. *The Apocryphal Jesus: Legends of the Early Church* (Oxford: OUP)

Elm, S. 1990. 'The *Sententiae ad Virginem* by Evagrius Ponticus and the Problem of Early Monastic Rules', *Augustinianum* 30: 393–404

———. 1991. 'Evagrius Ponticus' *Sententiae ad Virginem*', *Dumbarton Oaks Papers* 45: 97–120

Evelyn White, H.G. 1932. *The Monasteries of the Wâdi 'n Natrûn, Part II: The History of the Monasteries of Nitria and of Scetis* (New York: The Metropolitan Museum of Art)

Fabricius, J.A. and G. C. Harles. 1780–1809. *Bibliotheca graeca* (Hamburg: C.E. Bohn)

Florovsky, Georges. 1972. *Bible, Church, Tradition: An Eastern Orthodox View*, Collected Works, vol. 1 (Belmont, MA: Nordland)

Funk, W.-P. 1976. 'Ein doppelt überliefertes Stück spätägyptischer Weisheit', Zeitschrift für Ägyptische Sprache und Altertumskunde 103: 8–21

Geerard, M. 1974–98. *Corpus Christanorum Clavis Patrum Graecorum* (Turnhout: Brepols)

Géhin, P. 2004. 'Les développements récents de la recherche évagrienne', *OCP* 70: 103–25

Gendle, N. 1985. 'Cappadocian Elements in the Mystical Theology of Evagrius Ponticus', *SP* 16: 373–84

Goehring, J. 1986. *The Letter of Ammon and Pachomian Monasticism*, PTS 27

Gould, G. 1989. 'Moving on and staying put in the Apophthegmata Patrum', *SP* 20: 231–37

Guillaumont, A. 1961. 'Évagre et les anathématismes anti-origénistes de 553', *SP* 3 (= TU 78): 219–26

———. 1962. *Les Képhalaia Gnostica d'Évagre le Pontique et l'histoire de l'Origenisme chez les Grecs et chez les Syriens* (Paris: Éditions du Seuil)

———. 1984. 'La vision de l'intellect par lui-même', *Mélanges de l'Université Saint-Joseph* 50: 255–62; reprinted in his *Études sur la spiritualité de l'orient chrétien* (Bégrolles-en-Mauges: Abbaye de Bellefontaine, 1996): 143–50

——. 1985. 'Le rôle des versions orientales dans la récupération de l'oeuvre d'Évagre le Pontique', *Comptes Rendus des Séances de l'Académie des Inscriptions et Belles Lettres*, 1985: 64–74

——. 2004. *Un philosophe au désert: Évagre le Pontique* (Paris: Vrin)

Hadot, Pierre. 1995. *Philosophy as a Way of Life*, trans. M. Chase (London: Blackwell)

Hanson, R.P.C. 1954. *Origen's Doctrine of Tradition* (London: SPCK)

Harmless, W. 2004. *Desert Christians* (New York: OUP)

—— and R. Fitzgerald. 2001. 'The Sapphire Light of the Mind: The *Skemmata* of Evagrius Ponticus', *Theological Studies* 62: 498–529

Hausherr, I. 1933. 'Un écrit stoïcien sous le nom de Saint Antoine', in *De doctrina spirituali Christianorum Orientalium, OCA* 30 (Rome: PIOS)

——. 1934. 'La traité de l'oraison d'Evagre le Pontique (pseudo-Nil)', *Revue d'ascétique et de mystique* 15: 34–93, 113–70

——. 1936. 'Ignorance infinite', *OCP* 2: 351–62

——. 1939. 'Le *De Oratione* d'Évagre le Pontique en Syriaque et en Arabe'. *OCP* 5: 7–71

——. 1946. 'Le Métérikon de l'abbé Isaïe', *OCP* 12: 286–301

——. 1959. 'Ignorance infinie ou science infinie?', *OCP* 25: 44–52

Hombergen, D. 2001. *The Second Origenist Controversy*, SA 132

——. Forthcoming. 'Sixth-century Gazan Monasticism and Evagrian Origenism. What Happened with Evagrius in the Monastic Environment of Barsanuphius, John and Dorotheus of Gaza?' To appear in ed. A. Casiday, *Re-thinking Evagrius Ponticus* (Crestwood, NY: SVS Press)

Hunt, E.D. 1972. 'St Silvia of Aquitaine. The Role of a Theodosian Pilgrim in the Society of East and West', *Journal of Theological Studies* NS 23: 351–73

——. 1982. Holy Land Pilgrimage in the Later Roman Empire, AD 312–460 (Oxford: Clarendon)

von Ivánka, E. 1954. 'KEPHALAIA: eine byzantinische Literaturform und ihre antiken Wurzeln', *Byzantinische Zeitschrift* 47: 285–91.

Kaster, R. 1999. 'Education', in eds G.W. Bowersock *et al.*, *Late Antiquity: A Guide to the Post-Classical World* (Harvard: Belknap Press): 421–23

Kirchmeyer, J. 1958. 'Pseudo-Athanasiana', *OCP* 24: 383–84

Lackner, W. 1966. 'Zum profanen Bildung des Euagrios Pontikos', in *Hans Gerstinger. Festgabe zum 80. Geburtstag* (Graz: Akademische Druck- und Verlagsanstalt)

Leclercq, H. 1907–53. 'Ibora', in *Dictionnaire d'archéologie chrétienne et de liturgie* (Paris: Letouzy et Ané), 7: 4–9

Liddell, H.G. and R. Scott. 1968. *A Greek–English Lexicon* (Oxford: Clarendon)

Louth, A. 1981. *The Origins of the Christian Mystical Tradition* (Oxford: Clarendon)

——. 1996. *Maximus the Confessor* (London: Routledge)

——. 1998. *Wisdom of the Byzantine Church: Evagrios of Pontos and Maximos the Confessor* (Columbia, MO: Department of Religious Studies)

——. 2002. 'Evagrios on Prayer', in ed. James Hogg, *'Standing up to Godwards': Essays in Mystical and Monastic Theology in Honour of the Reverend John Clark on his Sixty-fifth Birthday*, Analecta Cartusiana 204 (Salzburg: Institut für Anglistik und Amerikanistik): 163–72

——. 2003. 'The Collectio Sabbaitica and Sixth Century Origenism', in ed. L. Perrone, *Origeniana Octava* (Leuven: Peeters): 1167–76

McGuckin, J. 1986. 'The Changing Forms of Jesus according to Origen', *Origeniana Quinta* (Innsbruck: Tyrolia Verlag): 215–22

——. 2001. *St Gregory of Nazianzus: An Intellectual Biography* (Crestwood, NY: SVS Press)

Marsili, S. 1936. *Giovanni Cassiano ed Evagrio Pontico*, SA 5

Mercati, Giovanni. 1914. 'Intorno ad uno scolio creduto di Evagrio', *Revue Biblique* NS 11: 534–42

Mikhail, M.S. and Tim Vivian. 1997. 'Life of Saint John the Little', *CCR* 18: 1–64

Miquel, P. 1986. *Lexique du désert: étude de quelques mots-clés du vocabulaire monastique grec ancien* (Bégrolles-en-Mauges: Abbaye de Bellefontaine)

Moine, N. 'Mélanie l'Ancienne', in *Dictionnaire de Spiritualité* 10: 955–60

Muyldermans, J. 1938. 'Evagriana. Le Vatic. Barb. Graec. 515', *Mus* 51: 191–226

——. 1940. 'Fragment arménien du *Ad virgines* d'Évagre', *Mus* 53: 77–87

——. 1963. 'Euagriana coptica', *Mus* 76: 271–76

O'Laughlin, M. 1997. 'Evagrius Ponticus in Spiritual Perspective', *SP* 30: 224–30

Perler, O. 1950. 'Arkandisziplin', *Reallexikon für Antike und Christentum* 1: 667–76

Pieper, Josef. 1957. *The Silence of St Thomas* (London: Faber & Faber)

Refoulé, F. 1961. 'La christologie d'Évagre et l'Origénisme', *OCP* 27: 221–66

——. 1967. 'Evagrius Ponticus', in *New Catholic Encyclopedia* (Washington, DC): 5: 644–45

Regnault, L. 1999. *The Day-to-Day Life of the Desert Fathers in Fourth-century Egypt*, trans. É. Poirier Jr (Petersham, MA: St Bede's Publications)

Rondeau, M.-J. 1960. 'Le commentaire sur les Psaumes d'Évagre le Pontique', *OCP* 26: 307–48

Rousseau, P. 1994. *Basil of Caesarea* (Berkeley, CA: University of California Press)

Rubenson, S. 1995. *The Letters of St Antony: Monasticism and the Making of a Saint* (Minneapolis, MN: Fortress Press)

Samir, Khalil. 1992. 'Évagre le Pontique dans la tradition arabo-copte', in *Actes du IVe Congrès Copte*, Publications de l'Institut Orientaliste de Louvain 41 (Louvain-la-Neuve: Institut Orientaliste de l'Université Catholique de Louvain): 2: 123–53

Sheridan, M. 1996. 'Review of Elizabeth A. Clark, *The Origenist Controversy*', *Collectanea Cisterciensia* 58: 38–42.

——. 2002. 'The Spiritual and Intellectual World of Early Egyptian Monasticism', *Coptica* 1: 1–51

Stern, Sacha. 2001. *Calendar and Community: A History of the Jewish Calendar, 2nd Century BCE–10th Century CE* (Oxford: OUP)

Viller, M. 1930. 'Aux Sources de la spiritualité de S. Maxime. Les oeuvres d'Évagre le Pontique', *Revue d'Ascétique et de Mystique* 11: 156–84; 239–68; 331–36

Viller, M. *et al.* eds. 1932–95. *Dictionnaire de spiritualité ascétique et mystique*, 17 vols (Paris: Beauchesne).

Vivian, T. 1997. 'Saint Paul of Tamma: Four Works Concerning Monastic Spirituality: "On Humility," "On Poverty," A Letter, and "An Untitled Work"', *CCR* 18: 105–16

——. 2004. *Four Desert Fathers: Pambo, Evagrius, Macarius of Egypt & Macarius of Alexandria* (Crestwood, NY: SUS Press)

Wright, William. 1871. *Catalogue of Syriac Manuscripts in the British Museum Acquired since the year 1838* (London: British Museum)

INDEX

angel 103, 142, 155, 198, 200;
definition of 47, 171; demons
disguised as 196; Devil as fallen
55; as intercessors and protectors
125, 139, 142, 176, 178, 189–90,
194, 196, 198, 235 n. 18, 236 n.
34; Jesus Christ, as less than 50–1;
Jesus Christ, as title for 54;
meditating upon 87; monks as
equal to 198, 237 n. 44; ranks of
145, 157; as sources of inspiration
94–5, 109–10
anger 62, 94, 97, 100, 101, 108,
109, 118, 141, 146, 147, 152,
170, 173, 174, 177, 178, 184,
189, 200, 217 n. 14, 237 n. 49
asceticism 13, 21–2, 27, 32, 35,
36–7, 50, 57, 83, 91, 109, 112,
115, 116, 127, 131, 137, 149,
156, 175, 187, 193, 218 n. 33
avarice 72, 91, 102–5, 116, 191

Balthasar, Hans Urs von 24, 25–7,
123, 153–4
Barsanuphius of Gaza 18–19
Basil the Great 3, 6–7, 23, 34–5,
45–6, 212 n. 29
body 109, 126, 140–1, 145, 174,
178–9, 195, 196; Christ's 134,
171, 182; demons acting upon
111, 175, 177, 193, 195; different
types of 57; God acts apart from
115, 193; meditating upon 87;
mental representations of 106–7,
127; needs of 84, 88, 112, 168,

197, 201; Origen's alleged
teaching on 14–15, 19; qualities
of 72–3; in relation to mind and
spirit 47, 52, 57, 67–75, 199; as
source of temptations 92–3
Book of Hierotheos 20, 29
Bunge, Gabriel 43–4, 59, 64, 151,
165–7

church 13, 131, 158, 169, 171
concept 90, 91, 92, 94, 100, 101,
102, 104, 105, 106, 114–16, 132,
139, 174, 177, 178, 188
concupiscence 101, 102, 108, 176,
189, 192
contemplation 56, 72, 100, 109,
126, 138, 142, 143, 155, 192,
195; as aim of Christian life 52–3,
114, 218 n. 33; as defence against
demons 102–3; example of 106–7;
as kingdom of heaven 57;
Evagrius' practice of 47; God as
object of 132; as mode of prayer
187; of nature 7, 13, 22, 27, 58,
65, 126, 131, 134, 135, 147, 164,
187, 192, 193, 218 n. 33;
preparation for 50, 127, 149, 175,
182, 200; superseded by prayer
115–16, 192
creation 15, 19, 28, 34–5, 55–6,
65–9, 122, 125, 126, 145, 214 n.
15
cross, sign of the 111, 118, 222
n. 5
Cyril of Scythopolis 18–20, 29

247

Gregory of Nazianzus, a complex and colourful figure in a crucial age (fourth century AD), when it was permissible for the first time to be a public Christian intellectual, was well placed to become one of the outstanding defenders and formulators of Church doctrine.

A gifted and skilled rhetorician, poet, and orator, as well as a profound theologian, Gregory was ordained a bishop and served, for almost two years, as head of the orthodox Christian community in Constantinople, where he played a crucial role in formulating the classical doctrines of the Trinity and the person of Christ. Under fire from opponents in the Church, the enigmatic Gregory eventually retreated into a quiet life of study and simple asceticism in his native Cappadocia, concentrating there on bringing the broad canon of his own writings to their present form. The body of his works, including poetry, letters, sermons and lectures on religious themes, and written with the precision and elegance of classical Greek literature, was recognized in the Byzantine age as equal in quality to the achievements of the greatest Greek writers.

A collection of new translations of a selection of these works, with an extensive introduction to Gregory's life, thought, and writings, Gregory of Nazianzus presents to us a vivid portrait of a fascinating character, who deserves to be regarded as one of the Christian tradition's outstanding theologians, and as the first true Christian humanist.

ISBN10:	0–415–12180–9 (hbk)
ISBN10:	0–415–12181–7 (pbk)
ISBN13:	978–0–415–12180–4 (hbk)
ISBN13:	978–0–415–12181–1 (pbk)

Related titles from Routledge

Gregory the Great
John Moorhead

Gregory's life culminated in his holding the office of pope (590–604). He is generally regarded as one of the outstanding figures in the long line of popes, and by the late ninth century had come to be known as 'the Great'. He played a critical role in the history of his time, and is regarded as one of the four great fathers of the Western Church, alongside Ambrose, Jerome and Augustine.

This volume provides an introduction to Gregory the Great's life and works and to the most fascinating areas of his thinking. It includes English translations of his influential writings on such topics as the interpretation of the Bible and human personality types. These works show Gregory communicating what seem to be abstruse ideas to ordinary people, and they remain highly current today.

ISBN10:   0–415–23389–5 (hbk)
ISBN10:   0–415–23390–9 (pbk)

ISBN13:   978–0–415–23389–7 (hbk)
ISBN13:   978–0–415–23390–3 (pbk)

Available at all good bookshops
For ordering and further information please visit:
www.routledge.com

Lightning Source UK Ltd.
Milton Keynes UK
UKHW021252181119
353758UK00015B/3640/P